LIGHT UP THE DAY

Bible readings for

every day of the year

ISBN-13:
978-1725648869

ISBN-10:
1725648865

Introduction and reading plan © Margaret Bolton, 2018
Extracts of the Holy Bible taken from various sources as shown.

INTRODUCTION

There are many ways to read the Holy Bible. Some like to read a few verses a day, others to read three or four chapters a day starting at Genesis and working through to the end of Revelation every year. Some people like the chronological approach, others prefer thematic. There is no right way but every Christian should be fully familiar with the Holy Scriptures. It is the Word of God given to us for our instruction and comfort and if we want to develop a living relationship with God, we need to read His Word and to do so daily. The purpose of this book is to provide a set of readings to take you through the year. Each week you have:

- Monday – teaching direct from Our Lord Jesus Christ
- Tuesday – a reading from the prophets
- Wednesday – a reading from the epistles
- Thursday – an extract of the Law
- Friday – a story taken from the Old Testament
- Saturday – a wisdom reading or psalm
- Sunday – an event from the life of Our Lord or His apostles taken from the New Testament

The variety is deliberate. Many people start reading the Holy Bible with the best of intentions but get disheartened when they face several days of passages which are either difficult to understand or seem rather uninteresting or even nauseating, such as long lists of genealogies or directions for animal sacrifices. This volume does not cover the entire Holy Bible but it includes readings from sixty of the books within, most being ten to twenty verses long though some are shorter and a few longer. The objective is to cover a wide cross-section of the teaching therein.

The readings are taken from a variety of public domain sources: Bible in Basic English (BBE), Webster's (WBS) or the New Heart (NHT). British spelling has been used.

Two principles underlie this work. The first is that the Holy Bible is the Word of God, not the product of human invention limited by whatever cultural norms existed at the time. Secondly, that God is one and that since English grammar has thou as the second person singular and you as the plural, it is appropriate that God is addressed as Thou.

HOW TO USE THIS BOOK

If you are starting the plan at the beginning of the year, start on the first Sunday with the Prologue. Thereafter, continue through the fifty-two weeks as shown. Otherwise, just commence the readings at the appropriate week. For leap years, a 366th day reading appears at the end.

Easter is not a fixed festival but the readings for week thirteen are designed to lead up to Easter Sunday and include an extra long passage for Good Friday. You may wish to swap this week's readings over according to when Easter comes in the year. The table below gives the dates for Easter and shows the week numbers otherwise. Week fifty-one includes Christmas readings.

For those who like to incorporate their reading in a more formal setting, a brief daily office is included based largely on the Book of Common Prayer.

Year	1st Sunday	Easter Sunday	Week
2019	January 6th	April 21st	15
2020	January 5th	April 12th	14
2021	January 3rd	April 4th	13
2022	January 2nd	April 17th	15
2023	January 1st	April 9th	14
2024	January 7th	March 31st	12
2025	January 5th	April 20th	15
2026	January 4th	April 5th	13
2027	January 3rd	March 28th	12
2028	January 2nd	April 16th	15

DAILY OFFICE

Almighty God, unto whom all hearts be open, all desires known, and from whom no secrets are hid; Cleanse the thoughts of my heart by the inspiration of thy Holy Spirit, that I may perfectly love thee, and worthily magnify thy holy Name; through Christ our Lord. Amen.

Have mercy upon me O God after Thy great goodness;
According to the multitude of Thy mercies do away mine offences
Wash me thoroughly from my wickedness and cleanse me from my sin
Make me a clean heart O God and renew a right spirit within me

Blessed Lord, who hast caused all holy Scriptures to be written for our learning; Grant that I may in such wise hear them, read, mark, learn, and inwardly digest them, that by patience and comfort of thy holy Word, I may embrace, and ever hold fast, the blessed hope of everlasting life, which thou hast given us in our Saviour Jesus Christ. Amen.

THE READING

Our Father, which art in heaven, Hallowed be thy Name. Thy kingdom come. Thy will be done, in earth as it is in heaven. Give us this day our daily bread. And forgive us our trespasses, As we forgive them that trespass against us. And lead us not into temptation; But deliver us from evil: For thine is the kingdom, The power, and the glory, For ever and ever. Amen.

Father I thank Thee for this day, my food and all Thy gifts which I receive of Thy bounteous liberality. Grant that I may take them for my comfort and use them in Thy service and give me grace that I may hereafter live a godly, righteous and sober life, though Jesus Christ our Lord. Amen

Teach me, Good Lord, to serve Thee as Thou deservest; to give and not to count the cost; to fight and not to heed the wounds; to toil and not seek for rest; to labour and not to ask for any reward save that of knowing that I do thy will.

Guide me O Lord in all my doings with Thy most gracious favour, and further me with Thy continual help, that all my works, begun, continued, and ended in Thee, may glorify Thy name and be acceptable in Thy sight now and forever.

Fulfil now, O Lord, the desires and petitions of thy servant, as may be most expedient for them; granting me in this world knowledge of thy truth, and in the world to come everlasting life.

Preserve me O Lord whilst waking and guard me whilst sleeping, that awake I might watch with Christ, and asleep may rest in His peace. Amen

✝

For those wishing to include a song, any hymn or worship song may be added or one of those that follows:

1)
O Lamb of God, that takest away the sins of the world have mercy upon us
O Lamb of God, that takest away the sins of the world, have mercy upon us
O Lamb of God, that takest away the sins of the world, grant us thy peace

2)
God be in my head and in my understanding
God be in my eyes, and in my looking;
God be in my mouth, and in my speaking;
God be in my heart, and in my thinking;
God be at my end, and at my departing

3)
Before the ending of the day,
Creator of the world we pray,
That with thy wonted favour thou
Wouldst be our guard and keeper now.

From all ill dreams defend our eyes,
From nightly fears and fantasies;
Tread underfoot our ghostly foe,
That no pollution we may know.

O Father, that we ask be done,
Through Jesus Christ, thine only Son;
Who, with the Holy Ghost and thee,
Doth live and reign eternally

4)
Before the starting of the day,
Creator of the world we pray,
That with thy wonted favour thou
Wouldst be our guard and keeper now.

'Gainst all temptation gird our arm
And keep us free from sin and harm;
Incline our hearts to do what's right
That we may walk in joy and light.

O Father, that we ask be done,
Through Jesus Christ, thine only Son;
Who, with the Holy Ghost and thee,
Doth live and reign eternally

5)
Harken O Lord, have mercy upon us
For we have sinned against Thee

THE READINGS

Prologue

Sunday

John 1:1-14 (WBS)
In the beginning was the Word, and the Word was with God, and the Word was God. The same was in the beginning with God. All things were made by him; and without him was not anything made that was made. In him was life; and the life was the light of men. And the light shineth in darkness; and the darkness comprehended it not. There was a man sent from God, whose name was John. The same came for a witness, to bear testimony of the Light, that all men through him might believe. He was not that Light, but was sent to bear testimony of that Light. That was the true Light, which lighteth every man that cometh into the world. He was in the world, and the world was made by him, and the world knew him not. He came to his own, and his own received him not. But as many as received him, to them he gave power to become the sons of God, even to them that believe on his name: who were born, not of blood, nor of the will of the flesh, nor of the will of man, but of God. And the Word was made flesh, and dwelt among us, and we beheld his glory, the glory as of the only begotten of the Father, full of grace and truth.

Week 1

Monday

Matt. 5:1-12 (BBE)
And seeing great masses of people he went up into the mountain; and when he was seated his disciples came to him and with these words he gave them teaching, saying,
Happy are the poor in spirit: for the kingdom of heaven is theirs.
Happy are those who are sad: for they will be comforted.
Happy are the gentle: for the earth will be their heritage.
Happy are those whose heart's desire is for righteousness: for they will have their desire.
Happy are those who have mercy: for they will be given mercy.
Happy are the clean in heart: for they will see God.
Happy are the peacemakers: for they will be named sons of God.
Happy are those who are attacked on account of righteousness: for the kingdom of heaven will be theirs.
Happy are you when men give you a bad name, and are cruel to you, and say all evil things against you falsely, because of me. Be glad and full of joy; for great is your reward in heaven: for so were the prophets attacked who were before you.

Tuesday

Isa 6:1-8 (NHT)

In the year that king Uzziah died, I saw the Lord sitting on a throne, high and lifted up; and his train filled the temple. Above him stood the seraphim. Each one had six wings. With two he covered his face. With two he covered his feet. With two he flew. One called to another, and said, "Holy, holy, holy, is the Lord of hosts. The whole earth is full of his glory." The foundations of the thresholds shook at the voice of him who called, and the house was filled with smoke. Then I said, "Woe is me. For I am undone, because I am a man of unclean lips, and I dwell in the midst of a people of unclean lips: for my eyes have seen the King, the Lord of hosts." Then one of the seraphim flew to me, having a live coal in his hand, which he had taken with the tongs from off the altar. He touched my mouth with it, and said, "Look, this has touched your lips; and your iniquity is taken away, and your sins forgiven." I heard the Lord's voice, saying, "Whom shall I send, and who will go for us?" Then I said, "Here I am. Send me."

Wednesday

Rom. 4:2-3,7-8,23-24; 5:1,3-8 (BBE)

For if Abraham got righteousness by works, he has reason for pride; but not before God. But what does it say in the holy Writings? And Abraham had faith in God, and it was put to his account as righteousness. Happy are those who have forgiveness for their wrongdoing, and whose sins are covered. Happy is the man against whom no sin is recorded by the Lord. Now, it was not because of him only that this was said, but for us in addition, to whose account it will be put, if we have faith in Him who made Jesus our Lord come back again from the dead, who was put to death for our evil-doing, and came to life again so that we might have righteousness. For which reason, because we have righteousness through faith, let us be at peace with God through our Lord Jesus Christ; And not only so, but let us have joy in our troubles: in the knowledge that trouble gives us the power of waiting; and waiting gives experience; and experience, hope: and hope does not put to shame; because our hearts are full of the love of God through the Holy Spirit which is given to us. for when we were still without strength, at the right time Christ gave his life for evil-doers. Now it is hard for anyone to give his life even for an upright man, though it might be that for a good man someone would give his life. But God has made clear his love to us, in that, when we were still sinners, Christ gave his life for us.

Thursday

Lev. 26: 3-4,6,9,11-12,14-18 (BBE)

If you are guided by my rules, and keep my laws and do them, then I will give you rain at the right time, and the land will give her increase and the trees of the field will give their fruit; and I will give you peace in the land, and you will take your rest and no one will give you cause for fear; and I will put an end to all evil beasts in the land, and no sword of war will go through your land. And I will have pleasure in you and make you fertile and greater in number; and I will keep my agreement with you. And I will put my holy House among you, and my soul will not be turned away from you in disgust. And I will be present among you and will be your God and you will be my people.

But if you do not give ear to me, and do not keep all these my laws; and if you go against my rules and if you have hate in your souls for my decisions and you do not do all my orders, but go against my agreement; this will I do to you: I will put fear in your hearts, even wasting disease and burning pain, drying up the eyes and making the soul feeble, and you will get no profit from your seed, for your haters will take it for food. and my face will be turned from you, and you will be broken before those who are against you, and your haters will become your rulers, and you will go in flight when no man comes after you. And if, even after these things, you will not give ear to me, then I will send you punishment seven times more for your sins.

Friday

Gen. 1:1–2:3 (BBE)
At the first God made the heaven and the earth. And the earth was waste and without form; and it was dark on the face of the deep: and the Spirit of God was moving on the face of the waters and God said, Let there be light: and there was light. And God, looking on the light, saw that it was good: and God made a division between the light and the dark, naming the light, Day, and the dark, Night. And there was evening and there was morning, the first day.

And God said, Let there be a solid arch stretching over the waters, parting the waters from the waters. And God made the arch for a division between the waters which were under the arch and those which were over it: and it was so. And God gave the arch the name of Heaven. And there was evening and there was morning, the second day.

And God said, Let the waters under the heaven come together in one place, and let the dry land be seen: and it was so. And God gave the dry land the name of Earth; and the waters together in their place were named Seas: and God saw that it was good. And God said, Let grass come up on the earth, and plants producing seed, and fruit-trees giving fruit, in which is their seed, after their sort: and it was so. And grass came up on the earth, and every plant producing seed of its sort, and every tree producing fruit, in which is its seed, of its sort: and God saw that it was good. And there was evening and there was morning, the third day.

And God said, Let there be lights in the arch of heaven, for a division between the day and the night, and let them be for signs, and for marking the changes of the year, and for days and for years:

And let them be for lights in the arch of heaven to give light on the earth: and it was so. And God made the two great lights: the greater light to be the ruler of the day, and the smaller light to be the ruler of the night: and he made the stars. and God put them in the arch of heaven, to give light on the earth; to have rule over the day and the night, and for a division between the light and the dark: and God saw that it was good. And there was evening and there was morning, the fourth day.

And God said, Let the waters be full of living things, and let birds be in flight over the earth under the arch of heaven. And God made great sea-beasts, and every sort of living and moving thing with which the waters were full, and every sort of winged bird: and God saw that it was good. And God gave them his blessing, saying, Be fertile and have increase, making all the waters of the seas full, and let the birds be increased in the earth. And there was evening and there was morning, the fifth day.

And God said, Let the earth give birth to all sorts of living things, cattle and all things moving on the earth, and beasts of the earth after their sort: and it was so. And God made the beast of the earth after its sort, and the cattle after their sort, and everything moving on the face of the earth after its sort: and God saw that it was good. And God said, Let us make man in our image, like us: and let him have rule over the fish of the sea and over the birds of the air and over the cattle and over all the earth and over every living thing which goes flat on the earth. And God made man in his image, in the image of God he made him: male and female he made them. and God gave them his blessing and said to them, Be fertile and have increase, and make the earth full and be masters of it; be rulers over the fish of the sea and over the birds of the air and over every living thing moving on the earth. And God said, See, I have given you every plant producing seed, on the face of all the earth, and every tree which has fruit producing seed: they will be for your food: and to every beast of the earth and to every bird of the air and every living thing moving on the face of the earth I have given every green plant for food: and it was so.

And God saw everything which he had made and it was very good. And there was evening and there was morning, the sixth day. And the heaven and the earth and all things in them were complete.

And on the seventh day God came to the end of all his work; and on the seventh day he took his rest from all the work which he had done. And God gave his blessing to the seventh day and made it holy: because on that day he took his rest from all the work which he had made and done.

Saturday

Ps. 1 (BBE)

Happy is the man who does not go in the company of sinners, or take his place in the way of evil-doers, or in the seat of those who do not give honour to the Lord. but whose delight is in the law of the Lord, and whose mind is on his law day and night. He will be like a tree planted by the rivers of water, which gives its fruit at the right time, whose leaves will ever be green; and he will do well in all his undertakings.

The evil-doers are not so; but are like the dust from the grain, which the wind takes away. For this cause there will be no mercy for sinners when they are judged, and the evil-doers will have no place among the upright, because the Lord sees the way of the upright, but the end of the sinner is destruction.

Sunday

Luke 2:21-35 (BBE)

And when, after eight days, the time came for his circumcision, he was named Jesus, the name which the angel had given to him before his birth.

And when the necessary days for making them clean by the law of Moses had come to an end, they took him to Jerusalem to give him to the Lord (as it says in the law of the Lord, every mother's first male child is to be holy to the Lord), and to make an offering, as it is ordered in the law of the Lord, of two doves or other young birds. And there was then in Jerusalem a man whose name was Simeon; and he was an upright man, fearing God and waiting for the comfort of Israel: and the Holy Spirit was on him and he had knowledge, through the Holy Spirit, that he would not see death till he had seen the Lord's Christ.

And full of the Spirit he came into the Temple; and when the father and mother came in with the child Jesus, to do with him what was ordered by the law, then he took him in his arms and gave praise to God and said, "Now you are letting your servant go in peace, O Lord, as you have said; For my eyes have seen your salvation, which you have made ready before the face of all nations; a light of revelation to the Gentiles, and the glory of your people Israel." And his father and mother were full of wonder at the things which were said about him. And Simeon gave them his blessing and said to Mary, his mother, "See, this child will be the cause of the downfall and the lifting up of great numbers of people in Israel, and he will be a sign against which hard words will be said; and a sword will go through your heart; so that the secret thoughts of men may come to light."

Week 2

Monday

Matt. 5:13-20 (BBE)

You are the salt of the earth; but if its taste goes from the salt, how will you make it salt again? It is then good for nothing but to be put out and crushed under foot by men.

You are the light of the world. A town put on a hill may be seen by all and a burning light is not put under a vessel, but on its table; so that its rays may be shining on all who are in the house. Even so let your light be shining before men, so that they may see your good works and give glory to your Father in heaven.

Let there be no thought that I have come to put an end to the law or the prophets. I have not come for destruction, but to make complete. Truly I say to you, Till heaven and earth come to an end, not the smallest letter or part of a letter will in any way be taken from the law, till all things are done. Whoever then goes against the smallest of these laws, teaching men to do the same, will be named least in the kingdom of heaven; but he who keeps the laws, teaching others to keep them, will be named great in the kingdom of heaven. For I say to you, If your righteousness is not greater than the righteousness of the scribes and Pharisees, you will never go into the kingdom of heaven.

Tuesday
Isa. 1:1-4,11,15-17 (BBE)

The vision of Isaiah, the son of Amoz, which he saw about Judah and Jerusalem, in the days of Uzziah, Jotham, Ahaz, and Hezekiah, kings of Judah. Give ear, O heavens, and you, O earth, to the word which the Lord has said: I have taken care of my children till they became men, but their hearts have been turned away from me. Even the ox has knowledge of its owner, and the ass of the place where its master puts its food: but Israel has no knowledge, my people give no thought to me. O nation full of sin, a people weighted down with crime, a generation of evil-doers, false-hearted children: they have gone away from the Lord, they have no respect for the Holy One of Israel, their hearts are turned back from him. What use to me is the number of the offerings which you give me? says the Lord; your burned offerings of sheep, and the best parts of fat cattle, are a weariness to me; I take no pleasure in the blood of oxen, or of lambs, or of he-goats and when your hands are stretched out to me, my eyes will be turned away from you: even though you go on making prayers, I will not give ear: your hands are full of blood. Be washed, make yourselves clean; put away the evil of your doings from before my eyes; let there be an end of sinning. Take pleasure in well-doing; let your ways be upright, keep down the cruel, give a right decision for the child who has no father, see to the cause of the widow.

Wednesday
Rom 6:4-14 (BBE)

We have been placed with him among the dead through baptism into death: so that as Christ came again from the dead by the glory of the Father, we, in the same way, might be living in new life. For, if we have been made like him in his death, we will, in the same way, be like him in his coming to life again; being conscious that our old man was put to death on the cross with him, so that the body of sin might be put away, and we might no longer be servants to sin because he who is dead is free from sin. But if we are dead with Christ, we have faith that we will be living with him; having knowledge that because Christ has come back from the dead, he will never again go down to the dead; death has no more power over him for his death was a death to sin, but his life now is a life which he is living to God. Even so see yourselves as dead to sin, but living to God in Christ Jesus. For this cause do not let sin be ruling in your body which is under the power of death, so that you give way to its desires; and do not give your bodies to sin as the instruments of wrongdoing, but give yourselves to God, as those who are living from the dead, and your bodies as instruments of righteousness to God. for sin may not have rule over you: because you are not under law, but under grace.

Thursday

Deut. 5:6-21 (NHT)

I am the Lord your God, who brought you out of the land of Egypt, out of the house of bondage. Do not have no other gods before me.

Do not make an engraved image for yourself, or any likeness of what is in heaven above, or on the earth below, or that is in the waters below the earth. You must not bow down yourself to them, nor serve them; for I, the Lord, your God, am a jealous God, visiting the iniquity of the fathers on the children, upon the third and upon the fourth generation of those who hate me; and showing loving kindness to thousands of those who love me and keep my commandments.

Do not take the name of the Lord your God in vain: for the Lord will not hold him guiltless who takes his name in vain.

Observe the Sabbath day, to keep it holy, as the Lord your God commanded you. Six days you may labour, and do all your work; but the seventh day is a Sabbath to the Lord your God. On it you must not do any work, you, your son, your daughter, your male servant, nor your female servant, your ox, nor your donkey, nor your livestock, your stranger who is within your gates; that your male servant and your female servant may rest as well as you. Remember that you were a slave in the land of Egypt, and the Lord your God brought you out of there by a mighty hand and by an outstretched arm: therefore the Lord your God commanded you to keep the Sabbath day.

Honour your father and your mother, as the Lord your God commanded you; that your days may be long, and that it may go well with you, in the land which the Lord your God gives you.

Do not commit adultery.
Do not murder.
Do not steal.

Do not give false testimony against your neighbour.

Do not covet your neighbour's wife. Do not crave your neighbour's house, his field, or his male servant, or his female servant, his ox, or his donkey, or anything that is your neighbour's.

Friday

Gen. 2:7-9,15-17,19-24 (BBE)

The Lord God made man from the dust of the earth, breathing into him the breath of life: and man became a living soul. And the Lord God made a garden in the east, in Eden; and there he put the man whom he had made and out of the earth the Lord made every tree to come, delighting the eye and good for food; and in the middle of the garden, the tree of life and the tree of the knowledge of good and evil. And the Lord God took the man and put him in the garden of Eden to do work in it and take care of it. And the Lord God gave the man orders, saying, "You may freely take of the fruit of every tree of the garden: but of the fruit of the tree of the knowledge of good and evil you may not take; for on the day when you take of it, death will certainly come to you." And from the earth the Lord God made every beast of the field and every bird of the air, and took them to the man to see what names he would give them: and whatever name he gave to any living thing, that was its name and the man gave names to all cattle and to the birds of the air and to every beast of the field; but Adam had no one like himself as a help. And the Lord God sent a deep sleep on the man, and took one of the bones from his side while he was sleeping, joining up the flesh again in its place and the bone which the Lord God had taken from the man he made into a woman, and took her to the man. And the man said, "this is now bone of my bone and flesh of my flesh: let her name be Woman because she was taken out of Man." For this cause will a man go away from his father and his mother and be joined to his wife; and they will be one flesh.

Saturday

Ps.2 (BBE)

Why are the nations so violently moved, and why are the thoughts of the people so foolish? The kings of the earth have taken their place, and the rulers are fixed in their purpose, against the Lord, and against the king of his selection, saying, let their chains be broken, and their cords taken from off us. Then he whose seat is in the heavens will be laughing: the Lord will make sport of them. Then will his angry words come to their ears, and by his wrath they will be troubled: But I have put my king on my holy hill of Zion. I will make clear the Lord's decision: he has said to me, "You are my son, this day have I given you being. Make your request to me, and I will give you the nations for your heritage, and the farthest limits of the earth will be under your hand. They will be ruled by you with a rod of iron; they will be broken like a potter's vessel." So now be wise, you kings: take his teaching, you judges of the earth. Give worship to the Lord with fear, kissing his feet and giving him honour for fear that he may be angry, causing destruction to come on you, because he is quickly moved to wrath. Happy are all those who put their faith in him.

Sunday

Matt.3:1-12 (BBE)

And in those days John the Baptist came preaching in the waste land of Judaea, saying, "Let your hearts be turned from sin; for the kingdom of heaven is near, for this is he of whom Isaiah the prophet said, The voice of one crying in the waste land, Make ready the way of the Lord, make his roads straight." Now John was clothed in camel's hair, with a leather band about him; and his food was locusts and honey. Then Jerusalem and all Judaea went out to him, and all the people from near Jordan; and they were given baptism by him in the river Jordan, saying openly that they had done wrong. But when he saw a number of the Pharisees and Sadducees coming to his baptism, he said to them, "Offspring of snakes, at whose word are you going in flight from the wrath to come? Let your change of heart be seen in your works: And say not to yourselves, We have Abraham for our father; because I say to you that God is able from these stones to make children for Abraham. And even now the axe is put to the root of the trees; every tree then which does not give good fruit is cut down, and put into the fire. Truly, I give baptism with water to those of you whose hearts are changed; but he who comes after me is greater than I, whose shoes I am not good enough to take up: He will give you baptism with the Holy Spirit and with fire: In whose hand is the instrument with which he will make clean his grain; he will put the good grain in his store, but the waste will be burned up in the fire which will never be put out."

Week 3

Monday

Matt. 5:21-26 (BBE)

You have knowledge that it was said in old times, 'You may not put to death'; and, whoever puts to death will be in danger of being judged: but I say to you that everyone who is angry with his brother will be in danger of being judged; and he who says to his brother, raca* will be in danger from the Sanhedrin; and whoever says, You foolish one, will be in danger of the hell of fire. If then you are making an offering at the altar and there it comes to your mind that your brother has something against you, while your offering is still before the altar, first go and make peace with your brother, then come and make your offering. Come to an agreement quickly with him who has a cause against you at law, while you are with him on the way, for fear that he may give you up to the judge and the judge may give you to the police and you may be put into prison. Truly I say to you, you will not come out from there till you have made payment of the very last farthing.

*Raca – empty headed

Tuesday

Isa. 1:18-20,25,27-28 (BBE)

Come now, and let us have an argument together, says the Lord: how may your sins which are red like blood be white as snow? how may their dark purple seem like wool? If you will give ear to my word and do it, the good things of the land will be yours; but if your hearts are turned against me, I will send destruction on you by the sword; so the Lord has said. And my hand will again be on you, washing away what is unclean as with soap, and taking away all your false metal; Upright acts will be the price of Zion's forgiveness, and by righteousness will men be living there. But a common destruction will overtake sinners and evil-doers together, and those who have gone away from the Lord will be cut off.

Wednesday

Rom. 7:12,14,18-23; 2:7-9,13 (BBE)

The law is holy, and its orders are holy, upright, and good. We are conscious that the law is of the spirit; but I am of the flesh, given into the power of sin for I am conscious that in me, that is, in my flesh, there is nothing good. I have the mind, but not the power, to do what is right; for the good which I have a mind to do, I do not: but the evil which I have no mind to do, that I do. But if I do what I have no mind to do, it is no longer I who do it, but the sin living in me. So I see a law that, though I have a mind to do good, evil is present in me. In my heart I take pleasure in the law of God but I see another law in my body, working against the law of my mind, and making me the servant of the law of sin which is in my flesh.

To those who go on with good works in the hope of glory and honour and salvation from death, he will give eternal life: but to those who, from a love of competition, are not guided by what is true, will come the heat of his wrath. Trouble and sorrow on all whose works are evil, to the Jew first and then to the Greek; for it is not the hearers of the law who will be judged as having righteousness before God, but only the doers:

Thursday

Deut. 6:4-7,13-14,17-18 (BBE)

Give ear, O Israel: the Lord our God is one Lord and the Lord your God is to be loved with all your heart and with all your soul and with all your strength. Keep these words, which I say to you this day, deep in your hearts; teaching them to your children with all care, talking of them when you are at rest in your house or walking by the way, when you go to sleep and when you get up. Let the fear of the Lord your God be in your hearts, and be his servants, taking your oaths by his name. Do not go after other gods, the gods of the peoples round about you. Keep with care the orders of the Lord your God, and his rules and his laws which he has given you and do what is upright and good in the eyes of the Lord your God, so that it may be well for you and you may go in and take for your heritage that good land which the Lord undertook by an oath to your fathers.

Friday
Gen. 3:1-12,16-19 (BBE)

Now the snake was wiser than any beast of the field which the Lord God had made. And he said to the woman, "Has God truly said that you may not take of the fruit of any tree in the garden?" And the woman said, "We may take of the fruit of the trees in the garden: but of the fruit of the tree in the middle of the garden, God has said,' If you take of it or put your hands on it, death will come to you.'" And the snake said, "Death will not certainly come to you: for God sees that on the day when you take of its fruit, your eyes will be open, and you will be as gods, having knowledge of good and evil." And when the woman saw that the tree was good for food, and a delight to the eyes, and to be desired to make one wise, she took of its fruit, and gave it to her husband. And their eyes were open and they were conscious that they had no clothing and they made themselves coats of leaves stitched together. There came to them the sound of the Lord God walking in the garden in the evening wind: and the man and his wife went to a secret place among the trees of the garden, away from the eyes of the Lord God and the voice of the Lord God came to the man, saying, "Where are you?" And he said, "Hearing your voice in the garden I was full of fear, because I was without clothing: and I kept myself from your eyes." And He said, "Who gave you the knowledge that you were without clothing? Have you taken of the fruit of the tree which I said you were not to take?" And the man said, "The woman whom you gave to be with me, she gave me the fruit of the tree and I took it." To the woman He said, "Great will be your pain in childbirth; in sorrow will your children come to birth; still your desire will be for your husband, but he will be your master." And to Adam He said," Because you gave ear to the voice of your wife and took of the fruit of the tree which I said you were not to take, the earth is cursed on your account; in pain you will get your food from it all your life. Thorns and waste plants will come up, and the plants of the field will be your food; with the hard work of your hands you will get your bread till you go back to the earth from which you were taken: for dust you are and to the dust you will go back."

Saturday

Ps. 5:1-8 (WBS)

Give ear to my words, O Lord, consider my meditation. Hearken to the voice of my cry, my King, and my God: for to thee will I pray. My voice shalt thou hear in the morning, O Lord; in the morning will I direct my prayer to thee, and will look up for thou art not a God that hath pleasure in wickedness: neither shall evil dwell with thee. The foolish shall not stand in thy sight: thou hatest all workers of iniquity. Thou shalt destroy them that speak falsehood: the Lord will abhor the bloody and deceitful man. But as for me, I will come into thy house in the multitude of thy mercy: and in thy fear will I worship towards thy holy temple. Lead me, O Lord, in thy righteousness, because of my enemies; make thy way straight before my face.

Sunday

Matt. 3:13-4:11 (NHT)

Then Jesus came from Galilee to the Jordan to John, to be baptized by him but John would have hindered him, saying, "I need to be baptized by you, and you come to me?" But Jesus, answering, said to him, "Allow it for now, for this is the fitting way for us to fulfil all righteousness." Then he allowed him.

And Jesus, when he was baptized, went up directly from the water; and look, the heavens were opened to him, and he saw the Spirit of God descending as a dove, and coming on him and look, a voice out of the heavens said, "This is my beloved Son, with whom I am well pleased."

Then Jesus was led up by the Spirit into the wilderness to be tempted by the devil and when he had fasted forty days and forty nights, he was hungry afterward. The tempter came and said to him, "If you are the Son of God, command that these stones become bread" but he answered and said, "It is written, 'Man does not live by bread alone, but by every word that proceeds out of the mouth of God.'"

Then the devil took him into the holy city. He set him on the pinnacle of the temple, and said to him, "If you are the Son of God, throw yourself down, for it is written, 'He will put his angels in charge of you.' and, 'In their hands they will lift you up, so that you will not strike your foot against a stone.'" Jesus said to him, "Again, it is written, 'Do not test the Lord your God.'" Again, the devil took him to a very high mountain, and showed him all the kingdoms of the world, and their glory and he said to him, "I will give you all of these things, if you will fall down and worship me." Then Jesus said to him, "Go away, Satan. For it is written, 'You are to worship the Lord your God, and serve him only.'" Then the devil left him, and look, angels came and served him.

Week 4

Monday

Matt 5:27-32 (BBE)

You have knowledge that it was said, "You may not have connection with another man's wife": but I say to you that everyone whose eyes are turned on a woman with desire has had connection with her in his heart.

If your right eye is a cause of trouble to you, take it out and put it away from you; because it is better to undergo the loss of one part, than for all your body to go into hell. And if your right hand is a cause of trouble to you, let it be cut off and put it away from you; because it is better to undergo the loss of one part, than for all your body to go into hell.

Again, it was said, Whoever puts away his wife has to give her a statement in writing for this purpose: but I say to you that everyone who puts away his wife for any other cause but the loss of her virtue, makes her false to her husband; and whoever takes her as his wife after she is put away, is no true husband to her.

Tuesday

Isa. 2:2-4, 22; 5:20-23 (NHT)

It shall happen in the latter days, that the mountain of the Lord's house shall be established on the top of the mountains, and shall be raised above the hills; and all nations shall flow to it. And many peoples shall come and say, "Come, let's go up to the mountain of the Lord, and to the house of the God of Jacob; and he will teach us of his ways, and we will walk in his paths." For out of Zion the law shall go forth, and the word of the Lord from Jerusalem. He will judge between the nations, and will decide concerning many peoples; and they shall beat their swords into ploughshares, and their spears into pruning hooks. Nation shall not lift up sword against nation, neither shall they learn war any more.

Stop trusting in man, whose breath is in his nostrils; for of what account is he?

Woe to those who call evil good, and good evil; who put darkness for light, and light for darkness; who put bitter for sweet, and sweet for bitter. Woe to those who are wise in their own eyes, and prudent in their own sight. Woe to those who are mighty to drink wine, and champions at mixing strong drink; who acquit the guilty for a bribe, but deny justice for the innocent.

Wednesday

Rom. 8:13-17; 11:17-21 (BBE)

For if you go in the way of the flesh, death will come on you; but if by the Spirit you put to death the works of the body, you will have life and all those who are guided by the Spirit of God are sons of God. For you did not get the spirit of servants again to put you in fear, but the spirit of sons was given to you, by which we say," Abba, Father." The Spirit is witness with our spirit that we are children of God and if we are children, we have a right to a part in the heritage; a part in the things of God, together with Christ; so that if we have a part in his pain, we will in the same way have a part in his glory. But if some of the branches were broken off, and you, an olive-tree of the fields, were put in among them, and were given a part with them in the root by which the olive-tree is made fertile, do not be uplifted in pride over the branches: because it is not you who are the support of the root, but it is by the root that you are supported. You will say," Branches were broken off so that I might be put in." Truly, because they had no faith they were broken off, and you have your place by reason of your faith. Do not be lifted up in pride, but have fear; for, if God did not have mercy on the natural branches, he will not have mercy on you.

Thursday

Deut. 15:7-8,10-11 (BBE)

If in any of your towns in the land which the Lord your God is giving you, there is a poor man, one of your countrymen, do not let your heart be hard or your hand shut to him; but let your hand be open to give him the use of whatever he is in need of. It is right for you to give to him, without grief of heart: for because of this, the blessing of the Lord your God will be on all your work and on everything to which you put your hand. For there will never be a time when there are no poor in the land; and so I give orders to you, Let your hand be open to your countrymen, to those who are poor and in need in your land.

Friday

Gen 6: 11-14; 7:1-5 (BBE)

The earth was evil in God's eyes and full of violent ways. And God, looking on the earth, saw that it was evil: for the way of all flesh had become evil on the earth. And God said to Noah, 'The end of all flesh has come; the earth is full of their violent doings, and now I will put an end to them with the earth. Make for yourself an ark of gopher wood with rooms in it, and make it safe from the water inside and out.' And the Lord said to Noah, 'Take all your family and go into the ark, for you only in this generation have I seen to be upright. Of every clean beast you will take seven males and seven females, and of the beasts which are not clean, two, the male and his female; and of the birds of the air, seven males and seven females, so that their seed may still be living on the face of the earth for after seven days I will send rain on the earth for forty days and forty nights, for the destruction of every living thing which I have made on the face of the earth.' And Noah did everything which the Lord said he was to do.

Saturday

Ps. 8 (WBS)

O Lord our Lord, how excellent is thy name in all the earth who hast set thy glory above the heavens. Out of the mouth of babes and sucklings hast thou ordained strength because of thy enemies, that thou mightest still the enemy and the avenger. When I consider thy heavens, the work of thy fingers; the moon and the stars, which thou hast ordained; What is man, that thou art mindful of him and the son of man, that thou visitest him? For thou hast made him a little lower than the angels, and hast crowned him with glory and honour. Thou hast made him to have dominion over the works of thy hands; thou hast put all things under his feet: All sheep and oxen, yes, and the beasts of the field; the fowl of the air, and the fish of the sea, and whatever passeth through the paths of the seas. O Lord our Lord, how excellent is thy name in all the earth!

Sunday

Gen. 7: 17,19, 23; 8: 6-12; 9:1-4,9,12-13 (BBE)

For forty days the waters were over all the earth; and the waters were increased so that the ark was lifted up high over the earth. And the waters overcame everything on the earth; and all the mountains under heaven were covered. Every living thing on the face of all the earth, man and cattle and things moving on the face of the earth, and birds of the air, came to destruction: only Noah and those who were with him in the ark, were kept from death. Then, after forty days, through the open window of the ark which he had made, Noah sent out a raven, which went this way and that till the waters were gone from the earth. And he sent out a dove, to see if the waters had gone from the face of the earth; but the dove saw no resting-place for her foot, and came back to the ark, for the waters were still over all the earth; and he put out his hand, and took her into the ark. And after waiting another seven days, he sent the dove out again; and the dove came back at evening, and in her mouth was an olive-leaf broken off: so Noah was certain that the waters had gone down on the earth. And after seven days more, he sent the dove out again, but she did not come back to him.

And God gave his blessing to Noah and his sons, and said, 'Be fertile, and have increase, and make the earth full. The fear of you will be strong in every beast of the earth and every bird of the air; everything which goes on the land, and all the fishes of the sea, are given into your hands. Every living and moving thing will be food for you; I give them all to you as before I gave you all green things, but flesh with the life-blood in it you may not take for food. Truly, I will make my agreement with you and with your seed after you.' And God said, This is the sign of the agreement which I make between me and you and every living thing with you, for all future generations: I will put my bow in the cloud and it will be for a sign of the agreement between me and the earth. And I will keep in mind the agreement between me and you and every living thing; and never again will there be a great flow of waters causing destruction to all flesh.'

Week 5

Monday

Matt 5: 33-42 (NHT)

Again you have heard that it was said to them of old time, 'Do not make false vows, but fulfil your vows to the Lord.' But I tell you, do not swear at all: neither by heaven, for it is the throne of God; nor by the earth, for it is the footstool of his feet; nor by Jerusalem, for it is the city of the great King. Neither should you swear by your head, for you cannot make one hair white or black but let your 'Yes' be 'Yes' and your 'No' be 'No.' Whatever is more than these is of the evil one.

You have heard that it was said, 'An eye for an eye, and a tooth for a tooth.' but I tell you, do not set yourself against the one who is evil. But whoever strikes you on your right cheek, turn to him the other also. And if anyone sues you to take away your coat, let him have your cloak also. And whoever compels you to go one mile, go with him two. Give to him who asks you, and do not turn away him who desires to borrow from you.

Tuesday

Isa 10: 1-3,23; 13:11-13 (BBE)

Cursed are those who make evil decisions, and the writers who make the records of their cruel acts: who do wrong to the poor in their cause, and take away the right of the crushed among my people, so that they may have the property of widows, and get under their power those who have no father. What will you do in the day of punishment, and in the destruction which is coming from far? To whom will you go for help, and what will become of your glory? For though your people, O Israel, are as the sand of the sea, only a small number will come back: for the destruction is fixed, overflowing in righteousness. For the Lord, the Lord of armies, is about to make destruction complete in all the land. The Lord says, 'I will send punishment on the world for its evil, and on the sinners for their wrongdoing; and I will put an end to all pride, and will make low the power of the cruel. I will make men so small in number, that a man will be harder to get than gold, even the best gold of Ophir.' For this cause the heavens will be shaking, and the earth will be moved out of its place, in the wrath of the Lord of armies, and in the day of his burning passion.

Wednesday

Rom. 8: 28-33, 38-39 (BBE)

We are conscious that all things are working together for good to those who have love for God, and have been marked out by his purpose, because those of whom he had knowledge before they came into existence, were marked out by him to be made like his Son, so that he might be the first among a band of brothers: and those who were marked out by him were named; and those who were named were given righteousness; and to those to whom he gave righteousness, in the same way he gave glory. What may we say about these things? If God is for us, who is against us? He who did not keep back his only Son, but gave him up for us all, will he not with him freely give us all things? Who will say anything against the saints of God? It is God who makes us clear from evil. For I am certain that not death, or life, or angels, or rulers, or things present, or things to come, or powers, or things on high, or things under the earth, or anything which is made, will be able to come between us and the love of God which is in Christ Jesus our Lord.

Thursday

Deut. 16:18-20; 19:15-19 (BBE)

You are to make judges and overseers in all your towns which the Lord your God gives you, for every tribe: and they are to be upright men, judging the people in righteousness. You are not to be moved in your judging by a man's position, you are not to take rewards; for rewards make the eyes of the wise man blind, and the decisions of the upright false. Let righteousness be your guide, so that you may have life, and take for your heritage the land which the Lord your God is giving you. One witness may not make a statement against a man in relation to any sin or wrongdoing which he has done: on the word of two or three witnesses a question is to be judged. If a false witness makes a statement against a man, saying that he has done wrong, then the two men, between whom the argument has taken place, are to come before the Lord, before the priests and judges who are then in power; and the judges will have the question looked into with care: and if the witness is seen to be false and to have made a false statement against his brother, then do to him what it was his purpose to do to his brother: and so put away the evil from among you.

Friday

Gen. 12:1-6; 15:1-6 (WBS)
Now the Lord had said to Abram, "Depart from thy country, and from thy kindred, and from thy father's house, to a land that I will show thee: And I will make of thee a great nation, and I will bless thee, and make thy name great; and thou shalt be a blessing: And I will bless them that bless thee, and curse him that curseth thee: and in thee shall all families of the earth be

blessed." So Abram departed, as the Lord had spoken to him, and Lot went with him: and Abram was seventy and five years old when he departed from Haran. And Abram took Sarai his wife, and Lot his brother's son, and all their substance that they had gathered, and the souls that they had gotten in Haran; and they went to go forth into the land of Canaan; and into the land of Canaan they came. And Abram passed through the land to the place of Shechem, to the plain of Moreh. And the Canaanite was then in the land. After these things the word of the Lord came to Abram in a vision, saying, "Fear not, Abram: I am thy shield, and thy exceeding great reward." And Abram said, "Lord GOD, what wilt thou give me, seeing I go childless, and the steward of my house is this Eliezer of Damascus?" And Abram said, "Behold, to me thou hast given no seed: and lo, one born in my house is my heir." And behold, the word of the Lord came to him, saying, "This shall not be thy heir; but he that shall come forth out of thy own bowels shall be thy heir." And he brought him forth abroad, and said, "Look now towards heaven, and tell the stars, if thou art able to number them:" and he said to him, "So shall thy seed be. And he believed in the Lord; and he counted it to him for righteousness.

Saturday

Ps. 95: 1-7 (BBE)

O come, let us make songs to the Lord; sending up glad voices to the Rock of our salvation. Let us come before his face with praises; and make melody with holy songs for the Lord is a great God, and a great King over all gods. The deep places of the earth are in his hand; and the tops of the mountains are his. The sea is his, and he made it; and the dry land was formed by his hands. O come, let us give worship, falling down on our knees before the Lord our Maker. For he is our God; and we are the people to whom he gives food, and the sheep of his flock. Today, if you would only give ear to his voice!

Sunday

Luke 5:1-11 (BBE)

Now it came about that while the people came pushing to be near him and to have knowledge of the word of God, he was by a wide stretch of water named Gennesaret. He saw two boats by the edge of the water, but the fishermen had gone out of them and were washing their nets. He got into one of the boats, the property of Simon, and made a request to him to go a little way out from the land and being seated he gave the people teaching from the boat. And when his talk was ended, he said to Simon, "Go out into deep water, and let down your nets for fish." And Simon, answering, said, "Master, we were working all night and we took nothing: but at your word I will let down the nets." And when they had done this, they got such a great number of fish that it seemed as if their nets would be broken. They made signs to their friends in the other boat to come to their help and they came, and the two boats were so full that they were going down.   But Simon, when he saw it, went down at the knees of Jesus and said, "Go away from me, O Lord, for I am a sinner."   For he was full of wonder and so were all those who were with him, at the number of fish which they had taken;   And so were James and John, the sons of Zebedee, who were working with Simon. And Jesus said to Simon," Have no fear; from this time forward you will be a fisher of men."   And when they had got their boats to the land, they gave up everything and went after him.

Week 6

Monday

Matt. 5: 43-48 (BBE)

You have knowledge that it was said, 'Have love for your neighbour, and hate for him who is against you:' but I say to you, Have love for those who are against you, and make prayer for those who are cruel to you so that you may be the sons of your Father in heaven; for his sun gives light to the evil and to the good, and he sends rain on the upright man and on the sinner. For if you have love for those who have love for you, what credit is it to you? do not the tax-farmers the same? And if you say, Good day, to your brothers only, what do you do more than others? do not even the Gentiles the same? Be then complete in righteousness, even as your Father in heaven is complete.

Tuesday

Isa. 12: 1-6 (NHT)

In that day you will say, "I will give thanks to you, the Lord; for you were angry with me, but your anger has turned away and you comfort me. Look, in the God of my salvation I will trust, and will not be afraid for the Lord is my strength and my song, and he has become my salvation." Therefore with joy you will draw water out of the wells of salvation. In that day you will say, "Give thanks to the Lord. Call on his name. Declare his doings among the peoples. Proclaim that his name is exalted. Sing to the Lord, for he has done excellent things. Let this be known in all the earth. Cry aloud and shout, you inhabitant of Zion; for the Holy One of Israel is great in the midst of you."

Wednesday

Rom. 12: 1-5,8 (BBE)

For this reason I make request to you, brothers, by the mercies of God, that you will give your bodies as a living offering, holy, pleasing to God, which is the worship it is right for you to give him. And let not your behaviour be like that of this world, but be changed and made new in mind, so that by experience you may have knowledge of the good and pleasing and complete purpose of God. But I say to every one of you, through the grace given to me, not to have an over-high opinion of himself, but to have wise thoughts, as God has given to every one a measure of faith. For, as we have a number of parts in one body, but all the parts have not the same use, so we, though we are a number of persons, are one body in Christ, and are dependent on one another. He who has the power of teaching, let him make use of it. He who has the power of comforting, let him do so; he who gives, let him give freely; he who has the power of ruling, let him do it with a serious mind; he who has mercy on others, let it be with joy.

Thursday
Deut. 21: 15-17; 22:5 (BBE)

If a man has two wives, one greatly loved and the other hated, and the two of them have had children by him; and if the first son is the child of the hated wife: then when he gives his property to his sons for their heritage, he is not to put the son of his loved one in the place of the first son, the son of the hated wife: but he is to give his first son his birth right, and twice as great a part of his property: for he is the first-fruits of his strength and the right of the first son is his.

It is not right for a woman to be dressed in man's clothing, or for a man to put on a woman's robe: whoever does such things is disgusting to the Lord your God.

Friday
Gen. 19: 1-13, 27-28 (NHT)

The two angels came to Sodom at evening. Lot sat in the gate of Sodom. Lot saw them, and rose up to meet them. He bowed himself with his face to the earth, and he said, "See now, my lords, please turn aside into your servant's house, stay all night, wash your feet, and you will rise up early, and go on your way." They said, "No, but we will stay in the street all night." He urged them greatly, and they came in with him, and entered into his house. He made them a feast, and baked unleavened bread, and they ate. But before they lay down, the men of the city, the men of Sodom, surrounded the house, both young and old, all the people from every quarter. They called to Lot, and said to him, "Where are the men who came in to you this night? Bring them out to us, that we may have sex with them." Lot went out to them to the door, and shut the door after him. He said, "Please, my brothers, do not act so wickedly. See now, I have two virgin daughters. Please let me bring them out to you, and you may do to them what seems good to you. Only do not do anything to these men, because they have come under the shadow of my roof." They said, "Stand back." They said, "This one fellow came in to live as a foreigner, and he appoints himself a judge. Now will we deal worse with you, than with them." They pressed hard on the man Lot, and drew near to break the door. But the men put forth their hand, and brought Lot into the house to them, and shut the door. They struck the men who were at the door of the house with blindness, both small and great, so that they wearied themselves to find the door. The men said to Lot, "Do you have anybody else here? Sons-in-law, your sons, your daughters, and whoever you have in the city, bring them out of the place: for we will destroy this place, because the outcry against them has grown great before the Lord that the Lord has sent us to destroy it." Abraham got up early in the morning to the place where he had stood before the Lord. He looked toward Sodom and Gomorrah, and toward all the land of the plain, and looked, and saw that the smoke of the land went up as the smoke of a furnace.

Saturday

Ps. 13 (WBS)

How long wilt thou forget me, O Lord? forever? How long wilt thou hide thy face from me? How long shall I take counsel in my soul, having sorrow in my heart daily? How long shall my enemy be exalted over me? Consider and hear me, O Lord my God lighten my eyes, lest I sleep the sleep of death; lest my enemy say,' I have prevailed against him'; and those that trouble me rejoice when I am moved. But I have trusted in thy mercy; my heart shall rejoice in thy salvation. I will sing to the Lord, because he hath dealt bountifully with me.

Sunday

Luke 4:14-30 (NHT)

Jesus returned in the power of the Spirit into Galilee, and news about him spread through all the surrounding area. He taught in their synagogues, being praised by all. He came to Nazareth, where he had been brought up. He entered, as was his custom, into the synagogue on the Sabbath day, and stood up to read. The scroll of the prophet Isaiah was handed to him. He opened the scroll, and found the place where it was written, "The Spirit of the Lord is upon me, because he has anointed me to preach good news to the poor. He has sent me to heal the broken hearted, to proclaim liberty to the captives, recovering of sight to the blind, to deliver those who are crushed, and to proclaim the acceptable year of the Lord." He closed the scroll, gave it back to the attendant, and sat down. The eyes of all in the synagogue were fastened on him. He began to tell them, "Today, this Scripture has been fulfilled in your hearing." All testified about him, and wondered at the gracious words which proceeded out of his mouth, and they said, "Is not this Joseph's son?" He said to them, "Doubtless you will tell me this parable, 'Physician, heal yourself. Whatever we have heard done at Capernaum, do also here in your hometown.'" He said, "Truly I tell you, no prophet is acceptable in his hometown. But truly I tell you, there were many widows in Israel in the days of Elijah, when the sky was shut up three years and six months, when a great famine came over all the land. Elijah was sent to none of them, except to Zarephath, in the land of Sidon, to a woman who was a widow. There were many lepers in Israel in the time of Elisha the prophet, yet not one of them was cleansed, except Naaman, the Syrian." They were all filled with wrath in the synagogue, as they heard these things. They rose up, threw him out of the city, and led him to the brow of the hill that their city was built on, that they might throw him off the cliff. But he, passing through the midst of them, went his way.

Week 7

Monday

Matt. 6: 1-4,16-18 (BBE)

Take care not to do your good works before men, to be seen by them; or you will have no reward from your Father in heaven. When then you give money to the poor, do not make a noise about it, as the false-hearted men do in the Synagogues and in the streets, so that they may have glory from men. Truly, I say to you, they have their reward. But when you give money, let not your left hand see what your right hand does so that your giving may be in secret; and your Father, who sees in secret, will give you your reward.

And when you go without food, be not sad-faced as the false-hearted are for they go about with changed looks, so that men may see that they are going without food. Truly I say to you, they have their reward. But when you go without food, put oil on your head and make your face clean so that no one may see that you are going without food, but your Father in secret; and your Father, who sees in secret, will give you your reward.

Tuesday

Isa. 14: 11-20 (BBE)

Your pride has gone down into the underworld, and the noise of your instruments of music; the worms are under you, and your body is covered with them. How great is your fall from heaven, O shining one, son of the morning! How are you cut down to the earth, low among the dead bodies! For you said in your heart,' I will go up to heaven, I will make my seat higher than the stars of God; I will take my place on the mountain of the meeting-place of the gods, in the inmost parts of the north. I will go higher than the clouds; I will be like the Most High.' But you will come down to the underworld, even to its inmost parts. Those who see you will be looking on you with care, they will be in deep thought, saying,' Is this the troubler of the earth, the shaker of kingdoms? Who made the world a waste, overturning its towns; who did not let his prisoners loose from the prison-house'. All the kings of the earth are at rest in glory, every man in his house, But you, like a birth before its time, are stretched out with no resting-place in the earth; clothed with the bodies of the dead who have been put to the sword, who go down to the lowest parts of the underworld; a dead body, crushed under foot. As for your fathers, you will not be united with them in their resting-place, because you have been the cause of destruction to your land, and of death to your people; the seed of the evil-doer will have no place in the memory of man.

Wednesday

Rom 12: 9-21 (BBE)

Let love be without deceit. Be haters of what is evil; keep your minds fixed on what is good. Be kind to one another with a brother's love, putting others before yourselves in honour. Be not slow in your work, but be quick in spirit, as the Lord's servants; being glad in hope, quiet in trouble, at all times given to prayer, giving to the needs of the saints, ready to take people into your houses. Give blessing and not curses to those who are cruel to you. Take part in the joy of those who are glad, and in the grief of those who are sorrowing. Be in harmony with one another. Do not have a high opinion of yourselves, but be in agreement with common people. Do not give yourselves an air of wisdom. Do not give evil for evil to any man. Let all your business be well ordered in the eyes of all men. As far as it is possible for you, be at peace with all men. Do not give punishment for wrongs done to you, dear brothers, but give way to the wrath of God; for it is said in the holy Writings, 'Punishment is mine, I will give reward', says the Lord. But if one who has hate for you is in need of food or of drink, give it to him, for in so doing you will put coals of fire on his head. Do not let evil overcome you, but overcome evil by good.

Thursday

Deut. 22: 13-22, 28-29 (BBE)

If any man takes a wife, and having had connection with her, has no delight in her, and says evil things about her and gives her a bad name, saying, I took this woman, and when I had connection with her it was clear to me that she was not a virgin: then let the girl's father and mother put before the responsible men of the town, in the public place, signs that the girl was a virgin: and let the girl's father say to the responsible men, 'I gave my daughter to this man for his wife, but he has no love for her; and now he has put shame on her, saying that she is not a virgin; but here is the sign that she is a virgin.' Then they are to put her clothing before the responsible men of the town. Then the responsible men of the town are to give the man his punishment. They will take from him a hundred shekels of silver, which are to be given to the father of the girl, because he has given an evil name to a virgin of Israel: she will go on being his wife, he may never put her away all his life. But if what he has said is true, and she is seen to be not a virgin, then they are to make the girl come to the door of her father's house and she will be stoned to death by the men of the town, because she has done evil and put shame on Israel, by acting as a loose woman in her father's house: so you are to put away evil from among you.

If a man is taken in the act of going in to a married woman, the two of them, the man as well as the woman, are to be put to death: so you are to put away the evil from Israel.

If a man sees a young virgin, who has not given her word to be married to anyone, and he takes her by force and has connection with her, and discovery is made of it; then the man will have to give the virgin's father fifty shekels of silver and make her his wife, because he has put shame on her; he may never put her away all his life.

Friday

Gen. 22: 1-13 (NHT)

It happened after these things, that God tested Abraham, and said to him, "Abraham, Abraham." He said, "Here I am." He said, "Now take your son, your only son, whom you love, even Isaac, and go into the land of Moriah. Offer him there for a burnt offering on one of the mountains which I will tell you of." Abraham rose early in the morning, and saddled his donkey, and took two of his young men with him, and Isaac his son. He split the wood for the burnt offering, and rose up, and went to the place of which God had told him. On the third day Abraham lifted up his eyes, and saw the place far off. Abraham said to his young men, "Stay here with the donkey. The boy and I will go yonder. We will worship, and come back to you." Abraham took the wood of the burnt offering and laid it on Isaac his son. He took in his hand the fire and the knife. They both went together. Isaac spoke to Abraham his father, and said, "My father?" He said, "Here I am, my son." He said, "Here is the fire and the wood, but where is the lamb for a burnt offering?" Abraham said, "God will provide himself the lamb for a burnt offering, my son." So they both went together. They came to the place which God had told him of. Abraham built the altar there, and laid the wood in order, bound Isaac his son, and laid him on the altar, on the wood. Abraham stretched forth his hand, and took the knife to kill his son. The angel of the Lord called to him out of the sky, and said, "Abraham, Abraham." He said, "Here I am." He said, "Do not lay your hand on the boy, neither do anything to him. For now I know that you fear God, seeing you have not withheld your son, your only son, from me." And Abraham lifted up his eyes and looked, and look, behind him was a ram caught in the thicket by his horns. Abraham went and took the ram, and offered him up for a burnt offering instead of his son.

Saturday

Ps. 98 (BBE)

O make a new song to the Lord, because he has done works of wonder; with his right hand, and with his holy arm, he has overcome. The Lord has given to all the knowledge of his salvation; he has made clear his righteousness in the eyes of the nations. He has kept in mind his mercy and his unchanging faith to the house of Israel; all the ends of the earth have seen the salvation of our God. Let all the earth send out a glad cry to the Lord; sounding with a loud voice, and praising him with songs of joy. Make melody to the Lord with instruments of music; with a corded instrument and the voice of song. With wind instruments and the sound of the horn, make a glad cry before the Lord, the King. Let the sea be thundering, with all its waters; the world, and all who are living in it; Let the streams make sounds of joy with their hands; let the mountains be glad together before the Lord, for he has come as judge of the earth; judging the world in righteousness, and giving true decisions for the peoples.

Sunday

Mark 2: 1-17 (NHT)

And when he entered again into Capernaum after some days, it was heard that he was in the house. Many were gathered together, so that there was no more room, not even around the door; and he spoke the word to them. Four people came, carrying a paralytic to him, and when they could not bring him because of the crowd, they removed the roof above him. When they had broken it up, they let down the mat that the paralytic was lying on. Jesus, seeing their faith, said to the paralytic, "Son, your sins are forgiven you." But there were some of the scribes sitting there, and reasoning in their hearts, "Why does this man speak like that? He is blaspheming; who can forgive sins but God alone?" And immediately Jesus, perceiving in his spirit that they so reasoned within themselves, said to them, "Why do you reason these things in your hearts? Which is easier, to tell the paralytic, 'Your sins are forgiven;' or to say, 'Arise, and take up your bed, and walk?' But that you may know that the Son of Man has authority on earth to forgive sins", he said to the paralytic, "I tell you, arise, take up your mat, and go to your house." And he arose immediately, and took up the mat, and went out in front of them all; so that they were all amazed, and glorified God, saying, "We never saw anything like this."

And Jesus went out again by the seaside. All the crowd came to him, and he taught them. As he passed by, he saw Levi, the son of Alphaeus, sitting at the tax office, and he said to him, "Follow me." And he arose and followed him.

It happened, that he was reclining at the table in his house, and many tax collectors and sinners sat down with Jesus and his disciples, for there were many, and they followed him. And the scribes of the Pharisees, when they saw him eating with the tax collectors and sinners, said to his disciples, "Why is it that he eats and drinks with tax collectors and sinners?" And when Jesus heard it, he said to them, "Those who are healthy have no need for a physician, but those who are sick. I came not to call the righteous, but sinners."

Week 8

Monday

Matt. 6: 5-15 (New Living Translation)

When you pray, don't be like the hypocrites who love to pray publicly on street corners and in the synagogues where everyone can see them. I tell you the truth, that is all the reward they will ever get. But when you pray, go away by yourself, shut the door behind you, and pray to your Father in private. Then your Father, who sees everything, will reward you. When you pray, don't babble on and on as the Gentiles do. They think their prayers are answered merely by repeating their words again and again. Don't be like them, for your Father knows exactly what you need even before you ask him! Pray like this:

> Our Father in heaven, may your name be kept holy.
> May your Kingdom come soon.
> May your will be done on earth, as it is in heaven.
> Give us today the food we need,
> and forgive us our sins, as we have forgiven those
> who sin against us.
> And don't let us yield to temptation, but rescue us from the evil one.

If you forgive those who sin against you, your heavenly Father will forgive you, but if you refuse to forgive others, your Father will not forgive your sins.

Tuesday

Isa 17:10a; 22:12-13; 24:1-3,17-18 (BBE)

You have not given honour to the God of your salvation, and have not kept in mind the Rock of your strength. In that day the Lord, the Lord of armies, was looking for weeping, and cries of sorrow, cutting off of the hair, and putting on the clothing of grief: but in place of these there was joy and delight, oxen and sheep were being made ready for food, there was feasting and drinking: men said, 'Now is the time for food and wine, for tomorrow death comes.'

See, the Lord is making the earth waste and unpeopled, he is turning it upside down, and sending the people in all directions. It will be the same for the people as for the priest; for the servant as for his master; and for the woman-servant as for her owner; the same for the one offering goods for a price as for him who takes them; the same for him who gives money at interest and for him who takes it; the same for him who lets others have the use of his property as for those who make use of it. The earth will be completely waste and without men; for this is the word of the Lord. Fear, and death, and the net, are come on you, O people of the earth. And it will be that he who goes in flight from the sound of fear will be overtaken by death; and he who gets free from death will be taken in the net: for the windows on high are open, and the bases of the earth are shaking.

Wednesday

Rom 13:8-10, 14;14-15,19-21 (NHT)

Owe no one anything, except to love one another; for he who loves his neighbour has fulfilled the law for the commandments, "Do not commit adultery," "Do not murder," "Do not steal," "Do not give false testimony," "Do not covet," and whatever other commandments there are, are all summed up in this saying, namely, "You are to love your neighbour as yourself." Love does not harm a neighbour. Love therefore is the fulfilment of the law. I know, and am persuaded in the Lord Jesus, that nothing is unclean of itself; except that to him who considers anything to be unclean, to him it is unclean, yet if because of food your brother is grieved, you walk no longer in love. Do not destroy with your food him for whom Christ died. So then, let us follow after things which make for peace, and things by which we may build one another up. Do not overthrow God's work for food's sake. All things indeed are clean, however it is evil for anyone who creates a stumbling block by eating. It is good to not eat meat, drink wine, or do anything by which your brother stumbles, or is offended, or is made weak.

Thursday

Deut 23: 21-24 (BBE)

When you take an oath to the Lord, do not be slow to give effect to it: for without doubt the Lord your God will make you responsible, and will put it to your account as sin, but if you take no oath, there will be no sin. Whatever your lips have said, see that you do it; for you gave your word freely to the Lord your God.

When you go into your neighbour's vine-garden, you may take of his grapes at your pleasure, but you may not take them away in your vessel.

Friday

Gen. 24: 1-7, 10-19, 22-25, 32-38, 50-51, 57-67 (NHT)

Abraham was old, and well stricken in age. The Lord had blessed Abraham in all things. Abraham said to his servant, the elder of his house, who ruled over all that he had, "Please put your hand under my thigh. I will make you swear by the Lord, the God of heaven and the God of the earth, that you shall not take a wife for my son of the daughters of the Canaanites, among whom I live but you shall go to my country, and to my relatives, and take a wife for my son Isaac." The servant said to him, "What if the woman isn't willing to follow me to this land? Must I bring your son again to the land you came from?" Abraham said to him, "Beware that you do not bring my son there again. The Lord, the God of heaven, who took me from my father's house, and from the land of my birth, who spoke to me, and who swore to me, saying, 'I will give this land to your offspring.' He will send his angel before you, and you shall take a wife for my son from there." The servant took ten camels, of his master's camels, and departed, having a variety of good things of his master's with him. He arose, and went to Mesopotamia, to the city of Nahor. He made the camels kneel down outside the city by the well of water at the time of evening, the time that women go out to draw water. He said, "O Lord, the God of my master Abraham, please give me success this day, and show kindness to my master Abraham. Look, I am standing by the spring of water. The daughters of the men of the city are coming out to draw water. Let it happen, that the young lady to whom I will say, 'Please let down your pitcher, that I may drink,' and she will say, 'Drink, and I will also give your camels a drink', let her be the one you have appointed for your servant Isaac. By this I will know that you have shown kindness to my master. "It happened, before he had finished speaking, that look, Rebekah came out, who was born to Bethuel the son of Milcah, the wife of Nahor, Abraham's brother, with her pitcher on her shoulder. The young lady was very beautiful to look at, a virgin, neither had any man known her. She went down to the spring, filled her pitcher, and came up. The servant ran to meet her, and said, "Please give me a drink, a little water from your pitcher." She said, "Drink, my lord." She hurried, and let down her pitcher on her hand, and gave him drink. When she had done giving him drink, she said, "I will also draw for your camels, until they have done drinking. "It happened, as the camels had finished drinking, that the man took a gold ring weighing a beka,* which he put on her nose, and two bracelets for her hands weighing ten shekels of gold and said, "Whose daughter are you? Please tell me. Is there room in your father's house for us to lodge in?" She said to him, "I am the daughter of Bethuel the son of Milcah, whom she bore to Nahor." She said moreover to him, "We have both straw and provender enough, and room to lodge in." The man came into the house, and he unloaded the camels. He gave straw and provender for the camels, and water to wash his feet and the feet of the men who were with him. Food was set before him to eat, but he said, "I will not eat until I have told my message." He said, "Speak on." He said, "I am Abraham's servant. The Lord has blessed my master greatly. He has become great. He has given him flocks and herds, silver and gold, male servants and female servants, and camels and donkeys. Sarah, my master's wife, bore a son to my master when she was old. He has given all that he has to him. My master made me swear, saying, 'You shall not take a wife for my son of the daughters of the Canaanites, in whose land I live, but you shall go to my father's house, and to my relatives, and take a wife for my son.' Then Laban and Bethuel answered, "The thing proceeds from the Lord. We can't speak to you bad or good. Look, Rebekah is before you. Take, and go, and let her be your master's son's wife, as the Lord has spoken." It happened that when Abraham's servant heard their words, he bowed himself down to the earth to the Lord. They said, "We will call the young lady, and ask her." They called Rebekah, and said to her, "Will you go with this man?" She said, "I will go." They sent away Rebekah, their sister, with her nurse, Abraham's servant, and his men. They blessed Rebekah, and said to her, "Our sister, may you be the mother of thousands of ten thousands, and let your descendants possess the gate of those who hate them." Rebekah arose with her ladies. They rode on the camels, and followed the man. The servant took Rebekah, and went his way. Isaac came from the way of Beer Lahai Roi, for he lived in the land of the Negev. Isaac went out to meditate in the field at the evening. He lifted up his eyes, and saw, and, look, there were camels coming. Rebekah lifted up her eyes, and when she saw Isaac, she dismounted from the camel. She said to the servant, "Who is the man who is walking in the field to meet us?" The servant said, "It is my master." She took her veil, and covered herself. The servant told Isaac all the things that he had done. Isaac brought her into his mother Sarah's tent, and took Rebekah, and she became his wife. He loved her. Isaac was comforted after his mother's death.

* Half a shekel, possibly around 122g

Saturday

Ps. 15 (WBS)

Lord, who shall abide in thy tabernacle? who shall dwell in thy holy hill? He that walketh uprightly, and worketh righteousness, and speaketh the truth in his heart. He that backbiteth not with his tongue, nor doeth evil to his neighbour, nor taketh up a reproach against his neighbour. In whose eyes a vile person is condemned; but he honoureth them that fear the Lord. He that sweareth to his own hurt, and changeth not. He that putteth not out his money to usury, nor taketh reward against the innocent. He that doeth these things shall never be moved.

Sunday

Mark 4: 35-41 (NHT)

And on that day, when evening had come, he said to them, "Let us go over to the other side." And leaving the crowd, they took him with them, even as he was, in the boat. And other boats were with him. And a big wind storm arose, and the waves beat into the boat, so much that the boat was already filled. And he himself was in the stern, asleep on the cushion, and they woke him up, and told him, "Teacher, do you not care that we are dying?" And he awoke, and rebuked the wind, and said to the sea, "Peace. Be still." And the wind ceased, and there was a great calm. And he said to them, "Why are you so afraid? Do you still have no faith?" And they were greatly afraid, and said to one another, "Who then is this, that even the wind and the sea obey him?"

Week 9

Monday

Matt.6:19-24 (BBE)

Make no store of wealth for yourselves on earth, where it may be turned to dust by worms and weather, and where thieves may come in by force and take it away, but make a store for yourselves in heaven, where it will not be turned to dust and where thieves do not come in to take it away: For where your wealth is, there will your heart be.

The light of the body is the eye; if then your eye is true, all your body will be full of light. But if your eye is evil, all your body will be dark. If then the light which is in you is dark, how dark it will be!

No man is able to be a servant to two masters: for he will have hate for the one and love for the other, or he will keep to one and have no respect for the other. You may not be servants of God and of wealth.

Tuesday

Isa.26:7-12,17-19; 33:2 (WBS)

The way of the just is uprightness: thou, most upright, dost weigh the path of the just. Yes, in the way of thy judgments, O Lord, have we waited for thee; the desire of our soul is to thy name, and to the remembrance of thee. With my soul have I desired thee in the night; yes, with my spirit within me will I seek thee early: for when thy judgments are in the earth, the inhabitants of the world will learn righteousness. Let favour be shown to the wicked, yet he will not learn righteousness: in the land of uprightness he will deal unjustly, and will not behold the majesty of the Lord. Lord, when thy hand is lifted up, they will not see: but they shall see, and be ashamed for their envy at the people; yes, the fire of thy enemies shall devour them. Lord, thou wilt ordain peace for us: for thou also hast wrought all our works in us. As a woman with child, that draweth near the time of her delivery, is in pain, and crieth out in her pangs; so have we been in thy sight, O Lord .We have been with child, we have been in pain, we have as it were brought forth wind; we have not wrought any deliverance on the earth; neither have the inhabitants of the world fallen. Thy dead men shall live, together with my dead body shall they arise. Awake and sing, ye that dwell in dust: for thy dew is as the dew of herbs, and the earth shall cast out the dead. O Lord, be gracious to us; we have waited for thee: be thou their arm every morning, our salvation also in the time of trouble.

Wednesday

I Cor.5:9-11; 6:9-12,13b,15-20 (NHT)

I wrote to you in my letter to have no company with sexual sinners; yet not at all meaning with the sexual sinners of this world, or with the covetous and extortioners, or with idolaters; for then you would have to leave the world. But as it is, I wrote to you not to associate with anyone who is called a brother who is a sexual sinner, or covetous, or an idolater, or a slanderer, or a drunkard, or an extortioner. Do not even eat with such a person, or do you not know that the unrighteous will not inherit the Kingdom of God? Do not be deceived. Neither the sexually immoral, nor idolaters, nor adulterers, nor effeminate, nor men who have sexual relations with men, nor thieves, nor covetous, nor drunkards, nor slanderers, nor swindlers, will inherit the Kingdom of God. Such were some of you, but you were washed. But you were sanctified. But you were justified in the name of the Lord Jesus Christ, and in the Spirit of our God. "All things are lawful for me," but not all things are expedient. "All things are lawful for me," but I will not be brought under the power of anything.

The body is not for sexual immorality, but for the Lord; and the Lord for the body. Do you not know that your bodies are members of Christ? Should I then take the members of Christ, and make them members of a prostitute? May it never be. Or do you not know that he who is joined to a prostitute is one body? For he says, "The two will become one flesh." But he who is joined to the Lord is one spirit. Flee sexual immorality. "Every sin that a person does is outside the body," but he who commits sexual immorality sins against his own body. Or do you not know that your body is a temple of the Holy Spirit which is in you, which you have from God? You are not your own, for you were bought with a price. Therefore glorify God in your body.

Thursday

Deut 24:10-15, 19 (BBE)

If you let your brother have the use of anything which is yours, do not go into his house and take anything of his as a sign of his debt; but keep outside till he comes out and gives it to you. If he is a poor man, do not keep his property all night; but be certain to give it back to him when the sun goes down, so that he may have his clothing for sleeping in, and will give you his blessing: and this will be put to your account as righteousness before the Lord your God. Do not be hard on a servant who is poor and in need, if he is one of your countrymen or a man from another nation living with you in your land. Give him his payment day by day, not keeping it back over night; for he is poor and his living is dependent on it; and if his cry against you comes to the ears of the Lord, it will be judged as sin in you. When you get in the grain from your field, if some of the grain has been dropped by chance in the field, do not go back and get it, but let it be for the man from a strange land, the child without a father, and the widow: so that the blessing of the Lord your God may be on all the work of your hands.

Friday

Gen.28:10-22 (BBE)

So Jacob went out from Beer-sheba to go to Haran and coming to a certain place, he made it his resting-place for the night, for the sun had gone down; and he took one of the stones which were there, and putting it under his head he went to sleep in that place. He had a dream, and in his dream he saw steps stretching from earth to heaven, and the angels of God were going up and down on them. And he saw the Lord by his side, saying, "I am the Lord, the God of Abraham your father, and the God of Isaac: I will give to you and to your seed this land on which you are sleeping. Your seed will be like the dust of the earth, covering all the land to the west and to the east, to the north and to the south: you and your seed will be a name of blessing to all the families of the earth. And truly, I will be with you, and will keep you wherever you go, guiding you back again to this land; and I will not give you up till I have done what I have said to you." And Jacob, awaking from his sleep, said, "Truly, the Lord is in this place and I was not conscious of it." And fear came on him, and he said, "This is a holy place; this is nothing less than the house of God and the doorway of heaven." And early in the morning Jacob took the stone which had been under his head, and put it up as a pillar and put oil on it. And he gave that place the name of Beth-el, but before that time the town was named Luz. Then Jacob took an oath, and said, "If God will be with me, and keep me safe on my journey, and give me food and clothing to put on, so that I come again to my father's house in peace, then I will take the Lord to be my God, And this stone which I have put up for a pillar will be God's house: and of all you give me, I will give a tenth part to you."

Saturday

Ps.16 (WBS)

Preserve me, O God: for in thee do I put my trust. O my soul, thou hast said to the Lord, Thou art my Lord: my goodness extendeth not to thee but to the saints that are in the earth, and to the excellent, in whom is all my delight. Their sorrows shall be multiplied that hasten after another god: their drink-offerings of blood will I not offer, nor take their names into my lips. The Lord is the portion of my inheritance and of my cup: thou maintainest my lot. The lines have fallen to me in pleasant places; yes, I have a goodly heritage. I will bless the Lord, who hath given me counsel: my reins* also instruct me in the night season. I have set the Lord always before me: because he is at my right hand, I shall not be moved. Therefore my heart is glad, and my glory rejoiceth: my flesh also shall rest in hope. For thou wilt not leave my

soul in hell; neither wilt thou suffer thy Holy One to see corruption. Thou wilt show me the path of life: in thy presence is fullness of joy; at thy right hand are pleasures for evermore.
*conscience

Sunday

Mark 5:21-43 (NHT)

And when Jesus had crossed back over in the boat to the other side, a large crowd was gathered to him; and he was by the sea. One of the rulers of the synagogue, Jairus by name, came; and seeing him, he fell at his feet, and pleaded with him repeatedly, saying, "My little daughter is at the point of death. Please come and lay your hands on her, that she may be made healthy, and live." And he went with him, and a large crowd followed him, and they pressed upon him on all sides. Now a woman, who had an issue of blood for twelve years, and had suffered many things by many physicians, and had spent all that she had, and was no better, but rather grew worse, having heard the things concerning Jesus, came up behind him in the crowd, and touched his clothes. For she said, "If I just touch his clothes, I will be made well." And immediately the flow of her blood was dried up, and she felt in her body that she was healed of her affliction. And immediately Jesus, perceiving in himself that the power had gone out from him, turned around in the crowd, and asked, "Who touched my clothes?" And his disciples said to him, "You see the crowd pressing against you, and you say, 'Who touched me?'" He looked around to see her who had done this thing. But the woman, fearing and trembling, knowing what had been done to her, came and fell down before him, and told him all the truth. And he said to her, "Daughter, your faith has made you well. Go in peace, and be cured of your disease." While he was still speaking, people came from the synagogue ruler's house saying, "Your daughter is dead. Why bother the Teacher any more?" But Jesus, overhearing the message spoken, said to the ruler of the synagogue, "Do not be afraid, only believe." And he allowed no one to follow him, except Peter, James, and John the brother of James. And they came to the synagogue ruler's house, and he saw an uproar, weeping, and great wailing. And when he had entered in, he said to them, "Why do you make an uproar and weep? The child is not dead, but is asleep. And they ridiculed him. But he, having put them all out, took the father of the child, her mother, and those who were with him, and went in where the child was. And taking the child by the hand, he said to her, "Talitha koum," which translated means, "Little girl, I tell you, get up." And immediately the girl rose up and walked, for she was twelve years old. And immediately they were overcome with amazement. And he strictly ordered them that no one should know this, and commanded that something should be given to her to eat.

Week 10

Monday

Matt.6:25-34 (BBE)

So I say to you, Take no thought for your life, about food or drink, or about clothing for your body. Is not life more than food, and the body more than its clothing? See the birds of heaven; they do not put seeds in the earth, they do not get in grain, or put it in storehouses; and your Father in heaven gives them food. Are you not of much more value than they? And which of you by taking thought is able to make himself a cubit taller? And why are you troubled about clothing? See the flowers of the field, how they come up; they do no work, they make no thread: but I say to you that even Solomon in all his glory was not clothed like one of these. If God gives such clothing to the grass of the field, which is here today and tomorrow is put into the oven, will he not much more give you clothing, O you of little faith? Then do not be full of care, saying, 'What are we to have for food or drink?' or, 'With what may we be clothed?' Because the Gentiles go in search of all these things: for your Father in heaven has knowledge that you have need of all these things: But let your first care be for his kingdom and his righteousness; and all these other things will be given to you in addition. Then have no care for tomorrow: tomorrow will take care of itself. Take the trouble of the day as it comes.

Tuesday

Isa.29:13-14; 30:12-13,15,18; 32:1-8 (BBE)

The Lord said, "Because this people come near to me with their mouths, and give honour to me with their lips, but their heart is far from me, and their fear of me is false, a rule given them by the teaching of men; for this cause I will again do a strange thing among this people, a thing to be wondered at: and the wisdom of their wise men will come to nothing, and the sense of their guides will no longer be seen." For this cause the Holy One of Israel says, "Because you will not give ear to this word, and are looking for help in ways of deceit and evil, and are putting your hope in them, this sin will be to you like a crack in a high wall, causing its fall suddenly and in a minute." For the Lord, the Holy One of Israel, said, "In quiet and rest is your salvation: peace and hope are your strength: but you would not have it so."

The Lord will be waiting, so that he may be kind to you; and he will be lifted up, so that he may have mercy on you; for the Lord is a God of righteousness: there is a blessing on all whose hope is in him. See, a king will be ruling in righteousness, and chiefs will give right decisions. A man will be as a safe place from the wind, and a cover from the storm; as rivers of water in a dry place, as the shade of a great rock in a waste land. And the eyes of those who see will not be shut, and those who have hearing will give ear to the word. The man of sudden impulses will become wise in heart, and he whose tongue is slow will get the power of talking clearly. The foolish man will no longer be named noble, and they will not say of the false man that he is a man of honour. For the foolish man will say foolish things, having evil thoughts in his heart, working what is unclean, and talking falsely about the Lord, to keep food from him who is in need of it, and water from him whose soul is desiring it. The designs of the false are evil, purposing the destruction of the poor man by false words, even when he is in the right, but the noble-hearted man has noble purposes, and by these he will be guided.

Wednesday
1Cor.7:8-11,28; 11:3-10; 14:34 (BBE)

I say to the unmarried and to the widows, it is good for them to be even as I am, but if they have not self-control let them get married; for married life is better than the burning of desire. But to the married I give orders, not I but the Lord, that the wife may not go away from her husband - or if she goes away from him, let her keep unmarried, or be united to her husband again- and that the husband may not go away from his wife. If you get married it is not a sin; and if an unmarried woman gets married it is not a sin. But those who do so will have trouble in the flesh. But I will not be hard on you.

It is important for you to keep this fact in mind, that the head of every man is Christ; and the head of the woman is the man, and the head of Christ is God.

Every man who takes part in prayer, or gives teaching as a prophet, with his head covered, puts shame on his head. But every woman who does so with her head unveiled, puts shame on her head: for it is the same as if her hair was cut off. For if a woman is not veiled, let her hair be cut off; but if it is a shame to a woman to have her hair cut off, let her be veiled. For it is not right for a man to have his head covered, because he is the image and glory of God: but the woman is the glory of the man. For the man did not come from the woman, but the woman from the man. And the man was not made for the woman, but the woman for the man. For this reason it is right for the woman to have a sign of authority on her head, because of the angels.

Let women keep quiet in the churches: for it is not right for them to be talking; but let them be under control, as it says in the law.

Thursday
Deut.24:16; 25:1-4 (BBE)

Fathers are not to be put to death for their children or children for their fathers: every man is to be put to death for the sin which he himself has done. If there is an argument between men and they go to law with one another, let the judges give their decision for the upright, and against the wrongdoer. And if the wrongdoer is to undergo punishment by whipping, the judge will give orders for him to go down on his face and be whipped before him, the number of the blows being in relation to his crime. He may be given forty blows, not more; for if more are given, your brother may be shamed before you.

Do not keep the ox from taking the grain when he is crushing it.

Friday

Gen.38:8-10; Num.15:32-36 (BBE)

Then Judah said to Onan, "Go in to your brother's wife and do what it is right for a husband's brother to do; make her your wife and get offspring for your brother." But Onan, seeing that the offspring would not be his, went in to his brother's wife, but let his seed go on to the earth, so that he might not get offspring for his brother. And what he did was evil in the eyes of the Lord, so that he put him to death, like his brother.

Now while the children of Israel were in the waste land, they saw a man who was getting sticks on the Sabbath day. And those who saw him getting sticks took him before Moses and Aaron and all the people. And they had him shut up, because they had no directions about what was to be done with him. Then the Lord said to Moses, "Certainly the man is to be put to death: let him be stoned by all the people outside the tent-circle." So all the people took him outside the tent-circle and he was stoned to death there, as the Lord gave orders to Moses.

Saturday

Ps.17:1,3-8 (WBS)

Hear the right, O Lord, attend to my cry, give ear to my prayer, that goeth not out of feigned lips. Thou hast proved my heart; thou hast visited me in the night; thou hast tried me, and shalt find nothing; I have purposed that my mouth shall not transgress. Concerning the works of men, by the word of thy lips I have kept me from the paths of the destroyer. Uphold my goings in thy paths, that my footsteps slip not. I have called upon thee, for thou wilt hear me, O God: incline thy ear to me, and hear my speech. Show thy wonderful loving-kindness, O thou that savest by thy right hand them who put their trust in thee from those that rise up against them. Keep me as the apple of the eye, hide me under the shade of thy wings.

Sunday

Mark 6:30-44 (NHT)

Then the apostles gathered themselves together to Jesus, and they told him all things, whatever they had done, and whatever they had taught. And he said to them, "Come away by yourselves to an isolated place, and rest awhile." For there were many coming and going, and they had no leisure so much as to eat. So they went away in the boat to an isolated place by themselves. But they saw them going, and many recognized him and ran there on foot from all the cities and they arrived before them. And he came out, saw a large crowd, and he had compassion on them, because they were like sheep without a shepherd, and he began to teach them many things. And when it was late in the day, his disciples came to him, and said, "This place is desolate, and it is late in the day. Send them away, that they may go into the surrounding country and villages, and buy themselves something to eat." But he answered them, "You give them something to eat." And they said to him, "Are we to go and buy two hundred denarii worth of bread, and give them something to eat?" He said to them, "How many loaves do you have? Go see." When they knew, they said, "Five, and two fish." He commanded them that everyone should sit down in groups on the green grass. They sat down in ranks, by hundreds and by fifties. He took the five loaves and the two fish, and looking up to heaven, he blessed and broke the loaves, and he gave to his disciples to set before them, and he divided the two fish among them all. They all ate, and were filled. They took up twelve baskets full of broken pieces and also of the fish. Those who ate the loaves were five thousand men.

Week 11

Monday

Matt.7:1-6 (BBE)

Be not judges of others, and you will not be judged, for as you have been judging, so you will be judged, and with your measure will it be measured to you. And why do you take note of the grain of dust in your brother's eye, but take no note of the bit of wood which is in your eye? Or how will you say to your brother, 'Let me take out the grain of dust from your eye', when you yourself have a bit of wood in your eye? You false one, first take out the bit of wood from your eye, then will you see clearly to take out the grain of dust from your brother's eye.

Do not give that which is holy to the dogs, or put your jewels before pigs, for fear that they will be crushed under foot by the pigs whose attack will then be made against you.

Tuesday

Isa.49:5-6; 50:4-6; 51:7-8 (NHT)

Now says the Lord who formed me from the womb to be his servant, to bring Jacob again to him, and that Israel be gathered to him; for I am honourable in the eyes of the Lord, and my God has become my strength. And he says, "It is too light a thing that you should be my servant to raise up the tribes of Jacob, and to restore the preserved of Israel; I will also give you as a light to the nations, that you may bring salvation to the farthest part of the earth." The Lord GOD has given me the tongue of those who are taught, that I may know how to sustain with a word him who is weary: he wakens morning by morning, he wakens my ear to hear as those who are taught. The Lord GOD has opened my ear, and I was not rebellious, neither turned away backward. I gave my back to those who strike, and my cheeks to those who tore out my beard; I did not cover my face from insults and spitting. "Listen to me, you who know righteousness, the people in whose heart is my law; do not fear the reproach of men, neither be dismayed at their insults. For the moth shall eat them up like a garment, and the worm shall eat them like wool; but my righteousness shall be forever, and my salvation to all generations."

Wednesday
1 Cor.10:16-17; 11:26-29; 10:21 (WBS)

The cup of blessing which we bless, is it not the communion of the blood of Christ? The bread which we break, is it not the communion of the body of Christ? For we being many are one bread, and one body: for we are all partakers of that one bread. For as often as ye eat this bread, and drink this cup, ye do show the Lord's death till he shall come. Wherefore, whoever shall eat this bread, and drink this cup of the Lord unworthily, shall be guilty of the body and blood of the Lord. But let a man examine himself, and so let him eat of that bread, and drink of that cup for he that eateth and drinketh unworthily, eateth and drinketh condemnation to himself, not discerning the Lord's body. Ye cannot drink the cup of the Lord, and the cup of demons: ye cannot be partakers of the Lord's table, and of the table of demons.

Thursday
Deut 7:26; 8:11-14,17-19 (BBE)

You may not take a disgusting thing into your house, and so become cursed with its curse: but keep yourselves from it, turning from it with fear and hate, for it is a cursed thing.

Take care that you are not turned away from the Lord your God and from keeping his orders and decisions and laws which I give you this day: and when you have taken food and are full, and have made fair houses for yourselves and are living in them; and when your herds and your flocks are increased, and your stores of silver and gold, and you have wealth of every sort; take care that your hearts are not lifted up in pride, giving no thought to the Lord your God who took you out of the land of Egypt, out of the prison-house; Say not then, in your hearts, 'My power and the strength of my hands have got me this wealth.' But keep in mind the Lord your God: for it is he who gives you the power to get wealth, so that he may give effect to the agreement which he made by his oath with your fathers, as at this day. And it is certain that if at any time you are turned away from the Lord your God, and go after other gods, to be their servants and to give them worship, destruction will overtake you.

Friday

Gen.39:1-20 (NHT)

Joseph was brought down to Egypt. Potiphar, an officer of Pharaoh's, the captain of the guard, an Egyptian, bought him from the hand of the Ishmaelites that had brought him down there. The Lord was with Joseph, and he was a prosperous man. He was in the house of his master the Egyptian. His master saw that the Lord was with him, and that the Lord made all that he did prosper in his hand. So Joseph found favour in the sight of his master, and served him, and he made him overseer over his house, and all that he had he put into his hand. It happened from the time that he made him overseer in his house, and over all that he had, that the Lord blessed the Egyptian's house for Joseph's sake; and the blessing of the Lord was on all that he had, in the house and in the field. He left all that he had in Joseph's hand. He did not concern himself with anything, except for the food which he ate. Joseph was well-built and handsome. It happened after these things, that his master's wife cast her eyes on Joseph; and she said, "Lie with me." But he refused, and said to his master's wife, "Look, my master doesn't know what is with me in the house, and he has put all that he has into my hand. He isn't greater in this house than I, neither has he kept back anything from me but you, because you are his wife. How then can I do this great wickedness, and sin against God?" As she spoke to Joseph day by day, he did not listen to her, to lie by her, or to be with her. About this time, he went into the house to do his work, and there were none of the men of the house inside. She caught him by his garment, saying, "Lie with me." He left his garment in her hand, and ran outside. When she saw that he had left his garment in her hand, and had run outside, she called to the men of her house, and spoke to them, saying, "Look, he has brought in a Hebrew to us to mock us. He came in to me to lie with me, and I cried with a loud voice. It happened, when he heard that I lifted up my voice and cried, that he left his garment by me, and ran outside." She left his garment by her, until his master came home. She spoke to him according to these words, saying, "The Hebrew servant, whom you have brought to us, came in to me to mock me, and said to me, "Let me lie with you." But when I raised my voice and cried out, he left his garment by me, and ran outside." It happened, when his master heard the words of his wife, which she spoke to him, saying, "This is what your servant did to me," that his anger burned. Joseph's master took him, and put him into the prison, the place where the king's prisoners were bound, and he was there in custody.

Saturday

Ps.18:1-6,16-19,46 (WBS)

I will love thee, O Lord, my strength. The Lord is my rock, and my fortress, and my deliverer; my God, my strength, in whom I will trust; my buckler, and the horn of my salvation, and my high tower. I will call upon the Lord, who is worthy to be praised: so shall I be saved from my enemies. The sorrows of death compassed me, and the floods of ungodly men made me afraid. The sorrows of hell encompassed me: the snares of death seized me. In my distress I called upon the Lord, and cried to my God: he heard my voice out of his temple, and my cry came before him, even into his ears. He sent from above, he took me, he drew me out of many waters. He delivered me from my strong enemy, and from them who hated me: for they were too strong for me. They attacked me in the day of my calamity: but the Lord was my stay. He brought me forth also in a large place; he delivered me, because he delighted in me. The Lord liveth; and blessed be my rock; and let the God of my salvation be exalted.

Sunday

Luke 10:38-42 (BBE)

Now, while they were on their way, he came to a certain town; and a woman named Martha took him into her house.: And she had a sister, by name Mary, who took her seat at the Lord's feet and gave attention to his words.: But Martha had her hands full of the work of the house, and she came to him and said, "Lord, is it nothing to you that my sister has let me do all the work? Say to her that she is to give me some help.": But the Lord, answering, said to her, "Martha, Martha, you are full of care and troubled about such a number of things. Little is needed, or even one thing only: for Mary has taken that good part, which will not be taken away from her."

Week 12

Monday

Matt:7:7-12 (NHT)

"Ask, and it will be given to you. Seek, and you will find. Knock, and it will be opened for you. For everyone who asks receives. He who seeks finds. To him who knocks it will be opened. Or who is there among you, who, if his son will ask him for bread, will give him a stone? Or if he will ask for a fish, who will give him a serpent? If you then, being evil, know how to give good gifts to your children, how much more will your Father who is in heaven give good things to those who ask him. Therefore whatever you desire for people to do to you, do also to them; for this is the Law and the Prophets.

Tuesday

Zech.9:9-11,16; 12:10; 14:9 (WBS)

Rejoice greatly, O daughter of Zion; shout, O daughter of Jerusalem: behold, thy King cometh to thee: he is just, and having salvation; lowly, and riding upon an ass, and upon a colt the foal of an ass. And I will cut off the chariot from Ephraim, and the horse from Jerusalem, and the battle-bow shall be cut off: and he shall speak peace to the heathen: and his dominion shall be from sea to sea, and from the river to the ends of the earth. As for thee also, by the blood of thy covenant I have sent forth thy prisoners out of the pit in which is no water. And the Lord their God will save them in that day as the flock of his people: for they shall be as the stones of a crown, lifted up as an ensign upon his land. And I will pour upon the house of David, and upon the inhabitants of Jerusalem, the spirit of grace and of supplications: and they shall look upon me whom they have pierced, and they shall mourn for him, as one mourneth for his only son, and shall be in bitterness for him, as one that is in bitterness for his first-born. And the Lord will be king over all the earth: in that day will there be one Lord, and his name one.

Wednesday

1 Cor.13 (BBE)

If I make use of the tongues of men and of angels, and have not love, I am like sounding brass, or a loud-tongued bell. And if I have a prophet's power, and have knowledge of all secret things; and if I have all faith, by which mountains may be moved from their place, but have not love, I am nothing. And if I give all my goods to the poor, and if I give my body to be burned, but have not love, it is of no profit to me. Love is never tired of waiting; love is kind; love has no envy; love has no high opinion of itself, love has no pride; Love's ways are ever fair, it takes no thought for itself; it is not quickly made angry, it takes no account of evil; It takes no pleasure in wrongdoing, but has joy in what is true; Love has the power of undergoing all things, having faith in all things, hoping all things. Though the prophet's word may come to an end, tongues come to nothing, and knowledge have no more value, love has no end. For our knowledge is only in part, and the prophet's word gives only a part of what is true: but when that which is complete is come, then that which is in part will be no longer necessary. When I was a child, I made use of a child's language, I had a child's feelings and a child's thoughts: now that I am a man, I have put away the things of a child. For now we see things in a glass, darkly; but then face to face: now my knowledge is in part; then it will be complete, even as God's knowledge of me. But now we still have faith, hope, love, these three; and the greatest of these is love.

Thursday

Lev.16:29-31,6-10,20-22 (BBE)

And let this be an order to you for ever: in the seventh month, on the tenth day, you are to keep yourselves from pleasure and do no sort of work, those who are Israelites by birth and those from other lands who are living among you: For on this day your sin will be taken away and you will be clean: you will be made free from all your sins before the Lord. It is a special Sabbath for you, and you are to keep yourselves from pleasure; it is an order for ever. Aaron is to give the ox of the sin-offering for himself, to make himself and his house free from sin. And he is to take the two goats and put them before the Lord at the door of the Tent of meeting. Aaron will make selection from the two goats by the decision of the Lord, one goat for the Lord and one for Azazel*, and the goat which is marked out for the Lord, let Aaron give for a sin-offering. But the goat for Azazel is to be placed living before the Lord, for the taking away of sin, that it may be sent away for Azazel into the waste land. And when he has done whatever is necessary to make the holy place and the Tent of meeting and the altar free from sin, let him put the living goat before the Lord; And Aaron, placing his two hands on the head of the living goat, will make a public statement over him of all the evil doings of the children of Israel and all their wrongdoing, in all their sins; and he will put them on the head of the goat and send him away, in the care of a man who will be waiting there, into the waste land. And the goat will take all their sins into a land cut off from men, and he will send the goat away into the waste land.

* a demon associated with the desert

Friday

Gen.41:1-7,15,25-27,39-40(BBE)

Now after two years had gone by, Pharaoh had a dream; and in his dream he was by the side of the Nile; and out of the Nile came seven cows, good-looking and fat, and their food was the river-grass. and after them seven other cows came out of the Nile, poor-looking and thin; and they were by the side of the other cows. And the seven thin cows made a meal of the seven fat cows. Then Pharaoh came out of his sleep. But he went to sleep again and had a second dream, in which he saw seven heads of grain, full and good, all on one stem. And after them came up seven other heads, thin and wasted by the east wind. And the seven thin heads made a meal of the good heads. And when Pharaoh was awake he saw it was a dream. And Pharaoh said to Joseph, "I have had a dream, and no one is able to give me the sense of it; now it has come to my ears that you are able to give the sense of a dream when it is put before you." Then Joseph said, "These two dreams have the same sense: God has made clear to Pharaoh what he is about to do. The seven fat cows are seven years, and the seven good heads of grain are seven years: the two have the same sense. The seven thin and poor-looking cows who came up after them are seven years; and the seven heads of grain, dry and wasted by the east wind, are seven years when there will be no food." And Pharaoh said to Joseph, "Seeing that God has made all this clear to you, there is no other man of such wisdom and good sense as you: You, then, are to be over my house, and all my people will be ruled by your word: only as king will I be greater than you."

Saturday
Ps.18:7-15,30-32 (WBS)

Then the earth shook and trembled; the foundations also of the hills moved and were shaken, because he was wroth. There went up a smoke out of his nostrils, and fire out of his mouth devoured: coals were kindled by it. He bowed the heavens also, and came down: and darkness was under his feet. And he rode upon a cherub, and flew; yes, he flew upon the wings of the wind. He made darkness his secret place; his pavilion around him were dark waters and thick clouds of the skies. At the brightness that was before him his thick clouds passed, hail stones and coals of fire. The Lord also thundered in the heavens, and the Highest gave his voice; hail stones and coals of fire. Yes, he sent out his arrows, and scattered them; and he shot out lightnings, and discomfited them. Then the channels of waters were seen, and the foundations of the world were uncovered at thy rebuke, O Lord, at the blast of the breath of thy nostrils. As for God, his way is perfect: the word of the Lord is tried. He is a buckler to all those that trust in him. For who is God save the Lord or who is a rock save our God? It is God that girdeth me with strength, and maketh my way perfect.

Sunday
Matt.21:1-13 (NHT)

When they drew near to Jerusalem, and came to Bethphage, to the Mount of Olives, then Jesus sent two disciples, saying to them, "Go into the village that is opposite you, and immediately you will find a donkey tied, and a colt with her. Untie them, and bring them to me. And if anyone says anything to you, you are to say, 'The Lord needs them,' and immediately he will send them." This took place that it might be fulfilled which was spoken through the prophet, saying, Say to the daughter of Zion, "Look, your King comes to you, humble, and riding on a donkey, on a colt, the foal of a donkey." The disciples went, and did just as Jesus directed them, and brought the donkey and the colt, and placed their clothes on them; and he sat on them. A very large crowd spread their clothes on the road. Others cut branches from the trees, and spread them on the road. The crowds who went before him, and who followed kept shouting, "Hosanna to the son of David. Blessed is he who comes in the name of the Lord. Hosanna in the highest." When he had come into Jerusalem, all the city was stirred up, saying, "Who is this?" The crowds said, "This is the prophet Jesus, from Nazareth of Galilee." Jesus entered into the temple, and drove out all of those who sold and bought in the temple, and overthrew the money changers' tables and the seats of those who sold the doves. He said to them, "It is written, 'My house will be called a house of prayer,' but you have made it a den of robbers."

Week 13 (leading to Easter Sunday)

Monday

John 15:9-17 (BBE)

Even as the Father has given me his love, so I have given my love to you: be ever in my love. If you keep my laws, you will be ever in my love, even as I have kept my Father's laws, and am ever in his love. I have said these things to you so that I may have joy in you and so that your joy may be complete. This is the law I give you: Have love one for another, even as I have love for you. Greater love has no man than this, that a man gives up his life for his friends. You are my friends, if you do what I give you orders to do. No longer do I give you the name of servants; because a servant is without knowledge of what his master is doing: I give you the name of friends, because I have given you knowledge of all the things which my Father has said to me. You did not take me for yourselves, but I took you for myself; and I gave you the work of going about and producing fruit which will be for ever; so that whatever request you make to the Father in my name he may give it to you. So this is my law for you: Have love one for another.

Tuesday

Isa.53:2-12 (WBS)

For he shall grow up before him as a tender plant, and as a root out of a dry ground: he hath no form nor comeliness; and when we shall see him, there is no beauty that we should desire him. He is despised and rejected by men; a man of sorrows, and acquainted with grief: and we hid as it were our faces from him; he was despised, and we esteemed him not. Surely he hath borne our griefs, and carried our sorrows: yet we did esteem him stricken, smitten by God, and afflicted. But he was wounded for our transgression, he was bruised for our iniquities: the chastisement of our peace was upon him; and with his stripes we are healed. All we like sheep have gone astray; we have turned every one to his own way; and the Lord hath laid on him the iniquity of us all. He was oppressed, and he was afflicted, yet he opened not his mouth; he is brought as a lamb to the slaughter, and as a sheep before her shearers is dumb, so he opened not his mouth. He was taken from prison and from judgment: and who shall declare his generation? for he was cut off from the land of the living: for the transgression of my people was he stricken. And he made his grave with the wicked, and with the rich in his death: because he had done no violence, neither was any deceit in his mouth. Yet it pleased the Lord to bruise him; he hath put him to grief: when thou shalt make his soul an offering for sin, he shall see his seed, he shall prolong his days, and the pleasure of the Lord shall prosper in his hand. He shall see of the travail of his soul, and shall be satisfied: by his knowledge shall my righteous servant justify many; for he shall bear their iniquities. Therefore I will divide to him a portion with the great, and he shall divide the spoil with the strong; because he hath poured out his soul to death: and he was numbered with the transgressors; and he bore the sin of many, and made intercession for the transgressors.

Wednesday

Phil 1:27, 2:5-11 (NHT)

Only let your manner of life be worthy of the Good News of Christ, that, whether I come and see you or am absent, I may hear of your state, that you stand firm in one spirit, with one soul striving for the faith of the Good News. Have this in your mind, which was also in Christ Jesus, who, existing in the form of God, did not consider equality with God a thing to be grasped, but emptied himself, taking the form of a servant, being made in the likeness of men. And being found in human form, he humbled himself, becoming obedient to death, yes, the death of the cross. Therefore God also highly exalted him, and gave to him the name which is above every name; that at the name of Jesus every knee should bow, of those in heaven, those on earth, and those under the earth, and that every tongue should confess that Jesus Christ is Lord, to the glory of God the Father.

Thursday

Matt 26:17-49 (NHT)

Now on the first day of unleavened bread, the disciples came to Jesus, saying, "Where do you want us to prepare for you to eat the Passover?" He said, "Go into the city to a certain person, and tell him, 'The Teacher says, "My time is near. I will keep the Passover at your house with my disciples."'" The disciples did as Jesus commanded them, and they prepared the Passover. Now when evening had come, he was reclining at the table with the twelve. As they were eating, he said, "Truly I tell you that one of you will betray me." And they were greatly distressed, and each one began to ask him, "It is not me, is it, Lord?" He answered, "He who dipped his hand with me in the dish, the same will betray me. The Son of Man goes, even as it is written of him, but woe to that man through whom the Son of Man is betrayed. It would be better for that man if he had not been born." Judas, who betrayed him, answered, "It is not me, is it, Rabbi?" He said to him, "You said it." As they were eating, Jesus took bread, gave thanks for it, and broke it. He gave to the disciples, and said, "Take, eat; this is my body." He took a cup, gave thanks, and gave to them, saying, "All of you drink it, for this is my blood of the new covenant, which is poured out for many for the remission of sins. But I tell you that I will not drink of this fruit of the vine from now on, until that day when I drink it anew with you in my Father's Kingdom."

When they had sung the hymn, they went out to the Mount of Olives. Then Jesus said to them, "All of you will be made to stumble because of me tonight, for it is written, 'I will strike the shepherd, and the sheep of the flock will be scattered.' But after I am raised up, I will go before you into Galilee." But Peter answered him, "Even if all will be made to stumble because of you, I will never be made to stumble." Jesus said to him, "Truly I tell you that tonight, before the rooster crows, you will deny me three times." Peter said to him, "Even if I must die with you, I will not deny you." All of the disciples also said likewise. Then Jesus came with them to a place called Gethsemane, and said to his disciples, "Sit here, while I go there and pray." He took with him Peter and the two sons of Zebedee, and began to be sorrowful and severely troubled. Then he said to them, "My soul is exceedingly sorrowful, even to death. Stay here, and watch with me." He went forward a little, fell on his face, and prayed, saying, "My Father, if it is possible, let this cup pass away from me; nevertheless, not what I desire, but what you desire." He came to the disciples, and found them sleeping, and said to Peter, "What, could you not watch with me for one hour? Watch and pray, that you do not enter into temptation. The spirit indeed is willing, but the flesh is weak." Again, a second time he went away, and prayed, saying, "My Father, if this cannot pass away unless I drink it, your desire be done." He came again and found them sleeping, for their eyes were heavy. He left them again, went away, and prayed a third time, saying the same words. Then he came to the disciples, and said to them, "Sleep on now, and take your rest. Look, the hour is near, and the Son of Man is betrayed into the hands of sinners. Arise, let us be going. Look, he who betrays me is near." While he was still speaking, look, Judas, one of the twelve, came, and with him a large crowd with swords and clubs, from the chief priests and elders of the people. Now he who betrayed him gave them a sign, saying, "Whoever I kiss, he is the one. Seize him." Immediately he came to Jesus, and said, "Hail, Rabbi." and kissed him.

Friday

Mark 15:15-23; Luke 23:33-34; Mark 15:26; Luke 23:39-43; Matt.27:39-40; John 19:25-27; Mark 15:33-34; John 19:28-30a; Luke 23:46; Mark 15:38-39 (NHT)

Pilate, wishing to please the crowd, released Barabbas to them, and handed over Jesus, when he had flogged him, to be crucified. The soldiers led him away within the court, which is the Praetorium; and they called together the whole cohort. They clothed him with purple, and weaving a crown of thorns, they put it on him. They began to salute him, "Hail, King of the Jews." They struck his head with a reed, and spat on him, and bowing their knees, did homage to him. When they had mocked him, they took the purple off of him, and put his own garments on him. They led him out to crucify him. And they forced one passing by, Simon of Cyrene, coming from the country, the father of Alexander and Rufus, to go with them, that he might carry his cross.

And they brought him to the place called Golgotha, which is translated, "The place of a skull." They offered him wine mixed with myrrh to drink, but he did not take it. They crucified him there with the criminals, one on the right and the other on the left. And Jesus said, "Father, forgive them, for they do not know what they are doing." Dividing his garments among them, they cast lots. The superscription of his accusation was written over him, "THE KING OF THE JEWS."

One of the criminals who hung there insulted him, saying, "Are you not the Messiah? Save yourself and us." But the other answered, and rebuking him said, "Do you not even fear God, seeing you are under the same condemnation? And we indeed justly, for we receive the due reward for our deeds; but this man has done nothing wrong." And he said, "Jesus, remember me when you come into your Kingdom." And he said to him, "Assuredly I tell you, today you will be with me in Paradise."

Those who passed by blasphemed him, wagging their heads, and saying, "You who destroy the temple, and build it in three days, save yourself. If you are the Son of God, come down from the cross."

But there were standing by the cross of Jesus his mother, and his mother's sister, Mary the wife of Cleopas, and Mary Magdalene. Therefore when Jesus saw his mother, and the disciple whom he loved standing there, he said to his mother, "Woman, look, your son." Then he said to the disciple, "Look, your mother." From that hour, the disciple took her to his own home.

When the sixth hour had come, there was darkness over the whole land until the ninth hour. At the ninth hour Jesus called out with a loud voice, saying, "Eloi, Eloi, lema sabachthani?" which is translated, "My God, my God, why have you forsaken me?" After this, Jesus, knowing that all things were now finished, that the Scripture might be fulfilled, said, "I am thirsty." Now a vessel full of vinegar was set there; so they put a sponge full of the vinegar on hyssop, and held it at his mouth. When Jesus therefore had received the vinegar, he said, "It is finished." He bowed his head. And Jesus, crying with a loud voice, said, "Father, into your hands I commit my spirit." Having said this, he breathed his last. The veil of the temple was torn in two from the top to the bottom. And when the centurion, who stood by opposite him, saw that he cried out like this and breathed his last, he said, "Truly this man was the Son of God."

Saturday

Ps.22:1-11 (WBS)

My God, my God, why hast thou forsaken me? why art thou so far from helping me, and from the words of my roaring? O my God, I cry in the day-time, but thou hearest not; and in the night season, and am not silent. But thou art holy, O thou that inhabitest the praises of Israel. Our fathers trusted in thee: they trusted, and thou didst deliver them. They cried to thee, and were delivered: they trusted in thee, and were not confounded. But I am a worm, and no man; a reproach of men, and despised by the people. All they that see me deride me: they shoot out the lip, they shake the head, saying, He trusted on the Lord that he would deliver him: let him deliver him, seeing he delighted in him. But thou art he that brought me forth into life: thou didst make me hope when I was upon my mother's breasts. I was cast upon thee from my birth: thou art my God from the time I was born. Be not far from me; for trouble is near; for there is none to help.

Sunday

Mark 16:1-16 (NHT)

When the Sabbath was past, Mary Magdalene, and Mary the mother of James, and Salome, bought spices, that they might come and anoint him. Very early on the first day of the week, they came to the tomb when the sun had risen. They were saying among themselves, "Who will roll away the stone from the door of the tomb for us?" for it was very big. Looking up, they saw that the stone was rolled back. Entering into the tomb, they saw a young man sitting on the right side, dressed in a white robe, and they were amazed. He said to them, "Do not be amazed. You seek Jesus, the Nazarene, who has been crucified. He has risen. He is not here. Look, the place where they put him. But go, tell his disciples and Peter, 'He goes before you into Galilee. There you will see him, as he said to you.'" They went out, and fled from the tomb, for trembling and astonishment had come on them. They said nothing to anyone; for they were afraid. Now when he had risen early on the first day of the week, he appeared first to Mary Magdalene, from whom he had cast out seven demons. She went and told those who had been with him, as they mourned and wept. When they heard that he was alive, and had been seen by her, they disbelieved. And after these things he appeared in another form to two of them, as they walked on their way into the country. And they went away and told it to the rest. They did not believe them, either. Afterward he was revealed to the eleven themselves as they were reclining, and he rebuked them for their unbelief and hardness of heart, because they did not believe those who had seen him after he had risen. And he said to them, "Go into all the world, and proclaim the Good News to the whole creation. He who believes and is baptized will be saved; but he who disbelieves will be condemned."

Week 14

Monday

Matt.7:13-20 (BBE)

Go in by the narrow door; for wide is the door and open is the way which goes to destruction, and great numbers go in by it. For narrow is the door and hard the road to life, and only a small number make discovery of it. Be on the watch for false prophets, who come to you in sheep's clothing, but inside they are cruel wolves. By their fruits you will get knowledge of them. Do men get grapes from thorns or figs from thistles? Even so, every good tree gives good fruit; but the bad tree gives evil fruit. It is not possible for a good tree to give bad fruit, and a bad tree will not give good fruit. Every tree which does not give good fruit is cut down and put in the fire. So by their fruits you will get knowledge of them.

Tuesday

Isa.35:1-10 (BBE)

The waste land and the dry places will be glad; the lowland will have joy and be full of flowers. It will be flowering like the rose; it will be full of delight and songs; the glory of Lebanon will be given to it; the pride of Carmel and Sharon: they will see the glory of the Lord, the power of our God. Make strong the feeble hands, give support to the shaking knees. Say to those who are full of fear, Be strong and take heart: see, your God will give punishment; the reward of God will come; he himself will come to be your saviour. Then the eyes of the blind will see, and the ears which are stopped will be open. Then will the feeble-footed be jumping like a roe, and the voice which was stopped will be loud in song: for in the waste land streams will be bursting out, and waters in the dry places. And the burning sand will become a pool, and the dry earth springs of waters: the fields where the sheep take their food will become wet land, and water-plants will take the place of grass. And a highway will be there; its name will be, The Holy Way; the unclean and the sinner may not go over it, and those who go on it will not be turned out of the way by the foolish. No lion will be there, or any cruel beast; they will not be seen there; but those for whom the Lord has given a price, Even those whom he has made free, will come back again; they will come with songs to Zion; on their heads will be eternal joy; delight and joy will be theirs, and sorrow and sounds of grief will be gone for ever.

Wednesday

I Cor 12:12-13,7,17-18,25-26; 3:16-17; 8:1b-3 (BBE)

For as the body is one, and has a number of parts, and all the parts make one body, so is Christ. For through the baptism of the one Spirit we were all formed into one body, Jews or Greeks, servants or free men, and were all made full of the same Spirit. And to every man some form of the

Spirit's working is given for the common good. If all the body was an eye, where would be the hearing? If all was hearing, where would be the smelling? But now God has put every one of the parts in the body as it was pleasing to him so that there might be no division in the body; but all the parts might have the same care for one another. And if there is pain in one part of the body, all the parts will be feeling it; or if one part is honoured, all the parts will be glad.

Do you not see that you are God's holy house, and that the Spirit of God has his place in you? If anyone makes the house of God unclean, God will put an end to him; for the house of God is holy, and you are his house.

We all seem to ourselves to have knowledge. Knowledge gives pride, but love gives true strength. If anyone seems to himself to have knowledge, so far he has not the right sort of knowledge about anything; but if anyone has love for God, God has knowledge of him

Thursday
Ex.21:12-17 (BBE)

He who gives a man a death-blow is himself to be put to death. But if he had no evil purpose against him, and God gave him into his hand, I will give you a place to which he may go in flight. But if a man makes an attack on his neighbour on purpose, to put him to death by deceit, you are to take him from my altar and put him to death. Any man who gives a blow to his father or his mother is certainly to be put to death. Any man who gets another into his power in order to get a price for him is to be put to death, if you take him in the act. Any man cursing his father or his mother is to be put to death.

Friday
Ex.1:6-2:10 (BBE)

Then Joseph came to his end, and all his brothers, and all that generation. And the children of Israel were fertile, increasing very greatly in numbers and in power; and the land was full of them. Now a new king came to power in Egypt, who had no knowledge of Joseph. And he said to his people, "See, the people of Israel are greater in number and in power than we are: Let us take care for fear that their numbers may become even greater, and if there is a war, they may be joined with those who are against us, and make an attack on us, and go up out of the land." So they put overseers of forced work over them, in order to make their strength less by the weight of their work. And they made store-towns for Pharaoh, Pithom and Raamses. But the more cruel they were to them, the more their number increased, till all the land was full of them. And the children of Israel were hated by the Egyptians. And they gave the children of Israel even harder work to do: And made their lives bitter with hard work, making building-material and bricks, and doing all sorts of work in the fields under the hardest conditions. And the king of Egypt said to the Hebrew women who gave help at the time of childbirth (the name of the one was Shiphrah and the name of the other Puah), "When you are looking after the Hebrew women in childbirth, if it is a son you are to put him to death; but if it is a daughter, she may go on living." But the women had the fear of God, and did not do as the king of Egypt said, but let the male children go on living. And the king of Egypt sent for the women, and said to them, "Why have you done this, and let the male children go on living?" And they said to Pharaoh, "Because the Hebrew women are not like the Egyptian women, for they are strong, and the birth takes place before we come to them." And the blessing of God was on these women: and the people were increased in number and became very strong. And because the women who took care of the Hebrew mothers had the fear of God, he gave them families. And Pharaoh gave orders to all his people, saying, "Every son who comes to birth is to be put into the river, but every daughter may go on living."

Now a man of the house of Levi took as his wife a daughter of Levi. And she became with child and gave birth to a Son; and when she saw that he was a beautiful child, she kept him secretly for three months. And when she was no longer able to keep him secret, she made him a basket out of the stems of water-plants, pasting sticky earth over it to keep the water out; and placing the baby in it she put it among the plants by the edge of the Nile. And his sister took her place at a distance to see what would become of him. Now Pharaoh's daughter came down to the Nile to take a bath, while her women were walking by the riverside; and she saw the basket among the river-plants, and sent her servant-girl to get it. And opening it, she saw the child, and he was crying. And she had pity on him, and said, This is one of the Hebrews' children. Then his sister said to Pharaoh's daughter, "May I go and get you one of the Hebrew women to give him the breast?" And Pharaoh's daughter said to her, "Go." And the girl went and got the child's mother. And Pharaoh's daughter said to her, "Take the child away and give it milk for me, and I will give you payment." And the woman took the child and gave it milk at her breast. And when the child was older, she took him to Pharaoh's daughter and he became her son, and she gave him the name Moses, because, she said, I took him out of the water.

Saturday
Ps.22:1,14-19 (WBS)

My God, my God, why hast thou forsaken me? why art thou so far from helping me, and from the words of my roaring? I am poured out like water, and all my bones are out of joint: my heart is like wax; it is melted in the midst of my bowels. My strength is dried up like a potsherd; and my tongue cleaveth to my jaws; and thou hast brought me into the dust of death. For dogs have compassed me: the assembly of the wicked have enclosed me: they pierced my hands and my feet. I may number all my bones: they look and stare upon me. They part my garments among them, and cast lots upon my vesture. But be not thou far from me, O Lord: O my strength, haste thee to help me.

Sunday

John 20:24-31 (NHT)

Thomas, one of the twelve, called Didymus, was not with them when Jesus came. The other disciples therefore said to him, "We have seen the Lord." But he said to them, "Unless I see in his hands the mark of the nails, and put my finger into the mark of the nails, and put my hand into his side, I will not believe." After eight days again his disciples were inside, and Thomas was with them. Jesus came, the doors being locked, and stood in the midst, and said, "Peace be to you." Then he said to Thomas, "Put your finger here, and observe my hands. Reach out your hand, and put it into my side; and do not be unbelieving, but believing." Thomas answered and said to him, "My Lord and my God." Jesus said to him, "Because you have seen me, you have believed. Blessed are those who have not seen, and have believed." Therefore Jesus did many other signs in the presence of his disciples, which are not written in this book; but these are written, that you may believe that Jesus is the Messiah, the Son of God, and that believing you may have life in his name.

Week 15

Monday

Matt.7:21-27 (BBE)

Not everyone who says to me, Lord, Lord, will go into the kingdom of heaven; but he who does the pleasure of my Father in heaven. A great number will say to me on that day, Lord, Lord, were we not prophets in your name, and did we not by your name send out evil spirits, and by your name do works of power? And then will I say to them, I never had knowledge of you: go from me, you workers of evil. Everyone, then, to whom my words come and who does them, will be like a wise man who made his house on a rock; And the rain came down and there was a rush of waters and the winds were driving against that house, but it was not moved; because it was based on the rock. And everyone to whom my words come and who does them not, will be like a foolish man who made his house on sand; And the rain came down and there was a rush of waters and the winds were driving against that house; and it came down and great was its fall.

Tuesday

Isa.38:9-19 (WBS)

The writing of Hezekiah king of Judah, when he had been sick, and had recovered from his sickness: I said in the cutting off of my days, I shall go to the gates of the grave: I am deprived of the residue of my years. I said, I shall not see the Lord, even the Lord, in the land of the living: I shall behold man no more with the inhabitants of the world. My age hath departed, and is removed from me as a shepherd's tent: I have cut off like a weaver my life: he will cut me off with pining sickness: from day even to night wilt thou make an end of me. I reckoned till morning, that, as a lion, so will he break all my bones: from day even to night wilt thou make an end of me. Like a crane or a swallow, so I chattered: I mourned as a dove: my eyes fail with looking upward: O Lord, I am oppressed; undertake for me. What shall I say? he hath both spoken to me, and himself hath done it: I shall go softly all my years in the bitterness of my soul. O Lord, by these things men live, and in all these things is the life of my spirit: so wilt thou recover me, and make me to live. Behold, for peace I had great bitterness: but thou hast in love to my soul delivered it from the pit of corruption: for thou hast cast all my sins behind thy back. For the grave cannot praise thee, death can not celebrate thee: they that go down into the pit cannot hope for thy truth. The living, the living, he shall praise thee, as I do this day: the father to the children shall make known thy truth.

Wednesday
1 Cor.15:20-22,42-44,50-53 (NHT)

But now Christ has been raised from the dead, the first fruits of those who are asleep. For since death came by man, the resurrection of the dead also came by man. For as in Adam all die, so also in Christ all will be made alive. There is one glory of the sun, another glory of the moon, and another glory of the stars; for one star differs from another star in glory. So also is the resurrection of the dead. It is sown in corruption; it is raised in incorruption. It is sown in dishonour; it is raised in glory. It is sown in weakness; it is raised in power. It is sown a natural body; it is raised a spiritual body. There is a natural body and there is also a spiritual body. Now I say this, brothers, that flesh and blood cannot inherit the Kingdom of God; neither does corruption inherit incorruption. Look, I tell you a mystery. We will not all sleep, but we will all be changed, in a moment, in the twinkling of an eye, at the last trumpet. For the trumpet will sound, and the dead will be raised incorruptible, and we will be changed. For this corruptible must put on incorruption, and this mortal must put on immortality.

Thursday
Ex.21:18-25 (BBE)

If, in a fight, one man gives another a blow with a stone, or with the shut hand, not causing his death, but making him keep in bed; If he is able to get up again and go about with a stick, the other will be let off; only he will have to give him payment for the loss of his time, and see that he is cared for till he is well. If a man gives his man-servant or his woman-servant blows with a rod, causing death, he is certainly to undergo punishment. But, at the same time, if the servant goes on living for a day or two, the master is not to get punishment, for the servant is his property. If men, while fighting, do damage to a woman with child, causing the loss of the child, but no other evil comes to her, the man will have to make payment up to the amount fixed by her husband, in agreement with the decision of the judges. But if damage comes to her, let life be given in payment for life, Eye for eye, tooth for tooth, hand for hand, foot for foot,25 Burning for burning, wound for wound, blow for blow.

Friday

Ex.3:1-11,13-14; 4:1-13 (NHT)

Now Moses was keeping the flock of Jethro, his father-in-law, the priest of Midian, and he led the flock to the back of the wilderness, and came to God's mountain, to Horeb. The angel of the Lord appeared to him in a flame of fire out of the midst of a bush. He looked, and look, the bush burned with fire, and the bush was not consumed. Moses said, "I will turn aside now, and see this great sight, why the bush is not burnt." When the Lord saw that he turned aside to see, God called to him out of the midst of the bush, and said, "Moses. Moses." He said, "Here I am." He said, "Do not come close. Take your sandals off of your feet, for the place you are standing on is holy ground." Moreover he said, "I am the God of your fathers, the God of Abraham, and the God of Isaac, and the God of Jacob." Moses hid his face; for he was afraid to look at God. The Lord said, "I have surely seen the affliction of my people who are in Egypt, and have heard their cry because of their taskmasters, for I know their sorrows. I have come down to deliver them out of the hand of the Egyptians, and to bring them up out of that land to a good and large land, to a land flowing with milk and honey; to the place of the Canaanites, and the Hittites, and the Amorites, and the Perizzites, and the Hivites, and the Jebusites. Now, look, the cry of the children of Israel has come to me. Moreover I have seen the oppression with which the Egyptians oppress them. Come now therefore, and I will send you to Pharaoh, that you may bring forth my people, the children of Israel, out of Egypt." And Moses said to God, "Who am I, that I should go to Pharaoh, and that I should bring forth the children of Israel out of Egypt?" And Moses said to God, "Look, when I come to the children of Israel, and tell them, 'The God of your fathers has sent me to you;' and they ask me, 'What is his name?' What should I tell them?" And God said to Moses, "I AM THAT I AM," and he said, "You shall tell the children of Israel this: 'I AM has sent me to you.'" Moses answered, "But, look, they will not believe me, nor listen to my voice; for they will say, 'The Lord has not appeared to you.'" The Lord said to him, "What is that in your hand?" He said, "A rod." He said, "Throw it on the ground." He threw it on the ground, and it became a serpent; and Moses ran away from it. The Lord said to Moses, "Put forth your hand, and take it by the tail." He put forth his hand, and laid hold of it, and it became a rod in his hand. "That they may believe that the Lord, the God of their fathers, the God of Abraham, the God of Isaac, and the God of Jacob, has appeared to you." The Lord said furthermore to him, "Now put your hand inside your cloak." He put his hand inside his cloak, and when he took it out, look, his hand was leprous, as white as snow. He said, "Put your hand inside your cloak again." He put his hand inside his cloak again, and when he took it out of his cloak, look, it had turned again as his other flesh. "It will happen, if they will neither believe you nor listen to the voice of the first sign, that they will believe the voice of the latter sign. It will happen, if they will not believe even these two signs, neither listen to your voice, that you shall take of the water of the river, and pour it on the dry land. The water which you take out of the river will become blood on the dry land." Moses said to the Lord, "Please, Lord, I am not eloquent, neither before now, nor since you have spoken to your servant; for I am slow of speech, and of a slow tongue." The Lord said to him, "Who made man's mouth? Or who makes one mute, or deaf, or seeing, or blind? Isn't it I, the Lord? Now therefore go, and I will be with your mouth, and teach you what you shall speak." He said, "Oh, Lord, please send someone else."

Saturday

Ps.19 (WBS)

The heavens declare the glory of God; and the firmament showeth the work of his hands. Day to day uttereth speech, and night to night showeth knowledge. There is no speech nor language, where their voice is not heard. Their line hath gone out through all the earth, and their words to the end of the world. In them hath he set a tabernacle for the sun, Which is as a bridegroom coming out of his chamber, and rejoiceth as a strong man to run a race. His going forth is from the end of the heaven, and his circuit to the ends of it: and there is nothing hid from his heat. The law of the Lord is perfect, converting the soul: the testimony of the Lord is sure, making wise the simple. The statutes of the Lord are right, rejoicing the heart: the commandment of the Lord is pure, enlightening the eyes. The fear of the Lord is clean, enduring for ever: the judgments of the Lord are true and righteous altogether. More to be desired are they than gold, yes, than much fine gold: sweeter also than honey and the honey-comb. Moreover, by them is thy servant warned: and in keeping of them there is great reward. Who can understand his errors? cleanse thou me from secret faults. Keep back thy servant also from presumptuous sins; let them not have dominion over me: then shall I be upright, and I shall be innocent from the great transgression. Let the words of my mouth, and the meditation of my heart, be acceptable in thy sight, O Lord, my strength, and my redeemer.

Sunday

John 21:1-17 (NHT)

After these things, Jesus revealed himself again to the disciples at the sea of Tiberias. He revealed himself this way. Simon Peter, Thomas called Didymus, Nathanael of Cana in Galilee, and the sons of Zebedee, and two others of his disciples were together. Simon Peter said to them, "I'm going fishing." They told him, "We are also coming with you." They went out, and entered into the boat. That night, they caught nothing. But when day had already come, Jesus stood on the beach, yet the disciples did not know that it was Jesus. Jesus therefore said to them, "Children, have you anything to eat?" They answered him, "No." He said to them, "Cast the net on the right side of the boat, and you will find some." They cast it therefore, and now they weren't able to draw it in for the multitude of fish. That disciple therefore whom Jesus loved said to Peter, "It's the Lord." So when Simon Peter heard that it was the Lord, he wrapped his coat around him (for he was naked), and threw himself into the sea. But the other disciples came in the little boat (for they were not far from the land, but about two hundred cubits away), dragging the net full of fish. So when they got out on the land, they saw a fire of coals there, and fish placed on it, and bread. Jesus said to them, "Bring some of the fish which you have just caught." Simon Peter went up, and drew the net to land, full of great fish, one hundred fifty-three; and even though there were so many, the net was not torn. Jesus said to them, "Come and eat breakfast." None of the disciples dared inquire of him, "Who are you?" knowing that it was the Lord. Then Jesus came and took the bread, gave it to them, and the fish likewise. This is now the third time that Jesus was revealed to his disciples, after he had risen from the dead. So when they had eaten their breakfast, Jesus said to Simon Peter, "Simon, son of John, do you love me more than these?" He said to him, "Yes, Lord; you know that I have affection for you." He said to him, "Feed my lambs." He said to him again a second time, "Simon, son of John, do you love me?" He said to him, "Yes, Lord; you know that I have affection for you." He said to him, "Tend my sheep." He said to him the third time, "Simon, son of John, do you have affection for me?" Peter was grieved because he asked him the third time, "Do you have affection for me?" He said to him, "Lord, you know everything. You know that I have affection for you." Jesus said to him, "Feed my sheep."

Week 16

Monday

Matt.12:30-37

Whoever is not with me is against me; and he who does not take part with me in getting people together, is driving them away. So I say to you, Every sin and every evil word against God will have forgiveness; but for evil words against the Spirit there will be no forgiveness. And whoever says a word against the Son of man, will have forgiveness; but whoever says a word against the Holy Spirit, will not have forgiveness in this life or in that which is to come. Make the tree good, and its fruit good; or make the tree bad, and its fruit bad; for by its fruit you will get knowledge of the tree. You offspring of snakes, how are you, being evil, able to say good things? because out of the heart's store come the words of the mouth. The good man out of his good store gives good things; and the evil man out of his evil store gives evil things. And I say to you that in the day when they are judged, men will have to give an account of every foolish word they have said. For by your words will your righteousness be seen, and by your words you will be judged.

Tuesday

Isa.40:1-8 (NHT)

"Comfort, comfort my people," says your God. "Speak tenderly to Jerusalem; and call out to her that her warfare is accomplished, that her iniquity is pardoned, that she has received of the Lord's hand double for all her sins." The voice of one who calls out in the wilderness, "Prepare the way of the Lord. Make his roads straight. Every valley will be filled, and every mountain and hill will be made low, and the uneven will be made level, and the rough places a plain. And the glory of the Lord will be revealed, and all flesh will see the salvation of God together; for the mouth of the Lord has spoken." The voice of one saying, "Cry." And I said, "What shall I cry?" "All flesh is like grass, and all its glory is like the flower of the field. The grass withers, the flower fades, because the Lord's breath blows on it. Surely the people are like grass. The grass withers, the flower fades, but the word of the Lord stands forever."

Wednesday

2 Cor.4:4-10, 16-18 (BBE)

The god of this world has made blind the minds of those who have not faith, so that the light of the good news of the glory of Christ, who is the image of God, might not be shining on them. For our preaching is not about ourselves, but about Christ Jesus as Lord, and ourselves as your servants through Jesus. Seeing that it is God who said, 'Let light be shining out of the dark', who has put in our hearts the light of the knowledge of the glory of God in the face of Jesus Christ. But we have this wealth in vessels of earth, so that it may be seen that the power comes not from us but from God; Troubles are round us on every side, but we are not shut in; things are hard for us, but we see a way out of them; We are cruelly attacked, but not without hope; we are made low, but we are not without help; In our bodies there is ever the mark of the death of Jesus, so that the life of Jesus may be seen in our bodies. For which cause we do not give way to weariness; but though our outer man is getting feebler, our inner man is made new day by day. For our present trouble, which is only for a short time, is working out for us a much greater weight of glory; While our minds are not on the things which are seen, but on the things which are not seen: for the things which are seen are for a time; but the things which are not seen are eternal.

Thursday

Ex.21:28-32 (BBE)

If an ox comes to be the cause of death to a man or a woman, the ox is to be stoned, and its flesh may not be used for food; but the owner will not be judged responsible. But if the ox has frequently done such damage in the past, and the owner has had word of it and has not kept it under control, so that it has been the cause of the death of a man or woman, not only is the ox to be stoned, but its owner is to be put to death. If a price is put on his life, let him make payment of whatever price is fixed. If the death of a son or of a daughter has been caused, the punishment is to be in agreement with this rule. If the death of a man-servant or of a woman-servant is caused by the ox, the owner is to give their master thirty shekels of silver, and the ox is to be stoned.

Friday

Ex.7:14-18,20;8:1-2,6,16-17,20-24; 9:1-6,8-10,13,17-18,25-26; 10:3-5,13-15,21-22; 11:4-5 (NHT)

The Lord said to Moses, "Pharaoh's heart is stubborn. He refuses to let the people go. Go to Pharaoh in the morning. Look, he goes out to the water; and you shall stand by the river's bank to meet him; and the rod which was turned to a serpent you shall take in your hand. You shall tell him, 'The Lord, God of the Hebrews, has sent me to you, saying, "Let my people go, that they may serve me in the wilderness:" and look, until now you haven't listened. Thus says the Lord, "In this you shall know that I am the Lord. Look, I will strike with the rod that is in my hand on the waters which are in the river, and they shall be turned to blood. The fish that are in the river shall die, and the river shall become foul; and the Egyptians shall loathe to drink water from the river."'" Moses and Aaron did so, as the Lord commanded; and he lifted up the rod, and struck the waters that were in the river, in the sight of Pharaoh, and in the sight of his servants; and all the waters that were in the river were turned to blood.

The Lord spoke to Moses, Go in to Pharaoh, and tell him, "This is what the Lord says, 'Let my people go, that they may serve me. If you refuse to let them go, look, I will plague all your borders with frogs: Aaron stretched out his hand over the waters of Egypt; and the frogs came up, and covered the land of Egypt.

The Lord said to Moses, "Tell Aaron, 'Stretch out your hand with your rod, and strike the dust of the earth, that it may become lice throughout all the land of Egypt.'" They did so; and Aaron stretched out his hand with his rod, and struck the dust of the earth, and there were lice on man, and on animal; all the dust of the earth became lice throughout all the land of Egypt.

The Lord said to Moses, "Rise up early in the morning, and stand before Pharaoh; look, he comes forth to the water; and tell him, 'This is what the Lord says, "Let my people go, that they may serve me. Else, if you will not let my people go, look, I will send swarms of flies on you, and on your servants, and on your people, and into your houses: and the houses of the Egyptians shall be full of swarms of flies, and also the ground whereon they are. I will set apart in that day the land of Goshen, in which my people dwell, that no swarms of flies shall be there; to the end you may know that I am the Lord in the midst of the earth. I will put a division between my people and your people: by tomorrow shall this sign be.'" The Lord did so; and there came grievous swarms of flies into the house of Pharaoh, and into his servants' houses: and in all the land of Egypt the land was corrupted by reason of the swarms of flies.

Then the Lord said to Moses, "Go in to Pharaoh, and tell him, 'This is what the Lord, the God of the Hebrews, says: "Let my people go, that they may serve me. For if you refuse to let them go, and hold them still, look, the hand of the Lord is on your livestock which are in the field, on the horses, on the donkeys, on the camels, on the herds, and on the flocks with a very grievous pestilence. The Lord will make a distinction between the livestock of Israel and the livestock of Egypt; and there shall nothing die of all that belongs to the children of Israel.'" The Lord appointed a set time, saying, "Tomorrow the Lord shall do this thing in the land." The Lord did that thing on the next day; and all the livestock of Egypt died, but of the livestock of the children of Israel, not one died.

The Lord said to Moses and to Aaron, "Take to you handfuls of ashes of the furnace, and let Moses sprinkle it toward the sky in the sight of Pharaoh. It shall become small dust over all the land of Egypt, and shall be a boil breaking forth with boils on man and on animal, throughout all the land of Egypt." They took ashes of the furnace, and stood before Pharaoh; and Moses sprinkled it up toward the sky; and it became a boil breaking forth with boils on man and on animal.

The Lord said to Moses, "Rise up early in the morning, and stand before Pharaoh, and tell him, 'This is what the Lord, the God of the Hebrews, says: "Let my people go, that they may serve me. as you still exalt yourself against my people, that you won't let them go. Look, tomorrow about this time I will cause it to rain a very grievous hail, such as has not been in Egypt since the day it was founded even until now. The hail struck throughout all the land of Egypt all that was in the field, both man and animal; and the hail struck every plant of the field, and broke every tree of the field. Only in the land of Goshen, where the children of Israel were, there was no hail.

Moses and Aaron went in to Pharaoh, and said to him, "This is what the Lord, the God of the Hebrews, says: 'How long will you refuse to humble yourself before me? Let my people go, that they may serve me. Or else, if you refuse to let my people go, look, tomorrow I will bring locusts into your country, and they shall cover the surface of the earth, so that one won't be able to see the earth. They shall eat the residue of that which has escaped, which remains to you from the hail, and shall eat every tree which grows for you out of the field. Moses stretched forth his rod over the land of Egypt, and the Lord brought an east wind on the land all that day, and all the night; and when it was morning, the east wind brought the locusts. The locusts went up over all the land of Egypt, and rested in all the borders of Egypt. They were very grievous. Before them there were no such locusts as they, neither after them shall be such. For they covered the surface of the whole earth, so that the land was destroyed, and they ate every plant of the land, and all the fruit of the trees which the hail had left. There remained nothing green, either tree or plant of the field, through all the land of Egypt.

The Lord said to Moses, "Stretch out your hand toward the sky, that there may be darkness over the land of Egypt, even darkness which may be felt." Moses stretched forth his hand toward the sky, and there was a thick darkness in all the land of Egypt three days.

And Moses said, "This is what the Lord says: 'About midnight I will go out into the midst of Egypt, and all the firstborn in the land of Egypt shall die, from the firstborn of Pharaoh who sits on his throne, even to the firstborn of the female servant who is behind the mill; and all the firstborn of livestock.

Saturday
Ps.23 (WBS)

The Lord is my shepherd; I shall not want. He maketh me to lie down in green pastures: he leadeth me beside the still waters. He restoreth my soul: he leadeth me in the paths of righteousness for his name's sake. Yes, though I walk through the valley of the shades of death, I will fear no evil: for thou art with me; thy rod and thy staff they comfort me Thou preparest a table before me in the presence of my enemies: thou anointest my head with oil; my cup runneth over. Surely goodness and mercy shall follow me all the days of my life: and I will dwell in the house of the Lord for ever.

Sunday
Mark 16:9-16,19-20 (NHT)

Now when he had risen early on the first day of the week, he appeared first to Mary Magdalene, from whom he had cast out seven demons. She went and told those who had been with him, as they mourned and wept. When they heard that he was alive, and had been seen by her, they disbelieved. And after these things he appeared in another form to two of them, as they walked on their way into the country. And they went away and told it to the rest. They did not believe them, either. Afterward he was revealed to the eleven themselves as they were reclining, and he rebuked them for their unbelief and hardness of heart, because they did not believe those who had seen him after he had risen. And he said to them, "Go into all the world, and proclaim the Good News to the whole creation. He who believes and is baptized will be saved; but he who disbelieves will be condemned. So then the Lord Jesus, after he had spoken to them, was taken up into heaven, and sat down at the right hand of God. And they went out and preached everywhere, the Lord working with them and confirming the message by the signs that followed.

Week 17

Monday

Matt.15:10,17-20 (BBE)

And he got the people together and said to them, Give ear, and let my words be clear to you: Do you not see that whatever goes into the mouth goes on into the stomach, and is sent out as waste? But the things which come out of the mouth come from the heart; and they make a man unclean. For out of the heart come evil thoughts, the taking of life, broken faith between the married, unclean desires of the flesh, taking of property, false witness, bitter words: These are the things which make a man unclean; but to take food with unwashed hands does not make a man unclean.

Tuesday

Isa.40:9-12,25-26,28-31 (NHT)

You who tell good news to Zion, go up on a high mountain. You who tell good news to Jerusalem, lift up your voice with strength. Lift it up. Do not be afraid. Say to the cities of Judah, "Look, your God." Look, the Lord GOD will come as a mighty one, and his arm will rule for him. Look, his reward is with him, and his recompense before him. He will feed his flock like a shepherd. He will gather the lambs in his arm, and carry them in his bosom. He will gently lead those who have their young. Who has measured the waters in the hollow of his hand, and marked off the sky with his span, and calculated the dust of the earth in a measure, and weighed the mountains in scales, and the hills in a balance? "To whom then will you liken me? Who is my equal?" says the Holy One. Lift up your eyes on high, and see who has created these, who brings out their host by number. He calls them all by name; by the greatness of his might, and because he is strong in power, not one is lacking. And now, haven't you known? Haven't you heard? The everlasting God, the Lord, the Creator of the farthest parts of the earth, doesn't faint. He isn't weary. His understanding is unsearchable. He gives power to the weak. He increases the strength of him who has no might. Even the youths faint and get weary, and the young men utterly fall; But those who wait for the Lord will renew their strength. They will mount up with wings like eagles. They will run, and not be weary. They will walk, and not faint.

Wednesday

2 Cor.5:1-7,17-21 (BBE)

For we are conscious that if this our tent of flesh is taken down, we have a building from God, a house not made with hands, eternal, in heaven. For in this we are crying in weariness, greatly desiring to be clothed with our house from heaven: So that our spirits may not be unclothed. For truly, we who are in this tent do give out cries of weariness, for the weight of care which is on us; not because we are desiring to be free from the body, but so that we may have our new body, and death may be overcome by life. Now he who has made us for this very thing is God, who has given us the Spirit as a witness of what is to come. So, then, we are ever without fear, and though conscious that while we are in the body we are away from the Lord, For we are walking by faith, not by seeing. So if any man is in Christ, he is in a new world: the old things have come to an end; they have truly become new. But all things are of God, who has made us at peace with himself through Christ, and has given to us the work of making peace; That is, that God was in Christ making peace between the world and himself, not putting their sins to their account, and having given to us the preaching of this news of peace. So we are the representatives of Christ, as if God was making a request to you through us: we make our request to you, in the name of Christ, be at peace with God. For him who had no knowledge of sin God made to be sin for us; so that we might become the righteousness of God in him.

Thursday

Ex.21:33-36 (BBE)

If a man makes a hole in the earth without covering it up, and an ox or an ass dropping into it comes to its death; The owner of the hole is responsible; he will have to make payment to their owner, but the dead beast will be his. And if one man's ox does damage to another man's ox, causing its death, then the living ox is to be exchanged for money, and division made of the price of it, and of the price of the dead one. But if it is common knowledge that the ox has frequently done such damage in the past, and its owner has not kept it under control, he will have to give ox for ox; and the dead beast will be his.

Friday

Ex.12:1-13,24-28 (BBE)

And the Lord said to Moses and Aaron in the land of Egypt, "Let this month be to you the first of months, the first month of the year. Say to all the children of Israel when they are come together, In the tenth day of this month every man is to take a lamb, by the number of their fathers' families, a lamb for every family: And if the lamb is more than enough for the family, let that family and its nearest neighbour have a lamb between them, taking into account the number of persons and how much food is needed for every man. Let your lamb be without a mark, a male in its first year: you may take it from among the sheep or the goats: Keep it till the fourteenth day of the same month, when everyone who is of the children of Israel is to put it to death between sundown and dark. Then take some of the blood and put it on the two sides of the door and over the door of the house where the meal is to be taken. And let your food that night be the flesh of the lamb, cooked with fire in the oven, together with unleavened bread and bitter-tasting plants. Do not take it uncooked or cooked with boiling water, but let it be cooked in the oven; its head with its legs and its inside parts. Do not keep any of it till the morning; anything which is not used is to be burned with fire. And take your meal dressed as if for a journey, with your shoes on your feet and your sticks in your hands: take it quickly: it is the Lord's Passover. For on that night I will go through the land of Egypt, sending death on every first male child, of man and of beast, and judging all the gods of Egypt: I am the Lord. And the blood will be a sign on the houses where you are: when I see the blood I will go over you, and no evil will come on you for your destruction, when my hand is on the land of Egypt. And you are to keep this as an order to you and to your sons for ever. And when you come into the land which the Lord will make yours, as he gave his word, you are to keep this act of worship. And when your children say to you, What is the reason of this act of worship? Then you will say, This is the offering of the Lord's Passover; for he went over the houses of the children of Israel in Egypt, when he sent death on the Egyptians, and kept our families safe." And the people gave worship with bent heads. And the children of Israel went and did so; as the Lord had given orders to Moses and Aaron, so they did.

Saturday
Ps.127:1; 24:1-5 (BBE)

If the Lord is not helping the builders, then the building of a house is to no purpose: if the Lord does not keep the town, the watchman keeps his watch for nothing. The earth is the Lord's, with all its wealth; the world and all the people living in it. For by him it was based on the seas, and made strong on the deep rivers. Who may go up into the hill of the Lord? and who may come into his holy place? He who has clean hands and a true heart; whose desire has not gone out to foolish things, who has not taken a false oath. He will have blessing from the Lord, and righteousness from the God of his salvation. This is the generation of those whose hearts are turned to you, even to your face, O God of Jacob. Let your heads be lifted up, O doors; be lifted up, O you eternal doors: that the King of glory may come in. Who is the

King of glory? The Lord of strength and power, the Lord strong in war. Let your heads be lifted up, O doors; let them be lifted up, O you eternal doors: that the King of glory may come in. Who is the King of glory? The Lord of armies, he is the King of glory.

Sunday

Acts 2:1-18 (BBE)

And when the day of Pentecost was come, they were all together in one place. And suddenly there came from heaven a sound like the rushing of a violent wind, and all the house where they were was full of it. And they saw tongues, like flames of fire, coming to rest on every one of them. And they were all full of the Holy Spirit, and were talking in different languages, as the Spirit gave them power. Now there were living at Jerusalem, Jews, God-fearing men, from every nation under heaven. And when this sound came to their ears, they all came together, and were greatly surprised because every man was hearing the words of the disciples in his special language. And they were full of wonder and said, "Are not all these men Galilaeans? How is it that every one of us is hearing their words in the language which was ours from our birth? Men of Parthia, Media, and Elam, and those living in Mesopotamia, in Judaea and Cappadocia, in Pontus and Asia, In Phrygia and Pamphylia, in Egypt and the parts of Libya about Cyrene, and those who have come from Rome, Jews by birth and others who have become Jews, Men of Crete and Arabia, to all of us they are talking in our different languages, of the great works of God." And they were all surprised and in doubt saying to one another, "What is the reason of this?" But others, making sport of them, said, "They are full of new wine." But Peter, getting up, with the eleven, said in a loud voice, "O men of Judaea, and all you who are living in Jerusalem, take note of this and give ear to my words. These men are not overcome with wine, as it seems to you, for it is only the third hour of the day; but this is the thing which was said by the prophet Joel; 'And it will come about, in the last days, says God, that I will send out my Spirit on all flesh; and your sons and your daughters will be prophets, and your young men will see visions, and your old men will have dreams: And on my men-servants and my women-servants I will send my Spirit, and they will be prophets.'"

Week 18

Monday

Matt.18:1-6 (BBE)

In that hour the disciples came to Jesus, saying, "Who is greatest in the kingdom of heaven?" And he took a little child, and put him in the middle of them, and said, "Truly, I say to you, If you do not have a change of heart and become like little children, you will not go into the kingdom of heaven. Whoever, then, will make himself as low as this little child, the same is the greatest in the kingdom of heaven. And whoever gives honour to one such little child in my name, gives honour to me: But whoever is a cause of trouble to one of these little ones who have faith in me, it would be better for him to have a great stone fixed to his neck, and to come to his end in the deep sea."

Tuesday

Isa.41:9b-13 (NHT)

You are my servant, I have chosen you and not rejected you. Do not be afraid, for I am with you. Do not be dismayed, for I am your God. I will strengthen you. Yes, I will help you. Yes, I will uphold you with the right hand of my righteousness. Look, all those who are incensed against you will be disappointed and confounded. Those who strive with you will be like nothing, and shall perish. You will seek them, and won't find them, even those who contend with you. Those who war against you will be as nothing, as a non-existent thing. For I, the Lord your God, will hold your right hand, saying to you, 'Do not be afraid. I will help you.'

Wednesday

2 Cor.6:14-18; 9:6-11 (BBE)

Do not keep company with those who have not faith: for what is there in common between righteousness and evil, or between light and dark? And what agreement is there between Christ and the Evil One? Or what part has one who has faith with one who has not? And what agreement has the house of God with images? For we are a house of the living God; even as God has said, I will be living among them, and walking with them; and I will be their God, and they will be my people. For which cause, come out from among them, and be separate, says the Lord, and let no unclean thing come near you; and I will take you for myself, and will be a Father to you; and you will be my sons and daughters, says the Lord, the Ruler of all. But in the Writings it says, He who puts in only a small number of seeds, will get in the same; and he who puts them in from a full hand, will have produce in full measure from them. Let every man do after the purpose of his heart; not giving with grief, or by force: for God takes pleasure in a ready giver. And God is able to give you all grace in full measure; so that ever having enough of all things, you may be full of every good work: As it is said in the Writings, He has sent out far and wide, he has given to the poor; his righteousness is for ever. And he who gives seed for putting into the field and bread for food, will take care of the growth of your seed, at the same time increasing the fruits of your righteousness; Your wealth being increased in everything, with a simple mind, causing praise to God through us.

Thursday

Ex.22:1-5 (BBE)

If a man takes without right another man's ox or his sheep, and puts it to death or gets a price for it, he is to give five oxen for an ox, or four sheep for a sheep, in payment: the thief will have to make payment for what he has taken; if he has no money, he himself will have to be exchanged for money, so that payment may be made. If a thief is taken in the act of forcing his way into a house, and his death is caused by a blow, the owner of the house is not responsible for his blood. But if it is after dawn, he will be responsible. If he still has what he had taken, whatever it is, ox or ass or sheep, he is to give twice its value. If a man makes a fire in a field or a vine-garden, and lets the fire do damage to another man's field, he is to give of the best produce of his field or his vine-garden to make up for it.

Friday

Ex.14:13-28 (BBE)

But Moses said, "Keep where you are and have no fear; now you will see the salvation of the Lord which he will give you today; for the Egyptians whom you see today you will never see again. The Lord will make war for you, you have only to keep quiet." And the Lord said to Moses, "Why are you crying out to me? give the children of Israel the order to go forward. And let your rod be lifted up and your hand stretched out over the sea, and it will be parted in two; and the children of Israel will go through on dry land. And I will make the heart of the Egyptians hard, and they will go in after them: and I will be honoured over Pharaoh and over his army, his war-carriages, and his horsemen. And the Egyptians will see that I am the Lord, when I get honour over Pharaoh and his war-carriages and his horsemen." Then the angel of God, who had been before the tents of Israel, took his place at their back; and the pillar of cloud, moving from before them, came to rest at their back: And it came between the army of Egypt and the army of Israel; and there was a dark cloud between them, and they went on through the night; but the one army came no nearer to the other all the night. And when Moses' hand was stretched out over the sea, the Lord with a strong east wind made the sea go back all night, and the waters were parted in two and the sea became dry land. And the children of Israel went through the sea on dry land: and the waters were a wall on their right side and on their left. Then the Egyptians went after them into the middle of the sea, all Pharaoh's horses and his war-carriages and his horsemen. And in the morning watch, the Lord, looking out on the armies of the Egyptians from the pillar of fire and cloud, sent trouble on the army of the Egyptians; And made the wheels of their war-carriages stiff, so that they had hard work driving them: so the Egyptians said, "Let us go in flight from before the face of Israel, for the Lord is fighting for them against the Egyptians." And the Lord said to

Moses, "Let your hand be stretched out over the sea, and the waters will come back again on the Egyptians, and on their war-carriages and on their horsemen." And when Moses' hand was stretched out over the sea, at dawn the sea came flowing back, meeting the Egyptians in their flight, and the Lord sent destruction on the Egyptians in the middle of the sea. And the waters came back, covering the war-carriages and the horsemen and all the army of Pharaoh which went after them into the middle of the sea; not one of them was to be seen.

Saturday
Ps.25:4-11,15-18 (WBS)

Show me thy ways, O Lord; teach me thy paths. Lead me in thy truth, and teach me: for thou art the God of my salvation; on thee do I wait all the day. Remember, O Lord, thy tender mercies and thy loving kindnesses; for they have been ever of old. Remember not the sins of my youth, nor my transgressions: according to thy mercy remember thou me for thy goodness' sake, O Lord. Good and upright is the Lord: therefore will he teach sinners in the way. The meek will he guide in judgment: and the meek will he teach his way. All the paths of the Lord are mercy and truth to such as keep his covenant and his testimonies. For thy name's sake, O Lord, pardon my iniquity; for it is great. My eyes are ever towards the Lord; for he will pluck my feet out of the net. Turn thee to me, and have mercy upon me; for I am desolate and afflicted. The troubles of my heart are enlarged: O bring thou me out of my distresses. Look upon my affliction and my pain; and forgive all my sins.

Sunday
Acts 3:1-16 (NHT)

Now Peter and John were going up into the temple at the hour of prayer, the ninth hour. A certain man who was lame from his mother's womb was being carried, whom they put daily at the door of the temple which is called Beautiful, to ask gifts for the needy of those who entered into the temple. Seeing Peter and John about to go into the temple, he asked to receive gifts for the needy. Peter, fastening his eyes on him, with John, said, "Look at us." He listened to them, expecting to receive something from them. But Peter said, "Silver and gold have I none, but what I have, that I give you. In the name of Jesus Christ the Nazorean, get up and walk." He took him by the right hand, and raised him up. Immediately his feet and his ankle bones received strength. Leaping up, he stood, and began to walk. He entered with them into the temple, walking, leaping, and praising God. All the people saw him walking and praising God. They recognized him, that it was he who used to sit begging for gifts for the needy at the Beautiful Gate of the temple. They were filled with wonder and amazement at what had happened to him. And as he held on to Peter and John, all the people ran together to them in the porch that is called Solomon's, greatly wondering. When Peter saw it, he responded to the people, "You men of Israel, why do you marvel at this? Why do you fasten your eyes on us, as though by our own power or godliness we had made him walk? The God of Abraham, Isaac, and Jacob, the God of our fathers, has glorified his Servant Jesus, whom you delivered up, and denied in the presence of Pilate, when he had determined to release him. But you denied the Holy and Righteous One, and asked for a man who was a murderer to be granted to you, and killed the Prince of life, whom God raised from the dead, to which we are witnesses. By faith in his name, his name has made this man strong, whom you see and know. Yes, the faith which is through him has given him this perfect soundness in the presence of you all.

Week 19

Monday

Matt.18:15-20 (BBE)

If your brother does wrong to you, go, make clear to him his error between you and him in private: if he gives ear to you, you have got your brother back again. But if he will not give ear to you, take with you one or two more, that by the lips of two or three witnesses every word may be made certain. And if he will not give ear to them, let it come to the hearing of the church: and if he will not give ear to the church, let him be to you as a Gentile and a tax-farmer. Truly I say to you, Whatever things are fixed by you on earth will be fixed in heaven: and whatever you make free on earth will be made free in heaven. Again, I say to you, that if two of you are in agreement on earth about anything for which they will make a request, it will be done for them by my Father in heaven. For where two or three are come together in my name, there am I among them.

Tuesday

Isa:42:1-7,16 (NHT)

"Look my servant, whom I uphold, my chosen one in whom my soul delights. I have put my Spirit on him; he will bring justice to the nations. He will not shout, nor raise his voice, nor cause it to be heard in the street. He won't break a bruised reed. And he won't extinguish a dimly burning wick. He will faithfully bring justice. He will not grow dim or be crushed, until he has established justice on the earth, and in his name the nations will hope." Thus says God, the Lord, he who created the heavens and stretched them out, he who spread out the earth and that which comes out of it, he who gives breath to its people and spirit to those who walk in it. "I, the Lord, have called you in righteousness, and will hold your hand, and will keep you, and make you a covenant for the people, as a light for the nations; to open the blind eyes, to bring the prisoners out of the dungeon, and those who sit in darkness out of the prison. I will bring the blind by a way that they do not know. I will lead them in paths that they do not know. I will make darkness light before them, and crooked places straight. I will do these things, and I will not forsake them.

Wednesday
Gal.3:10-11,26-29; 4:1-7 (BBE)

All who are of the works of the law are under a curse: because it is said in the Writings, "A curse is on everyone who does not keep on doing all the things which are ordered in the book of the law." Now that no man gets righteousness by the law in the eyes of God, is clear; because, "The upright will be living by faith." You are all sons of God through faith in Christ Jesus for all those of you who were given baptism into Christ did put on Christ. There is no Jew or Greek, servant or free, male or female: because you are all one in Jesus Christ. And if you are Christ's, then you are Abraham's seed, and yours is the heritage by the right of God's undertaking given to Abraham. But I say that as long as the son is a child, he is in no way different from a servant, though he is lord of all; but is under keepers and managers till the time fixed by the father. So we, when we were young, were kept under the first rules of the world; but when the time had come, God sent out his Son, made of a woman, made under the law, that he might make them free who were under the law, and that we might be given the place of sons. And because you are sons, God has sent out the Spirit of his Son into our hearts, saying, "Abba, Father." So that you are no longer a servant, but a son; and if a son, then the heritage of God is yours.

Thursday
Ex.22:6-15 (BBE)

If there is a fire and the flames get to the thorns at the edge of the field, causing destruction of the cut grain or of the living grain, or of the field, he who made the fire will have to make up for the damage. If a man puts money or goods in the care of his neighbour to keep for him, and it is taken from the man's house, if they get the thief, he will have to make payment of twice the value. If they do not get the thief, let the master of the house come before the judges and take an oath that he has not put his hand on his neighbour's goods. In any question about an ox or an ass or a sheep or clothing, or about the loss of any property which anyone says is his, let the two sides put their cause before God; and he who is judged to be in the wrong is to make payment to his neighbour of twice the value. If a man puts an ass or an ox or a sheep or any beast into the keeping of his neighbour, and it comes to death or is damaged or is taken away, without any person seeing it: If he takes his oath before the Lord that he has not put his hand to his neighbour's goods, the owner is to take his word for it and he will not have to make payment for it. But if it is taken from him by a thief, he is to make up for the loss of it to its owner. But if it has been damaged by a beast, and he is able to make this clear, he will not have to make payment for what was damaged. If a man gets from his neighbour the use of one of his beasts, and it is damaged or put to death when the owner is not with it, he will certainly have to make payment for the loss. If the owner is with it, he will not have to make payment: if he gave money for the use of it, the loss is covered by the payment.

Friday
Ex.16:2-3,11-31 NHT)

The whole congregation of the children of Israel murmured against Moses and against Aaron in the wilderness; and the children of Israel said to them, "We wish that we had died by the hand of the Lord in the land of Egypt, when we sat by the meat pots, when we ate our fill of bread, for you have brought us out into this wilderness, to kill this whole assembly with hunger." The Lord spoke to Moses, saying, "I have heard the murmurings of the children of Israel. Speak to them, saying, 'At evening you shall eat meat, and in the morning you shall be filled with bread: and you shall know that I am the Lord your God.'" It happened at evening that quail came up and covered the camp; and in the morning the dew lay around the camp. When the dew that lay had gone, look, on the surface of the wilderness was a small round thing, small as the frost on the ground. When the children of Israel saw it, they said one to another, "What is it?" For they did not know what it was. Moses said to them, "It is the bread which the Lord has given you to eat." This is the thing which the Lord has commanded: "Gather of it everyone according to his eating; an omer a head, according to the number of your persons, you shall take it, every man for those who are in his tent." The children of Israel did so, and gathered some more, some less. When they measured it with an omer, he who gathered much had nothing over, and he who gathered little had no lack. They gathered every man according to his eating. Moses said to them, "Let no one leave of it until the morning." Notwithstanding they did not listen to Moses, but some of them left of it until the morning, and it bred worms, and became foul: and Moses was angry with them. They gathered it morning by morning, everyone according to his eating. When the sun grew hot, it melted. It happened that on the sixth day they gathered twice as much bread, two omers for each one, and all the leaders of the congregation came and told Moses. He said to them, "This is that which the Lord has spoken, 'Tomorrow is a solemn rest, a holy Sabbath to the Lord. Bake that which you want to bake, and boil that which you want to boil; and all that remains over lay up for yourselves to be kept until the morning.'" They laid it up until the morning, as Moses asked, and it did not become foul, neither was there any worm in it. Moses said, "Eat that today, for today is a Sabbath to the Lord. Today you shall not find it in the field. Six days you shall gather it, but on the seventh day is the Sabbath. In it there shall be none." It happened on the seventh day, that some of the people went out to gather, and they found none. The Lord said to Moses, "How long do you refuse to keep my commandments and my laws? Look, because the Lord has given you the Sabbath, therefore he gives you on the sixth day the bread of two days. Everyone stay in his place. Let no one go out of his place on the seventh day." So the people rested on the seventh day. The house of Israel called its name Manna, and it was like coriander seed, white; and its taste was like wafers with honey.

Saturday

Ps.30:2,4-8,11-12 (WBS)

O Lord my God, I cried to thee, and thou hast healed me. Sing to the Lord, O ye saints of his, and give thanks at the remembrance of his holiness. For his anger endureth but a moment; in his favour is life: weeping may endure for a night, but joy cometh in the morning. And in my prosperity I said, I shall never be moved. Lord, by thy favour thou hast made my mountain to stand strong: thou didst hide thy face, and I was troubled. I cried to thee, O Lord; and to the Lord I made supplication. Thou hast turned for me my mourning into dancing: thou hast put off my sackcloth, and girded me with gladness; To the end that my glory may sing praise to thee, and not be silent. O Lord my God, I will give thanks to thee for ever.

Sunday

Acts 6:8-15; 7:1-2a,51-9 (BBE)

And Stephen, full of grace and power, did great wonders and signs among the people: But some of those who were of the Synagogue named that of the Libertines, and some of the men of Cyrene and of Alexandria and those from Cilicia and Asia, had arguments with Stephen: but they were not able to get the better of him, for his words were full of wisdom and of the Spirit: Then they got men to say, "He has said evil against Moses and against God, in our hearing." And the people, with the rulers and the scribes, were moved against him, and they came and took him before the Sanhedrin,: And they got false witnesses who said, "This man is for ever saying things against this holy place and against the law for he has said in our hearing that this Jesus of Nazareth will put this place to destruction and make changes in the rules which were handed down to us by Moses." And all those who were in the Sanhedrin, looking at him, saw that his face was like the face of an angel. Then the high priest said, "Are these things true?" And he said, "My brothers and fathers, give hearing. You whose hearts are hard and whose ears are shut to me; you are ever working against the Holy Spirit; as your fathers did, so do you: Which of the prophets was not cruelly attacked by your fathers? and they put to death those who gave them the news of the coming of the Upright One; whom you have now given up and put to death; You, to whom the law was given as it was ordered by angels, and who have not kept it." Hearing these things, they were cut to the heart and moved with wrath against him. But he was full of the Holy Spirit, and looking up to heaven, he saw the glory of God and Jesus at the right hand of God and he said, "Now I see heaven open, and the Son of man at the right hand of God." But with loud cries, and stopping their ears, they made an attack on him all together, driving him out of the town and stoning him, and the witnesses put their clothing at the feet of a young man named Saul. And Stephen, while he was being stoned, made prayer to God, saying, "Lord Jesus, take my spirit."

Week 20

Monday

Matt.18-21-35 (BBE)

Then Peter came and said to him, "Lord, what number of times may my brother do wrong against me, and I give him forgiveness? till seven times?" Jesus says to him," I say not to you, till seven times; but, till seventy times seven. For this reason the kingdom of heaven is like a king, who went over his accounts with his servants. And at the start, one came to him who was in his debt for ten thousand talents. And because he was not able to make payment, his lord gave orders for him, and his wife, and his sons and daughters, and all he had, to be given for money, and payment to be made. So the servant went down on his face and gave him worship, saying, 'Lord, give me time to make payment and I will give you all.' And the lord of that servant, being moved with pity, let him go, and made him free of the debt. But that servant went out, and meeting one of the other servants, who was in debt to him for one hundred pence, he took him by the throat, saying, 'Make payment of your debt.' So that servant went down on his face, requesting him and saying,' Give me time and I will make payment to you.' And he would not but went and put him into prison till he had made payment of the debt. So when the other servants saw what was done they were very sad, and came and gave word to their lord of what had been done. Then his lord sent for him and said, 'You evil servant; I made you free of all that debt, because of your request to me: Was it not right for you to have mercy on the other servant, even as I had mercy on you?' And his lord was very angry, and put him in the hands of those who would give him punishment till he made payment of all the debt. So will my Father in heaven do to you, if you do not everyone, from your hearts, give forgiveness to his brother."

Tuesday
Isa.43:1-3a,24b-25 (NHT)

But now thus says the Lord who created you, Jacob, and he who formed you, Israel: "Do not be afraid, for I have redeemed you. I have called you by your name. You are mine. When you pass through the waters, I will be with you; and through the rivers, they will not overflow you. When you walk through the fire, you will not be burned, and the flame will not scorch you. For I am the Lord your God, the Holy One of Israel, your Saviour. You have burdened me with your sins. You have wearied me with your iniquities. I, even I, am he who blots out your transgressions for my own sake; and I will not remember your sins.

Wednesday
Gal.5:16-23 (NHT)

Walk by the Spirit, and you will not carry out the desires of the flesh. For the flesh lusts against the Spirit, and the Spirit against the flesh; and these are contrary to one another, that you may not do the things that you desire. But if you are led by the Spirit, you are not under the law. Now the works of the flesh are obvious, which are: sexual immorality, uncleanness, lustfulness, idolatry, sorcery, hatred, strife, jealousies, outbursts of anger, rivalries, divisions, heresies, envyings, murders, drunkenness, orgies, and things like these; of which I forewarn you, even as I also forewarned you, that those who practice such things will not inherit the Kingdom of God. But the fruit of the Spirit is love, joy, peace, patience, kindness, goodness, faithfulness, gentleness, and self-control. Against such things there is no law.

Thursday
Ex.23:10-13 (BBE)

For six years put seed into your fields and get in the increase; But in the seventh year let the land have a rest and be unplanted; so that the poor may have food from it: and let the beasts of the field take the rest. Do the same with your vine-gardens and your olive-trees. For six days do your work, and on the seventh day keep the Sabbath; so that your ox and your ass may have rest, together with the son of your servant and the man from a strange land living among you. Take note of all these things which I have said to you, and let not the names of other gods come into your minds or from your lips. Three times in the year you are to keep a feast to me. You are to keep the feast of unleavened bread; for seven days let your bread be without leaven, as I gave you orders, at the regular time in the month Abib (for in it you came out of Egypt); and let no one come before me without an offering:

Friday

Ex.33:12-23; 34:5-8 (WBS)

And Moses said to the Lord, "See, thou sayest to me, Bring up this people: and thou hast not let me know whom thou wilt send with me. Yet thou hast said, I know thee by name, and thou hast also found grace in my sight. Now therefore, I pray thee, if I have found grace in thy sight, show me now thy way, that I may know thee, that I may find grace in thy sight: and consider that this nation is thy people. And he said, My presence shall attend thee, and I will give thee rest." And he said to him, "If thy presence shall not attend me, conduct us not hence. For wherein shall it be known here that I and thy people have found grace in thy sight? Is it not in that thou goest with us? So shall we be separated, I and thy people, from all the people that are upon the face of the earth." And the Lord said to Moses, "I will do this thing also that thou hast spoken: for thou hast found grace in my sight, and I know thee by name." And he said, "I beseech thee, show me thy glory." And He said, "I will make all my goodness pass before thee, and I will proclaim the name of the Lord before thee; and will be gracious to whom I will be gracious, and will show mercy on whom I will show mercy." And He said, "Thou canst not see my face: for there shall no man see me, and live." And the Lord said, "Behold, there is a place by me, and thou shalt stand upon a rock: And it shall come to pass, while my glory passeth by, that I will put thee in a cleft of the rock: and will cover thee with my hand while I pass by: And I will take away my hand, and thou shalt see my back parts: but my face shall not be seen." And the Lord descended in the cloud, and stood with him there, and proclaimed the name of the Lord. And the Lord passed by before him, and proclaimed, The Lord, The Lord God, merciful and gracious, long-suffering, and abundant in goodness and truth. Keeping mercy for thousands, forgiving iniquity and transgression and sin, and that will by no means clear the guilty; visiting the iniquity of the fathers upon the children, and upon the children's children, to the third and to the fourth generation. And Moses made haste, and bowed his head towards the earth, and worshiped.

Saturday

Ps.31:1-5,9-10,16 (WBS)

In thee, O Lord, do I put my trust; let me never be ashamed: deliver me in thy righteousness. Bow down thy ear to me; deliver me speedily: be thou my strong rock, for a house of defence to save me. For thou art my rock and my fortress; therefore for thy name's sake lead me, and guide me. Pull me out of the net that they have laid privily for me: for thou art my strength. Into thy hand I commit my spirit: thou hast redeemed me, O Lord God of truth. Have mercy upon me, O Lord, for I am in trouble: my eye is consumed with grief, yes, my soul and my belly. For my life is spent with grief, and my years with sighing: my strength faileth because of my iniquity, and my bones are consumed. Make thy face to shine upon thy servant: save me for thy mercies' sake.

Sunday

Acts 8:26-39 (NHT)

But an angel of the Lord spoke to Philip, saying, "Arise, and go toward the south to the way that goes down from Jerusalem to Gaza. This is a desert." And he arose and went; and look, there was a man from Ethiopia, a eunuch of great authority under Candace, queen of the Ethiopians, who was over all her treasure, who had come to Jerusalem to worship. He was returning and sitting in his chariot, and was reading the prophet Isaiah. The Spirit said to Philip, "Go near, and join yourself to this chariot." Philip ran to him, and heard him reading Isaiah the prophet, and said, "Do you understand what you are reading?" He said, "How can I, unless someone explains it to me?" He begged Philip to come up and sit with him. Now the passage of the Scripture which he was reading was this, "He was led as a sheep to the slaughter. As a lamb before his shearer is silent, so he does not open his mouth. In his humiliation his justice was taken away. Who will declare his generation? For his life is taken from the earth." The eunuch answered Philip, "Who is the prophet talking about? About himself, or about someone else?" Philip opened his mouth, and beginning from this Scripture, preached to him Jesus. As they went on the way, they came to some water, and the eunuch said, "Look, here is water. What is keeping me from being baptized?" He commanded the chariot to stand still, and they both went down into the water, both Philip and the eunuch, and he baptized him. When they came up out of the water, the Spirit of the Lord caught Philip away, and the eunuch did not see him anymore, for he went on his way rejoicing.

Week 21

Monday

Matt.19:1-12 (BBE)

And it came about that after saying these words, Jesus went away from Galilee, and came into the parts of Judaea on the other side of Jordan. And a great number went after him; and he made them well there. And certain Pharisees came to him, testing him, and saying, "Is it right for a man to put away his wife for every cause?" And he said in answer, "Have you not seen in the Writings, that he who made them at the first made them male and female, and said, For this cause will a man go away from his father and mother, and be joined to his wife; and the two will become one flesh? So that they are no longer two, but one flesh. Then let not that which has been joined by God be parted by man." They say to him, "Why then did Moses give orders that a husband might give her a statement in writing and be free from her?" He says to them, "Moses, because of your hard hearts, let you put away your wives: but it has not been so from the first. And I say to you, Whoever puts away his wife for any other cause than the loss of her virtue, and takes another, is a false husband: and he who takes her as his wife when she is put away, is no true husband to her." The disciples say to him, "If this is the position of a man in relation to his wife, it is better not to be married." But he said to them, "Not all men are able to take in this saying, but only those to whom it is given. For there are men who, from birth, were without sex: and there are some who were made so by men: and there are others who have made themselves so for the kingdom of heaven. He who is able to take it, let him take it."

Tuesday
Isa.45:5-9,22-25 (NHT)

I am the Lord, and there is no other. Besides me, there is no God. I will strengthen you, though you have not known me; that they may know from the rising of the sun, and from the west, that there is none besides me. I am the Lord, and there is no one else. I form the light, and create darkness. I make peace, and create calamity. I am the Lord, who does all these things. Distil, you heavens, from above, and let the skies pour down righteousness. Let the earth open, that it may bring forth salvation, and let it cause righteousness to spring up with it. I, the Lord, have created it. Woe to him who strives with his Maker, a clay pot among the clay pots of the earth. Shall the clay ask him who fashions it, 'What are you making?' or your work, 'He has no hands?' Look to me, and be saved, every part of the earth; for I am God, and there is no other. By myself have I sworn, the word is gone forth from my mouth in righteousness, and shall not return, that to me every knee shall bow, every tongue shall swear to God. Only in the Lord, it is said of me, is righteousness and strength; even to him shall men come; and all those who were incensed against him shall be disappointed. In the Lord shall all the descendants of Israel be justified, and shall glory.

Wednesday
Eph.2:1-10 (BBE)

And to you did he give life, when you were dead through your wrongdoing and sins, In which you were living in the past, after the ways of this present world, doing the pleasure of the lord of the power of the air, the spirit who is now working in those who go against the purpose of God; Among whom we all at one time were living in the pleasures of our flesh, giving way to the desires of the flesh and of the mind, and the punishment of God was waiting for us even as for the rest. But God, being full of mercy, through the great love which he had for us, Even when we were dead through our sins, gave us life together with Christ (by grace you have salvation), So that we came back from death with him, and are seated with him in the heavens, in Christ Jesus; That in the time to come he might make clear the full wealth of his grace in his mercy to us in Christ Jesus: Because by grace you have salvation through faith; and that not of yourselves: it is given by God: Not by works, so that no man may take glory to himself. For by his act we were given existence in Christ Jesus to do those good works which God before made ready for us so that we might do them.

Thursday
Ex.22:25-30; 23:4-5 (BBE)

If you let any of the poor among my people have the use of your money, do not be a hard creditor to him, and do not take interest. If ever you take your neighbour's clothing in exchange for the use of your money, let him have it back before the sun goes down: For it is the only thing he has for covering his skin; what is he to go to sleep in? and when his cry comes up to me, I will give ear, for my mercy is great.

You may not say evil of the judges, or put a curse on the ruler of your people.

Do not keep back your offerings from the wealth of your grain and your vines. The first of your sons you are to give to me. In the same way with your oxen and your sheep: for seven days let the young one be with its mother; on the eighth day give it to me.

If you come across the ox or the ass of one who is no friend to you wandering from its way, you are to take it back to him. If you see the ass of one who has no love for you bent down to the earth under the weight which is put on it, you are to come to its help, even against your desire.

Friday
Num.9:15-22 (BBE)

And on the day when the House was put up, the cloud came down on it, on the Tent of witness; and in the evening there was a light like fire over the House till the morning. And so it was at all times: it was covered by the cloud, and by a light as of fire by night. And whenever the cloud was taken up from over the House, then the children of Israel went journeying on; and in the place where the cloud came to rest, there the children of Israel put up their tents. At the order of the Lord the children of Israel went forward, and at the order of the Lord they put up their tents: as long as the cloud was resting on the House, they did not go away from that place. When the cloud was resting on the House for a long time the children of Israel, waiting for the order of the Lord, did not go on. Sometimes the cloud was resting on the House for two or three days; then, by the order of the Lord, they kept their tents in that place, and when the Lord gave the order they went on. And sometimes the cloud was there only from evening to morning; and when the cloud was taken up in the morning they went on their journey again: or if it was resting there by day and by night, whenever the cloud was taken up they went forward. Or if the cloud came to rest on the House for two days or a month or a year without moving, the children of Israel went on waiting there and did not go on; but whenever it was taken up they went forward on their journey.

Saturday
Ps.33:1-11 (BBE)

Be glad in the Lord, O doers of righteousness; for praise is beautiful for the upright. Give praise to the Lord on the corded instrument; make melody to him with instruments of music. Make a new song to him; playing expertly with a loud noise. For the word of the Lord is upright, and all his works are certain. His delight is in righteousness and wisdom; the earth is full of the mercy of the Lord. By the word of the Lord were the heavens made; and all the army of heaven by the breath of his mouth. He makes the waters of the sea come together in a mass; he keeps the deep seas in storehouses. Let the earth be full of the fear of the Lord; let all the people of the world be in holy fear of him. For he gave the word, and it was done; by his order it was fixed for ever. The Lord undoes the designs of the nations; he makes the thoughts of the peoples without effect. The Lord's purpose is eternal, the designs of his heart go on through all the generations of man.

Sunday
Acts 9:1-19 (BBE)

But Saul, still burning with desire to put to death the disciples of the Lord, went to the high priest, And made a request for letters from him to the Synagogues of Damascus, so that if there were any of the Way there, men or women, he might take them as prisoners to Jerusalem. And while he was journeying, he came near Damascus; and suddenly he saw a light from heaven shining round him; And he went down on the earth, and a voice said to him, "Saul, Saul, why are you attacking me so cruelly?" And he said, "Who are you, Lord?" And he said, "I am Jesus, whom you are attacking: But get up, and go into the town, and it will be made clear to you what you have to do." And the men who were with him were not able to say anything; hearing the voice, but seeing no one. And Saul got up from the earth, and when his eyes were open, he saw nothing; and he was guided by the hand into Damascus. And for three days he was not able to see, and he took no food or drink. Now there was a certain disciple at Damascus, named Ananias; and the Lord said to him in a vision, "Ananias"! and he said, "Here I am, Lord." And the Lord said to him, "Get up, and go to the street which is named Straight, and make search at the house of Judas for one named Saul of Tarsus: for he is at prayer; And he has seen a man named Ananias coming in and putting his hands on him, so that he may be able to see." But Ananias said, "Lord, I have had accounts of this man from a number of people, how much evil he has done to your saints at Jerusalem: And here he has authority from the chief priests to make prisoners all who give worship to your name." But the Lord said, "Go without fear: for he is a special vessel for me, to give to the Gentiles and kings and to the children of Israel the knowledge of my name: For I will make clear to him what troubles he will have to undergo for me." And Ananias went out and came to the house, and putting his hands on him, said, "Brother Saul, the Lord Jesus, whom you saw when you were on your journey, has sent me, so that you may be able to see, and be full of the Holy Spirit." And straight away it seemed as if a veil was taken from his eyes, and he was able to see; and he got up, and had baptism; And when he had taken food his strength came back. And for some days he kept with the disciples who were in Damascus.

Week 22

Monday

Matt.20:1-16 (BBE)

For the kingdom of heaven is like the master of a house, who went out early in the morning to get workers into his vine-garden. And when he had made an agreement with the workmen for a penny a day, he sent them into his vine-garden. And he went out about the third hour, and saw others in the market-place doing nothing; And he said to them, Go into the vine-garden with the others, and whatever is right I will give you. And they went to work. Again he went out about the sixth and the ninth hour, and did the same. And about the eleventh hour he went out and saw others doing nothing; and he says to them, Why are you here all the day doing nothing? They say to him, Because no man has given us work. He says to them, Go in with the rest, into the vine-garden. And when evening came, the lord of the vine-garden said to his manager, Let the workers come, and give them their payment, from the last to the first. And when those men came who had gone to work at the eleventh hour, they were given every man a penny. Then those who came first had the idea that they would get more; and they, like the rest, were given a penny. And when they got it, they made a protest against the master of the house, Saying, These last have done only one hour's work, and you have made them equal to us, who have undergone the hard work of the day and the burning heat. But he in answer said to one of them, Friend, I do you no wrong: did you not make an agreement with me for a penny? Take what is yours, and go away; it is my pleasure to give to this last, even as to you. Have I not the right to do as seems good to me in my house? or is your eye evil, because I am good? So the last will be first, and the first last.

Tuesday
Isa.55:6-12; 56:1-2 (NHT)

Seek the Lord while he may be found; call you on him while he is near: let the wicked forsake his way, and the unrighteous man his thoughts; and let him return to the Lord, and he will have mercy on him; and to our God, for he will abundantly pardon. "For my thoughts are not your thoughts, neither are your ways my ways," says the Lord. "For as the heavens are higher than the earth, so are my ways higher than your ways, and my thoughts than your thoughts. For as the rain comes down and the snow from the sky, and doesn't return there, but waters the earth, and makes it bring forth and bud, and gives seed to the sower and bread to the eater; so shall my word be that goes forth out of my mouth: it shall not return to me void, but it shall accomplish that which I please, and it shall prosper in the thing I sent it to do. For you shall go out with joy, and be led forth with peace: the mountains and the hills shall break forth before you into singing; and all the trees of the fields shall clap their hands. Thus says the Lord, "Keep justice, and do righteousness; for my salvation is near to come, and my righteousness to be revealed. Blessed is the man who does this, and the son of man who holds it fast; who keeps the Sabbath from profaning it, and keeps his hand from doing any evil."

Wednesday
Eph.3:12,14-21 (BBE)

By whom (Christ Jesus our Lord) we come near to God without fear through faith in him. For this cause I go down on my knees before the Father, From whom every family in heaven and on earth is named, That in the wealth of his glory he would make you strong with power through his Spirit in your hearts; So that Christ may have his place in your hearts through faith; and that you, being rooted and based in love, may have strength to see with all the saints how wide and long and high and deep it is, and to have knowledge of the love of Christ which is outside all knowledge, so that you may be made complete as God himself is complete. Now to him who is able to do in full measure more than all our desires or thoughts, through the power which is working in us, to him be the glory in the church and in Christ Jesus to all generations for ever and ever. So be it.

Thursday
Ex.23:1-3,6-8 (BBE)

Do not let a false statement go further; do not make an agreement with evil-doers to be a false witness. Do not be moved to do wrong by the general opinion, or give the support of your words to a wrong decision: But, on the other hand, do not be turned from what is right in order to give support to a poor man's cause. Let no wrong decisions be given in the poor man's cause. Keep yourselves far from any false business; never let the upright or him who has done no wrong be put to death: for I will make the evil-doer responsible for his sin. Take no rewards in a cause: for rewards make blind those who have eyes to see, and make the decisions of the upright false.

Friday
Josh.6:1-7,15-16,20,27 (BBE)

Now Jericho was all shut up because of the children of Israel: there was no going out or coming in. And the Lord said to Joshua, "See, I have given into your hands Jericho with its king and all its men of war. Now let all your fighting-men make a circle round the town, going all round it once. Do this for six days. And let seven priests go before the ark with seven loud-sounding horns in their hands: on the seventh day you are to go round the town seven times, the priests blowing their horns. And at the sound of a long note on the horns, let all the people give a loud cry; and the wall of the town will come down flat, and all the people are to go straight forward." Then Joshua, the son of Nun, sent for the priests and said to them, "Take up the ark of the agreement, and let seven priests take seven horns in their hands and go before the ark of the Lord." And he said to the people, "Go forward, circling the town, and let the armed men go before the ark of the Lord." Then on the seventh day they got up early, at the dawn of the day, and went round the town in the same way, but that day they went round it seven times. And the seventh time, at the sound of the priests' horns, Joshua said to the people, "Now give a loud cry; for the Lord has given you the town." So the people gave a loud cry, and the horns were sounded; and on hearing the horns the people gave a loud cry, and the wall came down flat, so that the people went up into the town, every man going straight before him, and they took the town. So the Lord was with Joshua; and news of him went through all the land.

Saturday
Ps.34:9-22 (BBE)

Keep yourselves in the fear of the Lord, all you his saints; for those who do so will have no need of anything. The young lions are in need and have no food; but those who are looking to the Lord will have every good thing. Come, children, give attention to me; I will be your teacher in the fear of the Lord. What man has a love of life, and a desire that his days may be increased so that he may see good? Keep your tongue from evil, and your lips from words of deceit. Be turned from evil, and do good; make a search for peace, desiring it with all your heart. The eyes of the Lord are on the upright, and his ears are open to their cry. The face of the Lord is against those who do evil, to take away the memory of them from the earth. The cry of the upright comes before the Lord, and he takes them out of all their troubles. The Lord is near the broken-hearted; he is the saviour of those whose spirits are crushed down. Great are the troubles of the upright: but the Lord takes him safely out of them all. He keeps all his bones: not one of them is broken. Evil will put an end to the sinner, and those who are haters of righteousness will come to destruction. The Lord will be the saviour of the souls of his servants, and no one who has faith in him will be put to shame.

Sunday

Acts 9:36-43 (BBE)

Now there was at Joppa a certain disciple named Tabitha, that is, Dorcas: this woman was given to good works and acts of mercy at all times. And it came about, in those days, that she got ill and came to her death: and when she had been washed, they put her in a room which was high up. And because Lydda was near Joppa, the disciples, having knowledge that Peter was there, sent two men to him, requesting him to come to them straight away. And Peter went with them. And when he had come, they took him into the room: and all the widows were there, weeping and putting before him the coats and clothing which Dorcas had made while she was with them. But Peter made them all go outside, and went down on his knees in prayer; and turning to the body, he said, "Tabitha, get up." And, opening her eyes, she saw Peter and got up. And he took her hand, lifting her up; and, sending for the saints and widows, he gave her to them, living. And news of it went all through Joppa, and a number of people had faith in the Lord. And he was living in Joppa for some time with Simon, a leather-worker.

Week 23

Monday

Matt.22:35-40 (BBE)

And one of them, a teacher of the law, put a question to him, testing him, and saying, "Master, which is the chief rule in the law?" And he said to him, "Have love for the Lord your God with all your heart, and with all your soul, and with all your mind. This is the first and greatest rule. And a second like it is this, Have love for your neighbour as for yourself. On these two rules all the law and the prophets are based."

Tuesday

Isa.58:9b-14 (NHT)

If you take away from the midst of you the yoke, the putting forth of the finger, and speaking wickedly; and if you draw out your soul to the hungry, and satisfy the afflicted soul: then your light shall rise in darkness, and your obscurity be as the noonday; and the Lord will guide you continually, and satisfy your soul in dry places, and make strong your bones; and you shall be like a watered garden, and like a spring of water, whose waters do not fail. Those who shall be of you shall build the old waste places; you shall raise up the foundations of many generations; and you shall be called The repairer of the breach, The restorer of paths to dwell in. "If you turn away your foot from the Sabbath, from doing your pleasure on my holy day; and call the Sabbath a delight, and the holy of the Lord honourable; and shall honour it, not doing your own ways, nor finding your own pleasure, nor speaking your own words: then you shall delight yourself in the Lord; and I will make you to ride on the high places of the earth; and I will feed you with the heritage of Jacob your father:" for the mouth of the Lord has spoken it.

Wednesday

Eph.4:22-32 (BBE)

You are to put away, in relation to your earlier way of life, the old man, which has become evil by love of deceit; And be made new in the spirit of your mind, And put on the new man, to which God has given life, in righteousness and a true and holy way of living. And so, putting away false words, let everyone say what is true to his neighbour: for we are parts one of another. Be angry without doing wrong; let not the sun go down on your wrath; And do not give way to the Evil One. Let him who was a thief be so no longer, but let him do good work with his hands, so that he may have something to give to him who is in need. Let no evil talk come out of your mouth, but only what is good for giving necessary teaching, and for grace to those who give ear. And do not give grief to the Holy Spirit of God, by whom you were marked for the day of salvation. Let all bitter, sharp and angry feeling, and noise, and evil words, be put away from you, with all unkind acts; And be kind to one another, full of pity, having forgiveness for one another, even as God in Christ had forgiveness for you.

Thursday

Ex.22:16-24

If a man takes a virgin, who has not given her word to another man, and has connection with her, he will have to give a bride-price for her to be his wife. If her father will not give her to him on any account, he will have to give the regular payment for virgins. Any woman using unnatural powers or secret arts is to be put to death. Any man who has sex connection with a beast is to be put to death. Complete destruction will come on any man who makes offerings to any other god but the Lord. Do no wrong to a man from a strange country, and do not be hard on him; for you yourselves were living in a strange country, in the land of Egypt. Do no wrong to a widow, or to a child whose father is dead. If you are cruel to them in any way, and their cry comes up to me, I will certainly give ear; And in the heat of my wrath I will put you to death with the sword, so that your wives will be widows and your children without fathers.

Friday

Ruth 1:1-17 (NHT)

It happened in the days when the judges judged, that there was a famine in the land. A certain man of Bethlehem Judah went to sojourn in the country of Moab, he, and his wife, and his two sons. The name of the man was Elimelech, and the name of his wife Naomi, and the name of his two sons Mahlon and Kilion, Ephrathites of Bethlehem Judah. They came into the country of Moab, and continued there. Elimelech, Naomi's husband, died; and she was left, and her two sons. And they took for themselves wives from the women of Moab; the name of the one was Orpah, and the name of the other Ruth: and they lived there about ten years. Mahlon and Kilion both died, and the woman was bereaved of her two children and of her husband. Then she arose with her daughters-in-law, that she might return from the country of Moab: for she had heard in the country of Moab how that the Lord had visited his people in giving them bread. She went forth out of the place where she was, and her two daughters-in-law with her; and they went on the way to return to the land of Judah. Naomi said to her two daughters-in-law, "Go, return each of you to her mother's house. May the Lord deal kindly with you, as you have dealt with the dead, and with me. The Lord grant you that you may find rest, each of you in the house of her husband." Then she kissed them, and they lifted up their voice, and wept. They said to her, "No, but we will return with you to your people." Naomi said, "Go back, my daughters. Why do you want to go with me? Do I still have sons in my womb, that they may be your husbands? Go back, my daughters, go your way; for I am too old to have a husband. If I should say, 'I have hope,' if I should even have a husband tonight, and should also bear sons; would you then wait until they were grown? Would you then refrain from having husbands? No, my daughters, for it grieves me much for your sakes, for the hand of the Lord has gone out against me." They lifted up their voice, and wept again: and Orpah kissed her mother-in-law and returned to her people, but Ruth clung to her. She said, "Look, your sister-in-law has gone back to her people, and to her god. Follow your sister-in-law. Ruth said, "Do not urge me to leave you, and to return from following after you, for where you go, I will go; and where you stay, I will stay; your people shall be my people, and your God my God; where you die, will I die, and there will I be buried. The Lord do so to me, and more also, if anything but death part you and me."

Saturday

Ps.37:1-11 (BBE)

Do not be angry because of the wrongdoers, or have envy of the workers of evil for they will quickly be cut down like grass, and become dry like the green plants. Have faith in the Lord, and do good; be at rest in the land, and go after righteousness. So will your delight be in the Lord, and he will give you your heart's desires. Put your life in the hands of the Lord; have faith in him and he will do it. And he will make your righteousness be seen like the light, and your cause like the shining of the sun. Take your rest in the Lord, waiting quietly for him; do not be angry because of the man who does well in his evil ways, and gives effect to his bad designs. Put an end to your wrath and be no longer bitter; do not give way to angry feeling which is a cause of sin. For the evil-doers will be cut off: but those who have faith in the Lord will have the earth for their heritage. For in a short time the evil-doer will be gone: you will go searching for his place, and it will not be there. But the gentle will have the earth for their heritage; they will take their delight in peace without measure.

Sunday

Acts 11:1-18 (NHT)

Now the apostles and the brothers who were in Judea heard that the Gentiles had also received the word of God. When Peter had come up to Jerusalem, those who were of the circumcision contended with him, saying, "You went in to uncircumcised men, and ate with them." But Peter began, and explained to them in order, saying, "I was in the city of Joppa praying, and in a trance I saw a vision: a certain container descending, like it was a great sheet let down from heaven by four corners. It came as far as me. When I had looked intently at it, I considered, and saw the four-footed animals of the earth, wild animals, crawling creatures, and birds of the sky. I also heard a voice saying to me, 'Rise, Peter, kill and eat.' But I said, 'Not so, Lord, for nothing unholy or unclean has ever entered into my mouth.' But a voice answered the second time out of heaven, 'What God has cleansed, do not call unclean.' This was done three times, and all were drawn up again into heaven. And look, immediately three men stood before the house where we were, having been sent from Caesarea to me. The Spirit told me to go with them, without discriminating. These six brothers also accompanied me, and we entered into the man's house. He told us how he had seen the angel standing in his house, and saying to him, 'Send to Joppa, and get Simon, whose surname is Peter, who will speak to you words by which you will be saved, you and all your house.' As I began to speak, the Holy Spirit fell on them, even as on us at the beginning. I remembered the word of the Lord, how he said, 'John indeed baptized in water, but you will be baptized in the Holy Spirit.' If then God gave to them the same gift as us, when we believed in the Lord Jesus Christ, who was I, that I could withstand God?" When they heard these things, they held their peace, and glorified God, saying, "Then God has also granted to the Gentiles repentance to life."

Week 24

Monday

Matt.25:1-13 (BBE)

Then the kingdom of heaven will be like ten virgins, the friends of the bride, who took their lights, and went out with the purpose of meeting the husband. And five of them were foolish, and five were wise. For the foolish, when they took their lights, took no oil with them. But the wise took oil in their vessels with their lights. Now the husband was a long time in coming, and they all went to sleep. But in the middle of the night there is a cry, "The husband comes! Go out to him. "Then all those virgins got up, and made ready their lights. And the foolish said to the wise, "Give us of your oil; for our lights are going out." But the wise made answer, saying, "There may not be enough for us and you; it would be better for you to go to the traders and get oil for yourselves." And while they went to get oil, the master came; and those who were ready went in with him to the feast: and the door was shut. After that the other virgins came, saying, "Lord, Lord, let us in." But he made answer and said, "Truly I say to you, I have no knowledge of you." Keep watch, then, because you are not certain of the day or of the hour.

Tuesday

Isa.59:12-13,15b,17-20 (WBS)

Our transgressions are multiplied before thee, and our sins testify against us: for our transgressions are with us; and as for our iniquities, we know them; In transgressing and lying against the Lord, and departing away from our God, speaking oppression and revolt, conceiving and uttering from the heart words of falsehood.

The Lord saw it, and it displeased him that there was no judgment. He put on righteousness as a breast-plate, and a helmet of salvation upon his head; and he put on the garments of vengeance for clothing, and was clad with zeal as a cloak. According to their deeds, accordingly he will repay, fury to his adversaries, recompense to his enemies; to the isles he will repay recompense. So shall they fear the name of the Lord from the west, and his glory from the rising of the sun. When the enemy shall come in like a flood, the Spirit of the Lord will lift up a standard against him. And the Redeemer will come to Zion, and to them that turn from transgression in Jacob, saith the Lord.

Wednesday

Eph.5:1-12,15-20 (BBE)

Let it then be your desire to be like God, as well-loved children; And be living in love, even as Christ had love for you, and gave himself up for us, an offering to God for a perfume of a sweet smell. But evil acts of the flesh and all unclean things, or desire for others' property, let it not even be named among you, as is right for saints; And let there be no low behaviour, or foolish talk, or words said in sport, which are not right, but in place of them the giving of praise. Being certain of this, that no man who gives way to the passions of the flesh, no unclean person, or one who has desire for the property of others, or who gives worship to images, has any heritage in the kingdom of Christ and God. Do not be turned from the right way by foolish words; for because of these things the punishment of God comes on those who do not put themselves under him. Have no part with such men; For you at one time were dark, but now are light in the Lord: let your behaviour be that of children of light (Because the fruit of the light is in all righteousness and in everything which is good and true), testing by experience what is well-pleasing to the Lord; And have no company with the works of the dark, which give no fruit, but make their true quality clear; for the things which are done by them in secret it is shame even to put into words. Take care then how you are living, not as unwise, but as wise; Making good use of the time, because the days are evil. For this reason, then, do not be foolish, but be conscious of the Lord's pleasure. And do not take overmuch wine by which one may be overcome, but be full of the Spirit; joining with one another in holy songs of praise and of the Spirit, using your voice in songs and making melody in your heart to the Lord; giving praise at all times for all things in the name of our Lord Jesus Christ, to God, even the Father

Thursday
Ex.34:10-14 (BBE)

And the Lord said, "See, this is what I will undertake: before the eyes of your people I will do wonders, such as have not been done in all the earth or in any nation: and all your people will see the work of the Lord, for what I am about to do for you is greatly to be feared. Take care to do the orders which I give you today; I will send out from before you the Amorite and the Canaanite and the Hittite and the Perizzite and the Hivite and the Jebusite. But take care, and do not make any agreement with the people of the land where you are going, for it will be a cause of sin to you. But their altars are to be overturned and their pillars broken and their images cut down: For you are to be worshippers of no other god: for the Lord is a God who will not give his honour to another."

Friday
Ruth 2:1-2,14-17; 4:13-17 (NHT)

Naomi had a kinsman of her husband's, a mighty man of wealth, of the family of Elimelech, and his name was Boaz. Ruth the Moabitess said to Naomi, "Let me now go to the field, and glean among the ears of grain after him in whose sight I shall find favour." She said to her, "Go, my daughter." At meal time Boaz said to her, "Come here, and eat of the bread, and dip your morsel in the vinegar." She sat beside the reapers, and they reached her parched grain, and she ate, and was satisfied, and left some of it. When she had risen up to glean, Boaz commanded his young men, saying, "Let her glean even among the sheaves, and do not reproach her. Also pull out some for her from the bundles, and leave it, and let her glean, and do not rebuke her." So she gleaned in the field until evening; and she beat out that which she had gleaned, and it was about an ephah of barley.

So Boaz took Ruth, and she became his wife; and he went in to her, and the Lord gave her conception, and she bore a son. The women said to Naomi, "Blessed be the Lord, who has not left you this day without a redeemer; and let his name be famous in Israel. He shall be to you a restorer of life, and sustain you in your old age, for your daughter-in-law, who loves you, who is better to you than seven sons, has borne him." Naomi took the child, and laid it in her bosom, and looked after him. The women, her neighbours, gave him a name, saying, "There is a son born to Naomi." And they named him Obed. He is the father of Jesse, the father of David.

Saturday

Ps.46 (NHT)

God is our refuge and strength, a very present help in trouble. Therefore we won't be afraid, though the earth changes, though the mountains are shaken into the heart of the seas; though its waters roar and are troubled, though the mountains tremble with their swelling. Selah. There is a river, the streams of which make the city of God glad, the holy place of the tents of the Most High. God is in her midst. She shall not be moved. God will help her at dawn. The nations raged. The kingdoms were moved. He lifted his voice, and the earth melted. The Lord of hosts is with us. The God of Jacob is our refuge. Come, see the Lord's works, what desolations he has made in the earth. He makes wars cease to the end of the earth. He breaks the bow, and shatters the spear. He burns the chariots in the fire. "Be still, and know that I am God. I will be exalted among the nations. I will be exalted in the earth." The Lord of hosts is with us. The God of Jacob is our refuge.

Sunday

Acts 12:1-11 (BBE)

Now, about that time, Herod the king made cruel attacks on the Christians. And he put James, the brother of John, to death with the sword. And when he saw that this was pleasing to the Jews he went on to take Peter in addition. This was at the time of the feast of unleavened bread. And having taken him, he put him in prison, with four bands of armed men to keep watch over him; his purpose being to take him out to the people after the Passover. So Peter was kept in prison: but the church made strong prayer to God for him. And when Herod was about to take him out, the same night Peter was sleeping in chains between two armed men, and the watchmen were keeping watch before the door of the prison. And a great light was seen shining in the room, and an angel of the Lord came to Peter and, touching him on his side so that he came out of his sleep, said, "Get up quickly." And his chains came off his hands. Then the angel said, "Put on your shoes and get ready to go." And he did so. And he said, Put your coat round you and come with me. And he went out after him; and he was not certain if what was done by the angel was a fact, for it seemed to him that he was seeing a vision. And when they had gone past the first and second watchmen they came to the iron door into the town, which came open by itself: and they went out and down one street; and then the angel went away. And when Peter came to his senses he said, "Now, truly, I am certain that the Lord has sent his angel and taken me out of the hands of Herod, against all the hopes of the Jews."

Week 25

Monday

Matt.25:14-30 (NHT)

For it is like a man, going on a journey, who called his own servants, and entrusted his goods to them. To one he gave five talents, to another two, to another one; to each according to his own ability. Then he went on his journey. Immediately the one who received the five talents went and traded with them, and made another five talents. In like manner he who got the two gained another two. But he who received the one went away and dug in the earth, and hid his lord's money. "Now after a long time the lord of those servants came, and reconciled accounts with them. And he who received the five talents came and brought another five talents, saying, 'Lord, you delivered to me five talents. See, I have gained another five talents.' "His lord said to him, 'Well done, good and faithful servant. You have been faithful over a few things, I will set you over many things. Enter into the joy of your lord.' "And he also who had the two talents came and said, 'Lord, you delivered to me two talents. See, I have gained another two talents.' "His lord said to him, 'Well done, good and faithful servant. You have been faithful over a few things, I will set you over many things. Enter into the joy of your lord.' "He also who had received the one talent came and said, 'Lord, I knew you that you are a hard man, reaping where you did not sow, and gathering where you did not scatter. I was afraid, and went away and hid your talent in the earth. See, you have what is yours.' "But his lord answered him, 'You wicked and slothful servant. You knew that I reap where I did not sow, and gather where I did not scatter. You ought therefore to have deposited my money with the bankers, and at my coming I should have received back my own with interest. Take away therefore the talent from him, and give it to him who has the ten talents. For to everyone who has will be given, and he will have abundance, but from him who does not have, even that which he has will be taken away. Throw out the unprofitable servant into the outer darkness, where there will be weeping and gnashing of teeth.

Tuesday

Isa.61:1-3,8-11 (NHT)

The Spirit of the Lord is upon me, because he has anointed me to preach good news to the poor. He has sent me to bind up the broken-hearted, to proclaim liberty to the captives, and an opening of the eyes to the blind; to proclaim the year of the Lord's favour, and the day of vengeance of our God; to comfort all who mourn; to appoint to those who mourn in Zion, to give to them a garland for ashes, the oil of joy for mourning, the garment of praise for the spirit of heaviness; that they may be called trees of righteousness, the planting of the Lord, that he may be glorified. "For I, the Lord, love justice, and I hate robbery with iniquity; and I will give them their recompense in truth, and I will make an everlasting covenant with them. Their offspring shall be known among the nations, and their descendants among the peoples; all who see them shall acknowledge them, that they are the offspring which the Lord has blessed." I will greatly rejoice in the Lord, my soul shall be joyful in my God; for he has clothed me with the garments of salvation, he has covered me with the robe of righteousness, as a bridegroom decks himself with a garland, and as a bride adorns herself with her jewels. For as the earth brings forth its bud, and as the garden causes the things that are sown in it to spring forth; so the Lord GOD will cause righteousness and praise to spring forth before all the nations.

Wednesday

Eph.5:24-27; 6:10-12,14-18 (BBE)

And as the church is under Christ's authority, so let wives be under the rule of their husbands in all things. Husbands, have love for your wives, even as Christ had love for the church, and gave himself for it; So that he might make it holy, having made it clean with the washing of water by the word, And might take it for himself, a church full of glory, not having one mark or fold or any such thing; but that it might be holy and complete. Lastly, be strong in the Lord, and in the strength of his power. Take up God's instruments of war, so that you may be able to keep your position against all the deceits of the Evil One. For our fight is not against flesh and blood, but against authorities and powers, against the world-rulers of this dark night, against the spirits of evil in the heavens. Take your place, then, having your body clothed with the true word, and having put on the breastplate of righteousness; Be ready with the good news of peace as shoes on your feet; And most of all, using faith as a cover to keep off all the flaming arrows of the Evil One. And take salvation for your head-dress and the sword of the Spirit, which is the word of God: With prayers and deep desires, making requests at all times in the Spirit, and keeping watch, with strong purpose, in prayer for all the saints.

Thursday
Lev.5:1-6 (BBE)

If anyone does wrong by saying nothing when he is put under oath as a witness of something he has seen or had knowledge of, then he will be responsible: If anyone becomes unclean through touching unconsciously some unclean thing, such as the dead body of an unclean beast or of unclean cattle or of any unclean animal which goes flat on the earth, he will be responsible: or if he becomes unclean through touching unconsciously any unclean thing of man, whatever it may be, when it is made clear to him he will be responsible: or if anyone, without thought, takes an oath to do evil or to do good, whatever he says without thought, with an oath, having no knowledge of what he is doing; when it becomes clear to him, he will be responsible for any of these things. And whoever is responsible for any such sin, let him make a statement openly of his wrongdoing; and take to the Lord the offering for the wrong which he has done, a female from the flock, a lamb or a goat, for a sin-offering, and the priest will take away his sin.

Friday
Judg.6:11-16,38-40 (WBS)

And there came an angel of the Lord, and sat under an oak which was in Ophrah, that pertained to Joash the Abiezrite: and his son Gideon thrashed wheat by the winepress, to hide it from the Midianites. And the angel of the Lord appeared to him, and said to him, "The Lord is with thee, thou mighty man of valour." And Gideon said to him, "O my Lord, if the Lord is with us, why then hath all this befallen us and where are all his miracles which our fathers told us of, saying, did not the Lord bring us up from Egypt? But now the Lord hath forsaken us, and delivered us into the hands of the Midianites." And the Lord looked upon him, and said, "Go in this thy might, and thou shalt save Israel from the hand of the Midianites: have not I sent thee?" And he said to him, "O my Lord, by what means shall I save Israel? Behold, my family is poor in Manasseh, and I am the least in my father's house." And the Lord said to him, "Surely I will be with thee, and thou shalt smite the Midianites as one man." And he said to him, "If now I have found grace in thy sight, then show me a sign that thou talkest with me." And Gideon said to God, "If thou wilt save Israel by my hand, as thou hast said, Behold, I will put a fleece of wool on the floor; and if the dew shall be on the fleece only, and it shall be dry upon all the earth besides, then shall I know that thou wilt save Israel by my hand, as thou hast said." And it was so: for he rose early on the morrow, and pressed the fleece, and wrung the dew out of the fleece, a bowl-full of water. And Gideon said to God, "Let not thy anger be hot against me, and I will speak but this once: Let me make trial, I pray thee, but this once with the fleece; let it now be dry only upon the fleece, and upon all the ground let there be dew." And God did so that night: for it was dry upon the fleece only, and there was dew on all the ground.

Saturday

Ps.51:1-12,15 (WBS)

Have mercy upon me, O God, according to thy loving-kindness: according to the multitude of thy tender mercies, blot out my transgressions. Wash me thoroughly from my iniquity, and cleanse me from my sin. For I acknowledge my transgressions: and my sin is ever before me. Against thee, thee only, have I sinned, and done this evil in thy sight: that thou mayest be justified when thou speakest, and be clear when thou judgest. Behold, I was shapen in iniquity; and in sin did my mother conceive me. Behold, thou desirest truth in the inward parts: and in the hidden part thou shalt make me to know wisdom. Purge me with hyssop, and I shall be clean: wash me, and I shall be whiter than snow. Make me to hear joy and gladness; that the bones which thou hast broken may rejoice. Hide thy face from my sins, and blot out all my iniquities. Create in me a clean heart, O God; and renew a right spirit within me. Cast me not away from thy presence; and take not thy holy spirit from me. Restore to me the joy of thy salvation; and uphold me with thy free spirit. O Lord, open thou my lips; and my mouth shall show forth thy praise.

Sunday

Acts 15:1,6-11,22-4,28-29 (BBE)

Now certain men came down from Judaea, teaching the brothers and saying that without circumcision, after the rule of Moses, there is no salvation. And the Apostles and the rulers of the church came together and gave thought to the question and when there had been much discussion, Peter got up and said to them, "My brothers, you have knowledge that some time back it was God's pleasure that by my mouth the good news might be given to the Gentiles so that they might have faith and God, the searcher of hearts, was a witness to them, giving them the Holy Spirit even as he did to us; making no division between them and us, but making clean their hearts by faith. Why then are you testing God, by putting on the neck of the disciples a yoke so hard that not even our fathers or we were strong enough for it? But we have faith that we will get salvation through the grace of the Lord Jesus in the same way as they." Then it seemed good to the Apostles and the rulers and all the church, to send men from among them to Antioch with Paul and Barnabas; Judas, named Barsabbas, and Silas, chief men among the brothers: And they sent a letter by them, saying, "The Apostles and the older brothers, to the brothers who are of the Gentiles in Antioch and

Syria and Cilicia, may joy be with you: Because we have knowledge that some who went from us have been troubling you with their words, putting your souls in doubt; to whom we gave no such order; it seemed good to the Holy Spirit and to us, to put on you nothing more than these necessary things; To keep from things offered to false gods, and from blood, and from things put to death in ways which are against the law, and from the evil desires of the body; if you keep yourselves from these, you will do well. May you be happy."

Week 26

Monday

Matt.25:31-46 (BBE)

But when the Son of man comes in his glory, and all the angels with him, then will he be seated in his glory: and before him all the nations will come together; and they will be parted one from another, as the sheep are parted from the goats by the keeper. And he will put the sheep on his right, but the goats on the left. Then will the King say to those on his right, "Come, you who have the blessing of my Father, into the kingdom made ready for you before the world was: for I was in need of food, and you gave it to me: I was in need of drink, and you gave it to me: I was wandering, and you took me in; I had no clothing, and you gave it to me: when I was ill, or in prison, you came to me." Then will the upright make answer to him, saying, "Lord, when did we see you in need of food, and give it to you? or in need of drink, and give it to you? And when did we see you wandering, and take you in? or without clothing, and give it to you? And when did we see you ill, or in prison, and come to you?" And the King will make answer and say to them, "Truly I say to you, because you did it to the least of these my brothers, you did it to me". Then will he say to those on the left, "Go from me, you cursed ones, into the eternal fire which is ready for the Evil One and his angels: for I was in need of food, and you gave it not to me; I was in need of drink, and you gave it not to me: I was wandering, and you took me not in; without clothing, and you gave me no clothing; ill, and in prison, and you came not to me." Then will they make answer, saying, "Lord, when did we see you in need of food or drink, or wandering, or without clothing, or ill, or in prison, and did not take care of you?" Then will he make answer to them, saying, "Truly I say to you, because you did it not to the least of these, you did it not to me." And these will go away into eternal punishment; but the upright into eternal life.

Tuesday

Isa.64:6-9; 65:8,11-14 (WBS)

We are all as an unclean thing, and all our righteousnesses are as filthy rags; and we all do fade as a leaf; and our iniquities, like the wind, have taken us away. And there is none that calleth upon thy name, that stirreth up himself to take hold of thee: for thou hast hid thy face from us, and hast consumed us, because of our iniquities. But now, O Lord, thou art our father; we are the clay, and thou our potter; and we all are the work of thy hand. Be not very wroth, O Lord, neither remember iniquity for ever: behold, see, we beseech thee, we are all thy people. Thus saith the Lord, As the new wine is found in the cluster, and one saith, Destroy it not; for a blessing is in it: so will I do for my servants' sake, that I may not destroy them all. But ye are they that forsake the Lord, that forget my holy mountain, that prepare a table for that troop, and that furnish the drink-offering to that number. Therefore will I number you to the sword, and ye shall all bow down to the slaughter: because when I called, ye did not answer; when I spoke, ye did not hear; but did evil before my eyes, and did choose that in which I delighted not. Therefore thus saith the Lord GOD, Behold, my servants shall eat, but ye shall be hungry: behold, my servants shall drink, but ye shall be thirsty: behold, my servants shall rejoice, but ye shall be ashamed: Behold, my servants shall sing for joy of heart, but ye shall cry for sorrow of heart, and shall howl for vexation of spirit.

Wednesday

Phil.2:14-15; 4:4-9 (NHT)

Do all things without murmurings and disputes, that you may become blameless and pure, children of God without blemish in the midst of a crooked and perverse generation, among whom you are seen as lights in the world, Rejoice in the Lord always. Again I will say, Rejoice. Let your gentleness be known to all people. The Lord is near. Do not be anxious about anything, but in everything, by prayer and petition with thanksgiving, let your requests be made known to God. And the peace of God, which surpasses all understanding, will guard your hearts and your thoughts in Christ Jesus. Finally, brothers, whatever things are true, whatever things are honest, whatever things are just, whatever things are pure, whatever things are lovely, whatever things are of good report; if there is any virtue, and if there is any praise, think on these things. And the things you learned and received and heard and saw in me, do these things. And the God of peace will be with you.

Thursday

Lev.6:1-5 (NHT)

The Lord spoke to Moses, saying, "If anyone sins, and commits a trespass against the Lord, and deals falsely with his neighbour in a matter of deposit, or of bargain, or of robbery, or has oppressed his neighbour, or has found what was lost and lies about it and swears falsely concerning any of the sinful things that a man may do; then it shall be, if he has sinned, and is guilty, he shall restore that which he took by robbery, or the thing which he has gotten by oppression, or the deposit which was committed to him, or the lost thing which he found, or anything about which he has sworn falsely; he shall restore it even in full, and shall add a fifth part more to it. To him to whom it belongs he shall give it, in the day of his being found guilty.

Friday

Judg.7:1-7a,16,19-22 (NHT)

Then Jerubbaal, who is Gideon, and all the people who were with him, rose up early, and camped beside the spring of Harod. And the camp of Midian was on the north side of them, by the hill of Moreh, in the valley. The Lord said to Gideon, "The people who are with you are too many for me to give the Midianites into their hand, lest Israel vaunt themselves against me, saying, 'My own hand has saved me.' Now therefore proclaim in the ears of the people, saying, 'Whoever is fearful and trembling, let him return and depart from Mount Gilead.' There returned of the people twenty-two thousand; but ten thousand remained. The Lord said to Gideon, "The people are yet too many; bring them down to the water, and I will try them for you there: and it shall be, that of whom I tell you, This shall go with you, the same shall go with you; and of whoever I tell you, This shall not go with you, the same shall not go. So he brought down the people to the water: and the Lord said to Gideon, "Everyone who laps of the water with his tongue, as a dog laps, you shall put to one side; likewise everyone who kneels down on his knees to drink shall be on the other side." The number of those who lapped, putting their hand to their mouth, was three hundred men: but all the rest of the people kneeled down on their knees to drink water. The Lord said to Gideon, "By the three hundred men who lapped will I save you, and deliver the Midianites into your hand; He divided the three hundred men into three companies, and he put into the hands of all of them trumpets, and empty pitchers, with torches within the pitchers. So Gideon and the hundred men who were with him came to the outermost part of the camp in the beginning of the middle watch, when they had but newly set the watch: and they blew the trumpets, and broke in pieces the pitchers that were in their hands. The three companies blew the trumpets, and broke the pitchers, and held the torches in their left hands, and the trumpets in their right hands with which to blow; and they called out, "The sword of the Lord and of Gideon.'" They each stood in his place every man around the camp; and all the army ran; and they shouted, and put them to flight. They blew the three hundred trumpets, and the Lord set every man's sword against his fellow, and against all the army; and the army fled as far as Beth Shittah toward Zererah, as far as the border of Abel Meholah, by Tabbath.

Saturday

Ps.55:1-2,5-8,16-18,22 (BBE)

Give hearing to my prayer, O God; and let not your ear be shut against my request. Give thought to me, and let my prayer be answered: I have been made low in sorrow; Fear and shaking have come over me, with deep fear I am covered. And I said, If only I had wings like a dove! for then I would go in flight from here and be at rest. I would go wandering far away, living in the waste land. I would quickly take cover from the driving storm and from the violent wind. As for me, I will make my prayer to God, and he will be my saviour. In the evening and in the morning and in the middle of the day I will make my prayer with sounds of grief; and my voice will come to his ears. He has taken my soul away from the attack which was made against me, and given it peace; for great numbers were against me. Put your cares on the Lord, and he will be your support; he will not let the upright man be moved.

Sunday

Acts 17:22-32 (NHT)

Paul stood in the middle of the Areopagus, and said, "You men of Athens, I perceive that you are very religious in all things. For as I passed along, and observed the objects of your worship, I found also an altar with this inscription: 'TO AN UNKNOWN GOD.' What therefore you worship in ignorance, this I announce to you. The God who made the world and all things in it, he, being Lord of heaven and earth, does not dwell in temples made with hands, neither is he served by human hands, as though he needed anything, seeing he himself gives to all life and breath, and all things. He made from one blood every nation of the human race to dwell on all the surface of the earth, having determined appointed seasons, and the boundaries of their dwellings, that they should seek God, if perhaps they might reach out for him and find him, though he is not far from each one of us. 'For in him we live, and move, and have our being.' As some of your own poets have said, 'For we are also his offspring.' Being then the offspring of God, we ought not to think that the Divine Nature is like gold, or silver, or stone, engraved by human art and design. The times of ignorance therefore God overlooked. But now he commands that all people everywhere should repent, because he has appointed a day in which he will judge the world in righteousness by the man whom he has ordained; of which he has given assurance to everyone by raising him from the dead." Now when they heard of the resurrection of the dead, some mocked; but others said, "We want to hear you again concerning this."

Week 27

Monday

Mark 4:21-25 (BBE)

    And he said to them, "When the light comes in, do people put it under a vessel, or under the bed, and not on its table? There is nothing covered which will not be seen openly, and nothing has been made secret which will not come to light. If any man has ears, let him give ear." And he said to them, "Take care what you give ear to: in the same measure as you give you will get, and more will be given to you. He who has, to him will be given: and he who has not, from him will be taken even that which he has".

Tuesday

Jer.1:4-9; 17:5-10 (BBE)

    Now the word of the Lord came to me, saying, "Before you were formed in the body of your mother I had knowledge of you, and before your birth I made you holy; I have given you the work of being a prophet to the nations." Then said I, "O Lord God see, I have no power of words, for I am a child." But the Lord said to me, "Do not say, I am a child: for wherever I send you, you are to go, and whatever I give you orders to say, you are to say. Have no fear because of them: for I am with you, to keep you safe," says the Lord. Then the Lord put out his hand, touching my mouth; and the Lord said to me, "See, I have put my words in your mouth: This is what the Lord has said: Cursed is the man who puts his faith in man, and makes flesh his arm, and whose heart is turned away from the Lord for he will be like the brushwood in the upland, and will not see when good comes; but his living-place will be in the dry places in the waste land, in a salt and unpeopled land. A blessing is on the man who puts his faith in the Lord, and whose hope the Lord is for he will be like a tree planted by the waters, pushing out its roots by the stream; he will have no fear when the heat comes, but his leaf will be green; in a dry year he will have no care, and will go on giving fruit. The heart is a twisted thing, not to be searched out by man: who is able to have knowledge of it? I the Lord am the searcher of the heart, the tester of the thoughts, so that I may give to every man the reward of his ways, in keeping with the fruit of his doings."

Wednesday

Col.1:12-23 (BBE)

    Praise to the Father who has given us a part in the heritage of the saints in light; who has made us free from the power of evil and given us a place in the kingdom of the Son of his love; in whom we have our salvation, the forgiveness of sins: who is the image of the unseen God coming into existence before all living things; for by him all things were made, in heaven and on earth, things seen and things unseen, authorities, lords, rulers, and powers; all things were made by him and for him; He is before all things, and in him all things have being. And he is the head of the body, the church: the starting point of all things, the first to come again from the dead; so that in all things he might have the chief place. For God in full measure was pleased to be in him; through him uniting all things with himself, having made peace through the blood of his cross; through him, I say, uniting all things which are on earth or in heaven. And you, who in the past were cut off and at war with God in your minds through evil works, he has now made one in the body of his flesh through death, so that you might be holy and without sin and free from all evil before him if you keep yourselves safely based in the faith, not moved from the hope of the good news which came to you, and which was given to every living being under heaven

Thursday
Ex.34:21,26-31 (NHT)

"Six days you shall work, but on the seventh day you shall rest: in ploughing time and in harvest you shall rest. You shall bring the first of the first fruits of your ground to the house of the Lord your God. You shall not boil a young goat in its mother's milk." The Lord said to Moses, "Write you these words: for in accordance with these words I have made a covenant with you and with Israel." He was there with the Lord forty days and forty nights; he neither ate bread, nor drank water. He wrote on the tablets the words of the covenant, the ten commandments. It happened, when Moses came down from Mount Sinai with the two tablets of the testimony in Moses' hand, when he came down from the mountain, that Moses did not know that the skin of his face shone by reason of his speaking with him. When Aaron and all the children of Israel saw Moses, look, the skin of his face shone; and they were afraid to come near him. Moses called to them, and Aaron and all the leaders of the congregation returned to him; and Moses spoke to them.

Friday
1Sam.1:1-11,19-20 (NHT)

Now there was a certain man of Ramathaim, a Zuphite of the hill country of Ephraim, and his name was Elkanah, the son of Jeroham, the son of Elihu, the son of Tohu, the son of Zuph, an Ephraimite. And he had two wives; the name of the one was Hannah, and the name of other Peninnah. And Peninnah had children, but Hannah had no children. This man went up out of his city from year to year to worship and to sacrifice to the Lord of hosts in Shiloh. The two sons of Eli, Hophni and Phinehas, priests of the Lord, were there. When the day came that Elkanah sacrificed, he gave to Peninnah his wife, and to all her sons and her daughters, portions: but to Hannah he gave a double portion; for he loved Hannah, but the Lord had shut up her womb. Her rival taunted her severely, to irritate her, because the

Lord had shut up her womb. As he did so year by year, when she went up to the house of the Lord, so she taunted her; therefore she wept, and did not eat. Elkanah her husband said to her, "Hannah, why do you weep? Why do you not eat? Why is your heart grieved? Am I not better to you than ten sons?" So Hannah rose after eating and drinking in Shiloh, and stood before the Lord. Now Eli the priest was sitting on the seat by the doorpost of the temple of the Lord. She was in bitterness of soul, and prayed to the Lord, and wept bitterly. She vowed a vow, and said, "Lord of hosts, if you will indeed look on the affliction of your handmaid, and remember me, and not forget your handmaid, but will give to your handmaid a son, then I will set him before you as a Nazirite until the day of his death. And he will not drink wine or strong drink, and no razor will come on his head." They rose up in the morning early, and worshiped before the Lord, and returned, and came to their house to Ramah: and Elkanah knew Hannah his wife; and the Lord remembered her. It happened, when the time had come, that Hannah conceived, and bore a son; and she named him Samuel, saying, "Because I have asked him of the Lord."

Saturday

Ps.69:1-4a,13-17 (WBS)

Save me, O God; for the waters are come in to my soul. I sink in deep mire, where there is no standing: I am come into deep waters, where the floods overflow me. I am weary of my crying: my throat is dried: my eyes fail while I wait for my God. They that hate me without a cause are more than the hairs of my head But as for me, my prayer is to thee, O Lord, in an acceptable time: O God, in the multitude of thy mercy hear me, in the truth of thy salvation. Deliver me out of the mire, and let me not sink: let me be delivered from them that hate me, and out of the deep waters. Let not the water-flood overflow me, neither let the deep swallow me up, and let not the pit shut her mouth upon me. Hear me, O Lord; for thy loving-kindness is good: turn to me according to the multitude of thy tender mercies. And hide not thy face from thy servant; for I am in trouble: hear me speedily.

Sunday

Acts 20:22-38 (BBE)

And now, as you see, I am going to Jerusalem, a prisoner in spirit, having no knowledge of what will come to me there: Only that the Holy Spirit makes clear to me in every town that prison and pains are waiting for me. But I put no value on my life, if only at the end of it I may see the work complete which was given to me by the Lord Jesus, to be a witness of the good news of the grace of God. And now I am conscious that you, among whom I have gone about preaching the kingdom, will not see my face again. And so I say to you this day that I am clean from the blood of all men. For I have not kept back from you anything of the purpose of God. Give attention to yourselves, and to all the flock which the Holy Spirit has given into your care, to give food to the church of God, for which he gave his blood. I am conscious that after I am gone, evil wolves will come in among you, doing damage to the flock; And from among yourselves will come men who will give wrong teaching, turning away the disciples after them. So keep watch, having in mind that for three years without resting I was teaching every one of you, day and night, with weeping. And now, I give you into the care of God and the word of his grace, which is able to make you strong and to give you your heritage among all the saints. I have had no desire for any man's silver or gold or clothing. You yourselves have seen that with these hands I got what was necessary for me and those who were with me. In all things I was an example to you of how, in your lives, you are to give help to the feeble, and keep in memory the words of the Lord Jesus, how he himself said, There is a greater blessing in giving than in getting. And having said these words, he went down on his knees in prayer with them all. And they were all weeping, falling on Paul's neck and kissing him, Being sad most of all because he had said that they would not see his face again. And so they went with him to the ship.

Week 28

Monday

Mark 4:26-32; Luke 17:20-21 (BBE)

And he said, Such is the kingdom of God, as if a man put seed in the earth, And went to sleep and got up, night and day, and the seed came to growth, though he had no idea how. The earth gives fruit by herself; first the leaf, then the head, then the full grain. But when the grain is ready, he quickly sends men to get it cut, because the time for cutting has come. And he said, What picture may we give of the kingdom of God, or with what story may we make it clear? It is like a grain of mustard seed, which, when it is put in the earth, is smaller than all the seeds on the earth, But when it is planted, it comes up, and becomes taller than all the plants, and puts out great branches, so that the birds of heaven are able to take rest in its shade.

And when the Pharisees put questions to him about when the kingdom of God would come, he gave them an answer and said, "The kingdom of God will not come through observation: And men will not say, See, it is here! or, There for the kingdom of God is among you."

Tuesday

Jer.17:21-25,27; 18:1-6 (BBE)

This is what the Lord has said: See to yourselves, that you take up no weight on the Sabbath day, or take it in through the doors of Jerusalem;

And take no weight out of your houses on the Sabbath day, or do any work, but keep the Sabbath day holy, as I gave orders to your fathers; But they gave no attention and would not give ear, but they made their necks stiff so that they might not give ear and might not get teaching. And it will be, that if with all care you give ear to me, says the Lord, and take no weight through the doorways of this town on the Sabbath day, but keep the Sabbath day holy and do no work in it; Then through the doors of this town there will come kings and princes, seated on the seat of David, going in carriages and on horseback, they and their princes, and the men of Judah and the people of Jerusalem: and this town will keep its place for ever. But if you do not give ear to me, to keep the Sabbath day holy, and to let no weight be lifted and taken through the doors of Jerusalem on the Sabbath day: then I will put a fire in its doorways, burning up the great houses of Jerusalem, and it will never be put out.

The word which came to Jeremiah from the Lord, saying, Up! go down to the potter's house, and there I will let my words come to your ears. Then I went down to the potter's house, and he was doing his work on the stones. And when the vessel, which he was forming out of earth, got damaged in the hand of the potter, he made it again into another vessel, as it seemed good to the potter to make it. Then the word of the Lord came to me, saying, O Israel, am I not able to do with you as this potter does? says the Lord. See, like earth in the potter's hand are you in my hands, O Israel.

Wednesday

Col.2:6-15 (BBE)

As, then, you took Christ Jesus the Lord, so go on in him, rooted and based together in him, strong in the faith which the teaching gave you, giving praise to God at all times. Take care that no one takes you away by force, through man's wisdom and deceit, going after the beliefs of men and the theories of the world, and not after Christ: for in him all the wealth of God's being has a living form, and you are complete in him, who is the head of all rule and authority: in whom you had a circumcision not made with hands, in the putting off of the body of the flesh, in the circumcision of Christ; having been put to death with him in baptism, by which you came to life again with him, through faith in the working of God, who made him come back from the dead. And you, being dead through your sins and the evil condition of your flesh, to you, I say, he gave life together with him, and forgiveness of all our sins; having put an end to the handwriting of the law which was against us, taking it out of the way by nailing it to his cross; Having made himself free from the rule of authorities and powers, he put them openly to shame, glorying over them in it.

Thursday

Lev.10:8-11 (NHT)

      The Lord spoke to Aaron, saying, "Drink no wine nor strong drink, you, nor your sons with you, when you go into the Tent of Meeting, that you do not die: it shall be a statute forever throughout your generations: and that you are to make a distinction between the holy and the common, and between the unclean and the clean; and that you are to teach the children of Israel all the statutes which the Lord has spoken to them by Moses."

Friday

1 Sam.3:1-17 (NHT)

      The child Samuel ministered to the Lord before Eli. The word of the Lord was rare in those days; there was no frequent vision. It happened at that time, when Eli was lying down in his place (now his eyes had begun to grow dim, so that he could not see), and the lamp of God hadn't yet gone out, and Samuel was lying down in the Lord's temple, where the ark of God was; that the Lord called, "Samuel. Samuel." And he said, "Here I am." He ran to Eli, and said, "Here I am; for you called me." He said, "I did not call; lie down again." He went and lay down. The Lord called yet again, "Samuel. Samuel." And he arose and went to Eli, and said, "Here I am; for you called me." He answered, "I did not call, my son; lie down again." Now Samuel did not yet know the Lord, neither was the word of the Lord yet revealed to him. The Lord called Samuel again the third time. He arose and went to Eli, and said, "Here I am; for you called me." Eli perceived that the Lord had called the child. Therefore Eli said to Samuel, "Go, lie down: and it shall be, if he calls you, that you shall say, 'Speak, Lord; for your servant hears.'" So Samuel went and lay down in his place. The Lord came, and stood, and called as at other times, "Samuel. Samuel." Then Samuel said, "Speak; for your servant hears." The Lord said to Samuel, "Look, I will do a thing in Israel, at which both the ears of everyone who hears it shall tingle. In that day I will perform against Eli all that I have spoken concerning his house, from the beginning even to the end. For I have told him that I will judge his house forever, for the iniquity which he knew, because his sons were cursing God, and he did not restrain them. Therefore I have sworn to the house of Eli, that the iniquity of Eli's house shall not be removed with sacrifice nor offering forever." And Samuel lay there until the morning, and in the morning he got up and opened the doors of the house of the Lord. And Samuel was afraid to tell Eli the vision. Then Eli called Samuel, and said, "Samuel, my son." He said, "Here I am." He said, "What is the thing that he has spoken to you? Please do not hide it from me. God do so to you, and more also, if you hide anything from me of all the things that he spoke to you in your ears."

Saturday

Ps.71;1-6,9,12,16-18,20-21 (WBS)

In thee, O Lord, do I put my trust: let me never be put to confusion. Deliver me in thy righteousness, and cause me to escape: incline thy ear to me, and save me. Be thou my strong habitation, to which I may continually resort: thou hast given commandment to save me; for thou art my rock and my fortress. Deliver me, O my God, from the hand of the wicked, from the hand of the unrighteous and cruel man. For thou art my hope, O Lord GOD: thou art my trust from my youth. By thee have I been sustained from my birth: thou art he that brought me into life: my praise shall be continually of thee Cast me not off in the time of old age; forsake me not when my strength faileth. O God, be not far from me: O my God, make haste for my help. I will go in the strength of the Lord GOD: I will make mention of thy righteousness, even of thine only. O God, thou hast taught me from my youth: and hitherto have I declared thy wondrous works. Now also when I am old and grey-headed, O God, forsake me not; until I have shown thy strength to this generation, and thy power to everyone that is to come Thou, who hast shown me great and severe troubles, wilt revive me again, and wilt bring me again from the depths of the earth. Thou wilt increase my greatness, and comfort me on every side.

Sunday

Luke 7:1-10 (BBE)

After he had come to the end of all his words in the hearing of the people, he went into Capernaum. And a certain captain had a servant who was very dear to him; this servant was ill and near to death. And when news of Jesus came to his ears, he sent to him rulers of the Jews, requesting that he would come and make his servant well. And they, when they came to Jesus, made their request warmly, saying, "It is right for you to do this for him, because he is a friend to our nation, and himself has put up a Synagogue for us." And Jesus went with them. And when he was not far from the house, the man sent friends to him, saying, "Lord, do not give yourself trouble: for I am not important enough for you to come into my house: And I had the feeling that I was not even good enough to come to you: but say the word only, and my servant will be well. For I, myself, am a man under authority, having men under me; and I say to this one, Go, and he goes; and to another, Come, and he comes; and to my servant, Do this, and he does it." And when these things were said to Jesus, he was surprised, and, turning to the mass of people coming after him, said, "I have not seen such great faith, no, not in Israel." And when those who were sent came back to the house they saw that the servant was well.

Week 29

Monday

Luke 8:1-15 (BBE)

And it came about, after a short time, that he went through town and country giving the good news of the kingdom of God, and with him were the twelve, And certain women who had been made free from evil spirits and diseases, Mary named Magdalene, from whom seven evil spirits had gone out, And Joanna, the wife of Chuza, Herod's chief house-servant, and Susanna and a number of others, who gave him of their wealth for his needs. And when a great number of people came together, and men from every town went out to him, he gave them teaching in the form of a story: "A man went out to put in seed, and while he was doing it, some was dropped by the wayside and it was crushed under foot, and was taken by the birds of heaven. And some went on the rock, and when it came up it became dry and dead because it had no water. And some went among thorns, and the thorns came up with it and it had no room for growth. And some falling on good earth, came up and gave fruit a hundred times as much." And with these words he said in a loud voice, "He who has ears, let him give ear." And his disciples put questions to him about the point of the story. And he said, "To you is given knowledge of the secrets of the kingdom of God; but to the others, they are given in stories, so that seeing, they may not see, and though they give hearing, the sense will not be clear to them. Now this is the point of the story: The seed is the word of God. Those by the side of the road are those who have given hearing; then the Evil One comes and takes away the word from their hearts, so that they may not have faith and get salvation. And those on the rock are those who with joy give hearing to the word; but having no root, they have faith for a time, and when the test comes they give up. And those which went among thorns are those who have given hearing, and go on their way, but they are overcome by cares and wealth and the pleasures of life, and they give no fruit. And those in the good earth are those who, having given ear to the word, keep it with a good and true heart, and in quiet strength give fruit."

Tuesday

Jer.31:31-34 (BBE)

See, the days are coming, says the Lord, when I will make a new agreement with the people of Israel and with the people of Judah: not like the agreement which I made with their fathers, on the day when I took them by the hand to be their guide out of the land of Egypt; which agreement was broken by them, and I gave them up, says the Lord. But this is the agreement which I will make with the people of Israel after those days, says the Lord; I will put my law in their inner parts, writing it in their hearts; and I will be their God, and they will be my people. And no longer will they be teaching every man his neighbour and every man his brother, saying, get knowledge of the Lord: for they will all have knowledge of me, from the least of them to the greatest of them, says the Lord: for they will have my forgiveness for their evil-doing, and their sin will go from my memory for ever.

Wednesday

Col.3:1-17; 4:2,5-6(BBE)

If then you have a new life with Christ, give your attention to the things of heaven, where Christ is seated at the right hand of God. Keep your mind on the higher things, not on the things of earth for your life on earth is done, and you have a secret life with Christ in God. At the coming of Christ who is our life, you will be seen with him in glory. Then put to death your bodies which are of the earth; wrong use of the flesh, unclean things, passion, evil desires and envy, which is the worship of strange gods; Because of which the wrath of God comes on those who go against his orders; among whom you were living in the past, when you did such things. But now it is right for you to put away all these things; wrath, passion, bad feeling, curses, unclean talk. Do not make false statements to one another; because you have put away the old man with all his doings, and have put on the new man, which has become new in knowledge after the image of his maker; where there is no Greek or Jew, no one with circumcision or without circumcision, no division between nations, no servant or free man: but Christ is all and in all. As saints of God, then, holy and dearly loved, let your behaviour be marked by pity and mercy, kind feeling, a low opinion of yourselves, gentle ways, and a power of undergoing all things; being gentle to one another and having forgiveness for one another, if anyone has done wrong to his brother, even as the Lord had forgiveness for you: And more than all, have love; the only way in which you may be completely joined together. And let the peace of Christ be ruling in your hearts, as it was the purpose of God for you to be one body; and give praise to God at all times. Let the word of Christ be in you in all wealth of wisdom; teaching and helping one another with songs of praise and holy words, making melody to God with grace in your hearts. And whatever you do, in word or in act, do all in the name of the Lord Jesus, giving praise to God the Father through him. Give yourselves to prayer at all times, keeping watch with praise; Be wise in your behaviour to those who are outside, making good use of the time. Let your talk be with grace, mixed with salt, so that you may be able to give an answer to everyone.

Thursday

Lev.12:1-8 (NHT)

The Lord spoke to Moses, saying, "Speak to the children of Israel, saying, 'If a woman conceives, and bears a male child, then she shall be unclean seven days; as in the days of her monthly period she shall be unclean. In the eighth day the flesh of his foreskin shall be circumcised. She shall continue in the blood of purification thirty-three days. She shall not touch any holy thing, nor come into the sanctuary, until the days of her purifying are completed. But if she bears a female child, then she shall be unclean two weeks, as in her period; and she shall continue in the blood of purification sixty-six days. "'When the days of her purification are completed, for a son, or for a daughter, she shall bring to the priest at the door of the Tent of Meeting, a year old lamb for a burnt offering, and a young pigeon, or a turtledove, for a sin offering: and he shall offer it before the Lord, and make atonement for her; and she shall be cleansed from the fountain of her blood. "'This is the law for her who bears, whether a male or a female. If she cannot afford a lamb, then she shall take two turtledoves, or two young pigeons; the one for a burnt offering, and the other for a sin offering: and the priest shall make atonement for her, and she shall be clean.'"

Friday
1 Sam.17:1-9,32-37,45,48-49,51 (BBE)

Now the Philistines got their armies together for war, and came together at Socoh in the land of Judah, and took up their position between Socoh and Azekah in Ephes-dammim. And Saul and the men of Israel came together and took up their position in the valley of Elah, and put their forces in order against the Philistines. The Philistines were stationed on the mountain on one side and Israel on the mountain on the other side: and there was a valley between them. And a fighter came out from the tents of the Philistines, named Goliath of Gath; he was more than six cubits tall. He had a head-dress of brass on his head, and he was dressed in a coat of metal, the weight of which was five thousand shekels of brass. His legs were covered with plates of brass and hanging on his back was a javelin of brass. The stem of his spear was as long as a cloth-worker's rod, and its head was made of six hundred shekels' weight of iron: and one went before him with his body-cover. He took up his position and in a loud voice said to the armies of Israel, "Why have you come out to make war? Am I not a Philistine and you servants of Saul? Send out a man for yourselves and let him come down to me. If he is able to have a fight with me and overcome me, then we will be your servants: but if I am able to overcome him, then you will be our servants and do work for us." And David said to Saul, "Let no man's heart become feeble because of him; I, your servant, will go out and have a fight with this Philistine." And Saul said to David, "You are not able to go out against this Philistine and have a fight with him: for you are only a boy, and he has been a man of war from his earliest days." And David said to Saul, "Your servant has been keeper of his father's sheep; and if a lion or a bear came and took a lamb from the flock, I went out after him, and overcame him, and took it out of his mouth: and if, turning on me, he came at me, I took him by the hair and overcame him and put him to death. Your servant has overcome lion and bear: and the fate of this Philistine, who is without circumcision, will be like theirs, seeing that he has put shame on the armies of the living God." And David said, "The Lord, who kept me safe from the grip of the lion and the bear, will be my saviour from the hands of this Philistine." And Saul said to David, "Go! and may the Lord be with you." Then David said to the Philistine, "You come to me with a sword and a spear and a javelin: but I come to you in the name of the Lord of armies, the God of the armies of Israel on which you have put shame." Now when the Philistine made a move and came near to David, David quickly went at a run in the direction of the army, meeting the Philistine face to face. And David put his hand in his bag and took out a stone and sent it from his leather band straight at the Philistine, and the stone went deep into his brow, and he went down to the earth, falling on his face. So running up to the Philistine and putting his foot on him, David took his sword out of its cover, and put him to death, cutting off his head with it. And when the Philistines saw that their fighter was dead, they went in flight.

Saturday
Ps.86:3-8,11-13,16-17 (WBS)

Be merciful to me, O Lord: for I cry to thee daily. Rejoice the soul of thy servant: for to thee, O Lord, do I lift up my soul. For thou, Lord, art good, and ready to forgive; and abundant in mercy to all them that call upon thee. Give ear, O Lord, to my prayer; and attend to the voice of my supplications. In the day of my trouble I will call upon thee: for thou wilt answer me. Among the gods there is none like thee, O Lord; neither are there any works like thy works. Teach me thy way, O Lord; I will walk in thy truth: unite my heart to fear thy name. I will praise thee, O Lord my God, with all my heart: and I will glorify thy name for evermore. For great is thy mercy towards me: and thou hast delivered my soul from the lowest hell. O turn to me, and have mercy upon me; give thy strength to thy servant, and save the son of thy handmaid. Show me a token for good; that they who hate me may see it, and be ashamed: because thou, Lord, hast helped me, and comforted me.

Sunday
Luke 7:11-17 (BBE)

And it came about, after a little time, that he went to a town named Nain; and his disciples went with him, and a great number of people. Now when he came near the door of the town, a dead man was being taken out, the only son of his mother, who was a widow: and a great number of people from the town were with her. And when the Lord saw her, he had pity on her and said to her, "Be not sad." And he came near, and put his hand on the stretcher where the dead man was: and those who were moving it came to a stop. And he said, "Young man, I say to you, Get up." And the dead man got up, and words came from his lips. And he gave him to his mother. And fear came on all, and they gave praise to God, saying, "A great prophet is among us": and, "God has given thought to his people". And this story about him went through all Judaea and the places round about.

Week 30

Monday

Luke 10:25-37 (BBE)

And a certain teacher of the law got up and put him to the test, saying, "Master, what have I to do so that I may have eternal life?" And he said to him, "What does the law say, in your reading of it?" And he, answering, said, "Have love for the Lord your God with all your heart and with all your soul and with all your strength and with all your mind; and for your neighbour as for yourself." And he said, "You have given the right answer: do this and you will have life." But he, desiring to put himself in the right, said to Jesus, "And who is my neighbour?" And Jesus, answering him, said, "A certain man was going down from Jerusalem to Jericho, and he got into the hands of thieves, who took his clothing and gave him cruel blows, and when they went away, he was half dead. And by chance a certain priest was going down that way: and when he saw him, he went by on the other side. And in the same way, a Levite, when he came to the place and saw him, went by on the other side. But a certain man of Samaria, journeying that way, came where he was, and when he saw him, he was moved with pity for him, And came to him and put clean linen round his wounds, with oil and wine; and he put him on his beast and took him to a house and took care of him. And the day after he took two pennies and gave them to the owner of the house and said, Take care of him; and if this money is not enough, when I come again I will give you whatever more is needed. Which of these three men, in your opinion, was neighbour to the man who came into the hands of thieves?" And he said, "The one who had mercy on him." And Jesus said, "Go and do the same."

Tuesday

Lam.3:1-7,21-26,31-33 (BBE)

I am the man who has seen trouble by the rod of his wrath. By him I have been made to go in the dark where there is no light. Truly against me his hand has been turned again and again all the day. My flesh and my skin have been used up by him and my bones broken. He has put up a wall against me, shutting me in with bitter sorrow. He has kept me in dark places, like those who have been long dead. He has put a wall round me, so that I am not able to go out; he has made great the weight of my chain. This I keep in mind, and because of this I have hope. It is through the Lord's love that we have not come to destruction, because his mercies have no limit. They are new every morning; great is your good faith. I said to myself, The Lord is my heritage; and because of this I will have hope in him. The Lord is good to those who are waiting for him, to the soul which is looking for him. It is good to go on hoping and quietly waiting for the salvation of the Lord. For the Lord does not give a man up for ever. For though he sends grief, still he will have pity in the full measure of his love, for he has no pleasure in troubling and causing grief to the children of men.

Wednesday
1Thes.4:3-9,11-12 (BBE)

For the purpose of God for you is this: that you may be holy, and may keep yourselves from the desires of the flesh; So that every one of you may keep his body holy and in honour; Not in the passion of evil desires, like the Gentiles, who have no knowledge of God; And that no man may make attempts to get the better of his brother in business: for the Lord is the judge in all these things, as we said to you before and gave witness. Because it is God's purpose that our way of life may be not unclean but holy. Whoever, then, goes against this word, goes against not man but God, who gives his Holy Spirit to you. But about loving the brothers, there is no need for me to say anything to you in this letter: for you have the teaching of God that love for one another is right and necessary; And that you may take pride in being quiet and doing your business, working with your hands as we gave you orders; That you may be respected by those who are outside, and may have need of nothing.

Thursday
Lev.15:1-2,16-18 (NHT)

The Lord spoke to Moses and to Aaron, saying, "Speak to the children of Israel, and tell them, 'When any man has a discharge from his body, because of his discharge he is unclean. '"If any man has an emission of semen, then he shall bathe all his flesh in water, and be unclean until the evening. Every garment, and every skin, whereon the semen is, shall be washed with water, and be unclean until the evening. If a man lies with a woman and there is an emission of semen, they shall both bathe themselves in water, and be unclean until the evening.

Friday
1 Sam.18:20-28; 19:11-16 (BBE)

And Saul's daughter Michal was in love with David: and Saul had word of it and was pleased. And Saul said, I will give her to him, so that she may be a cause of danger to him, and so that the hands of the Philistines may be against him. So Saul said to David, "Today you are to become my son-in-law for the second time." And Saul gave his servants orders saying,

"Have talk with David secretly and say to him, 'See how the king has delight in you, and how you are loved by all his servants: then be the king's son-in-law.'" And Saul's servants said these things to David. And David said, "Does it seem to you a small thing to be the king's son-in-law, seeing that I am a poor man, of no great name?" And the servants of Saul gave him an account of what David had said. And Saul said, then say to David, "The king has no desire for any bride-price, but only for the private parts of a hundred Philistines so that the king may get the better of his haters." But it was in Saul's mind that David might come to his end by the hands of the Philistines. And when his servants said these words to David, he was well pleased to be the son-in-law of the king. And the days were still not past. So David and his men got up and went, and put to death two hundred of the Philistines; and David took their private parts and gave the full number of them to the king, so that he might be the king's son-in-law. And Saul gave him his daughter Michal for his wife. And it was clear to Saul that the Lord was with David; and he was loved by all Israel. Then in that night Saul sent men to David's house to keep watch on him so as to put him to death in the morning: and David's wife Michal said to him, "If you do not go away to a safe place tonight you will be put to death in the morning." So Michal let David down through the window, and he went in flight and got away. Then Michal took the image and put it in the bed, with a cushion of goat's hair at its head, and she put clothing over it. And when Saul sent men to take David, she said, "He is ill." And Saul sent his men to see David, saying, "Do not come back without him, take him in his bed, so that I may put him to death." And when the men came in, there was the image in the bed, with the cushion of goat's hair at its head

Saturday
Ps.91 (BBE)

Happy is he whose resting-place is in the secret of the Lord, and under the shade of the wings of the Most High; who says of the Lord, He is my safe place and my tower of strength: he is my God, in whom is my hope. He will take you out of the bird-net, and keep you safe from wasting disease. You will be covered by his feathers; under his wings you will be safe: his good faith will be your salvation. You will have no fear of the evil things of the night, or of the arrow in flight by day, or of the disease which takes men in the dark, or of the destruction which makes waste when the sun is high. You will see a thousand falling by your side, and ten thousand at your right hand; but it will not come near you. Only with your eyes will you see the reward of the evil-doers. Because you have said, I am in the hands of the Lord, the Most High is my safe resting-place; no evil will come on you, and no disease will come near your tent for he will give you into the care of his angels to keep you wherever you go. In their hands they will keep you up, so that your foot may not be crushed against a stone. You will put your foot on the lion and the snake; the young lion and the great snake will be crushed under your feet. Because he has given me his love, I will take him out of danger: I will put him in a place of honour, because he has kept my name in his heart. When his cry comes up to me, I will give him an answer: I will be with him in trouble; I will make him free from danger and give him honour. With long life will he be rewarded; and I will let him see my salvation.

Sunday

Luke 7:36-50 (BBE)

And one of the Pharisees made a request that he would take a meal with him. And he went into the Pharisee's house and took his seat at the table. And there was a woman in the town who was a sinner; and when she had news that he was a guest in the Pharisee's house, she took a bottle of perfume, And went in and took her place at the back of him, near his feet, weeping, so that his feet were washed with the drops from her eyes, and with her hair she made them dry, and kissing his feet she put the perfume on them. Now when the Pharisee in whose house he was saw it, he said to himself, "This man, if he was a prophet, would be conscious what sort of woman this is who has put her hands on him, that she is a sinner." And Jesus, answering, said, "Simon, I have something to say to you." And he said, "Master, say on." And he said, "Two men were in debt to a certain man of business: one had a debt of five hundred pence, and the other of fifty. When they were unable to make payment, he made the two of them free of their debts. Which of them, now, will have the greater love for him?" Simon, in answer, said, "It seems he whose debt was greater." And he said, "Your decision is right." And turning to the woman he said to Simon, "You see this woman? I came into your house; you did not give me water for my feet: but she has been washing my feet with the drops from her eyes, and drying them with her hair. You did not give me a kiss: but she, from the time when I came in, has gone on kissing my feet. You put no oil on my head: but she has put perfume on my feet. And so I say to you, She will have forgiveness for her sins which are great in number, because of her great love: but he who has small need of forgiveness gives little love." And he said to her, "You have forgiveness for your sins." And those who were seated at table with him said to themselves, "Who is this who even gives forgiveness of sins?" And he said to the woman, "By your faith you have salvation; go in peace."

Week 31

Monday

Luke 12:13-21 (BBE)

And one of the people said to him, "Master, give an order to my brother to make division of the heritage with me." But he said, "Man, who made me a judge or a maker of decisions for you?" And he said to them,

"Take care to keep yourselves free from the desire for property; for a man's life is not made up of the number of things which he has." And he said to them, in a story, "The land of a certain man of great wealth was very fertile: And he said to himself, 'What is to be done for I have no place in which to put all my fruit.' And he said, 'This I will do: I will take down my store-houses and make greater ones, and there I will put all my grain and my goods. And I will say to my soul, Soul, you have a great amount of goods in store, enough for a number of years; be at rest, take food and wine and be happy.' But God said to him, 'You foolish one, tonight I will take your soul from you, and who then will be the owner of all the things which you have got together?' So that is what comes to the man who gets wealth for himself, and has not wealth in the eyes of God."

Tuesday
Ezek.18:5-13,20-23,32

But if a man is upright, living rightly and doing righteousness, And has not taken flesh with the blood for food, or given worship to the images of the children of Israel; if he has not had connection with his neighbour's wife, or come near to a woman at the time when she is unclean; And has done no wrong to any, but has given back to the debtor what is his, and has taken no one's goods by force, and has given food to him who was in need of it, and clothing to him who was without it; And has not given his money out at interest or taken great profits, and, turning his hand from evil-doing, has kept faith between man and man, And has been guided by my rules and has kept my laws and done them: he is upright, life will certainly be his, says the Lord. If he has a son who is a thief, a taker of life, who does any of these things, Who has taken flesh with the blood as food, and has had connection with his neighbour's wife, Has done wrong to the poor and to him who is in need, and taken property by force, and has not given back to one in his debt what is his, and has given worship to images and has done disgusting things, And has given out his money at interest and taken great profits: he will certainly not go on living: he has done all these disgusting things: death will certainly be his fate; his blood will be on him. The soul which does sin will be put to death: the son will not be made responsible for the evil-doing of the father, or the father for the evil-doing of the son; the righteousness of the upright will be on himself, and the evil-doing of the evil-doer on himself. But if the evil-doer, turning away from all the sins which he has done, keeps my rules and does what is ordered and right, life will certainly be his; death will not be his fate. Not one of the sins which he has done will be kept in memory against him: in the righteousness which he has done he will have life. Have I any pleasure in the death of the evil-doer? says the Lord: am I not pleased if he is turned from his way so that he may have life? For I have no pleasure in the death of him on whom death comes, says the Lord: be turned back then, and have life.

Wednesday

1 Thes 4:13-18 (BBE)

But it is our desire, brothers, that you may be certain about those who are sleeping; so that you may have no need for sorrow, as others have who are without hope. For if we have faith that Jesus underwent death and came back again, even so those who are sleeping will come again with him by God's power. For this we say to you by the word of the Lord, that we who are still living at the coming of the Lord, will not go before those who are sleeping. Because the Lord himself will come down from heaven with a word of authority, with the voice of the chief angel, with the sound of a horn: and the dead in Christ will come to life first; Then we who are still living will be taken up together with them into the clouds to see the Lord in the air: and so will we be for ever with the Lord. So then, give comfort to one another with these words.

Thursday

Lev.15:19-24 (NHT)

If a woman has a discharge, and her discharge in her flesh is blood, she shall be in her impurity seven days: and whoever touches her shall be unclean until the evening. Everything that she lies on in her impurity shall be unclean. Everything also that she sits on shall be unclean. Whoever touches her bed shall wash his clothes, and bathe himself in water, and be unclean until the evening. Whoever touches anything that she sits on shall wash his clothes, and bathe himself in water, and be unclean until the evening. If it is on the bed, or on anything whereon she sits, when he touches it, he shall be unclean until the evening. If any man lies with her, and her monthly flow is on him, he shall be unclean seven days; and every bed whereon he lies shall be unclean.

Friday

1 Sam.25:4-14,18-19,23-25,28,32-42 (BBE)

And David had word in the waste land that Nabal was cutting the wool of his sheep. And David sent ten young men, and said to them, "Go up to Carmel and go to Nabal, and say kind words to him in my name; And say this to my brother, 'May all be well for you: peace be to you and your house and all you have. I have had word that you have wool cutters: now the keepers of your sheep have been with us, and we have done them no evil, and taken nothing of theirs while they were in Carmel. If your young men are questioned they will say the same thing. So now, let my young men have grace in your eyes, for we are come at a good time; please give anything you may have by you to your servants and to your son David.'" And when David's young men came, they said all this to Nabal, in David's name, and said nothing more. And Nabal gave them his answer and said, "Who is David?

who is the son of Jesse? there are a number of servants in these days running away from their masters. Am I to take my bread and my wine and the meat I have got ready for my wool cutters and give it to men coming from I have no idea where?" So David's young men, turning away, went back and gave him an account of everything he had said. And David said to his men, "Put on your swords, every one of you." And every man put on his sword; and David did the same; and about four hundred men went up with David, and two hundred kept watch over their goods. But one of the young men said to Nabal's wife Abigail, "David sent men from the waste land to say kind words to our master, and he gave them a rough answer." Then Abigail quickly took two hundred cakes of bread and two skins full of wine and five sheep ready for cooking and five measures of dry grain and a hundred parcels of dry grapes and two hundred cakes of figs, and put them on asses. And she said to her young men, "Go on in front of me and I will come after you." But she said nothing to her husband Nabal. And when Abigail saw David, she quickly got off her ass, falling down on her face before him. And falling at his feet she said, "May the wrong be on me, my lord, on me: let your servant say a word to you, and give ear to the words of your servant. Let my lord give no attention to Nabal, that good-for-nothing: for as his name is, so is he, a man without sense: but I, your servant, did not see the young men whom my lord sent. And may the sin of your servant have forgiveness: for the Lord will certainly make your family strong, because my lord is fighting in the Lord's war; and no evil will be seen in you all your days." And David said to Abigail, "May the Lord, the God of Israel, be praised, who sent you to me today: A blessing on your good sense and on you, who have kept me today from the crime of blood and from taking into my hands the punishment for my wrongs. For truly, by the living Lord, the God of Israel, who has kept me from doing you evil, if you had not been so quick in coming to me and meeting me, by dawn there would not have been in Nabal's house so much as one male living." Then David took from her hands her offering: and he said to her, "Go back to your house in peace; see, I have given ear to your voice, and taken your offering with respect." And Abigail went back to Nabal; and he was feasting in his house like a king; and Nabal's heart was full of joy, for he had taken much wine; so she said nothing to him till dawn came. And in the morning, when the effect of the wine was gone, Nabal's wife gave him an account of all these things, and all the heart went out of him, and he became like stone. And about ten days after, the Lord sent disease on Nabal and death came to him. And David, hearing that Nabal was dead, said, "May the Lord be praised, who has taken up my cause against Nabal for the shame which he put on me, and has kept back his servant from evil, and has sent on Nabal's head the reward of his evil-doing." And David sent word to Abigail, desiring to take her as his wife. And when David's servants came to Carmel, to Abigail, they said to her, "David has sent us to you to take you to him as his wife." And she got up, and going down on her face to the earth, said, "See, I am ready to be a servant-girl, washing the feet of the servants of my lord." Then Abigail got up quickly and went on her ass, with five of her young women, after the men whom David had sent; and she became David's wife.

Saturday
Ps.100 (BBE)

Make a glad sound to the Lord, all the earth. Give worship to the Lord with joy; come before him with a song. Be certain that the Lord is God; it is he who has made us, and we are his; we are his people, and the sheep to whom he gives food. Come into his doors with joy, and into his house with praise; give him honour, blessing his name. For the Lord is good, and his mercy is never-ending; his faith is unchanging through all generations.

Sunday
John 2:13-17 (NHT)

The Jewish Passover was near, and Jesus went up to Jerusalem. And he found in the temple those who sold oxen, sheep, and doves, and the money changers sitting. And he made a whip of cords, and threw all out of the temple, both the sheep and the oxen; and he poured out the changers' money, and overthrew their tables. To those who sold the doves, he said, "Take these things out of here. Do not make my Father's house a marketplace." His disciples remembered that it was written, "Zeal for your house will consume me."

Week 32
Monday
Luke 15:1-7 (BBE)

Now all the tax-farmers and sinners came near to give ear to him. And the Pharisees and scribes were angry, saying, "This man gives approval to sinners, and takes food with them." And he made a story for them, saying, "What man of you, having a hundred sheep, if one of them gets loose and goes away, will not let the ninety-nine be in the waste land by themselves, and go after the wandering one, till he sees where it is? And when he has got it again, he takes it in his arms with joy. And when he gets back to his house, he sends for his neighbours and friends, saying to them, Be glad with me, for I have got back my sheep which had gone away. I say to you that even so there will be more joy in heaven when one sinner is turned away from his wrongdoing, than for ninety-nine good men, who have no need of a change of heart."

Tuesday

Ezek.22:1-2,7-12,22 (BBE)

And the word of the Lord came to me, saying, "And you, son of man, will you be a judge, will you be a judge of the town of blood? Then make clear to her all her disgusting ways. In you they have had no respect for father and mother; in you they have been cruel to the man from a strange land; in you they have done wrong to the child without a father and to the widow. You have made little of my holy things, and have made my Sabbaths unclean. In you there are men who say evil of others, causing death; in you they have taken the flesh with the blood for food; in your streets they have put evil designs into effect. In you they have let the shame of their fathers be seen. In you they have done wrong to a woman at the time when she was unclean and in you one man has done what was disgusting with his neighbour's wife; and another has made his daughter-in-law unclean; and another has done wrong to his sister, his father's daughter. In you they have taken rewards as the price of blood. You have taken interest and great profits, and have taken away your neighbours' goods by force, and have not kept me in mind," says the Lord. "As silver becomes soft in the oven, so you will become soft in it; and you will be certain that I the Lord have let loose my passion on you."

Wednesday

1Thes.5:5-23 (BBE)

For you are all sons of light and of the day: we are not of the night or of the dark. So then, let us not take our rest as the others do, but let us be self-controlled and awake. For those who are sleeping do so in the night; and those who are the worse for drink are so in the night; But let us, who are of the day, be serious, putting on the breastplate of faith and love, and on our heads, the hope of salvation. For God's purpose for us is not wrath, but salvation through our Lord Jesus Christ, Who was put to death for us, so that, awake or sleeping, we may have a part in his life. So then, go on comforting and building up one another, as you have been doing. But we make this request to you, my brothers: give attention to those who are working among you, who are over you in the Lord to keep order among you; And have a high opinion of them in love because of their work. Be at peace among yourselves. And our desire is that you will keep control over those whose lives are not well ordered, giving comfort to the feeble-hearted, supporting those with little strength, and putting up with much from all. Let no one give evil for evil; but ever go after what is good, for one another and for all. Have joy at all times. Keep on with your prayers. In everything give praise: for this is the purpose of God in Christ Jesus for you. Do not put out the light of the Spirit; Do not make little of the words of the prophets; Let all things be tested; keep to what is good; Keep from every form of evil. And may the God of peace himself make you holy in every way; and may your spirit and soul and body be free from all sin at the coming of our Lord Jesus Christ.

Thursday
Lev.17:10-12 (BBE)

And if any man of Israel, or any other living among them, takes any sort of blood for food, my wrath will be turned against that man and he will be cut off from among his people. For the life of the flesh is in its blood; and I have given it to you on the altar to take away your sin: for it is the blood which makes free from sin because of the life in it. For this reason I have said to the children of Israel, No man among you, or any others living with you, may take blood as food.

Friday
2 Sam.11:2-6,14-17,26-27 (BBE)

Now one evening, David got up from his bed, and while he was walking on the roof of the king's house, he saw from there a woman bathing; and the woman was very beautiful. And David sent to get knowledge who the woman was. And one said, Is this not Bath-sheba, the daughter of Eliam and wife of Uriah the Hittite? And David sent and took her; and she came to him, and he took her to his bed: (for she had been made clean;) then she went back to her house. And the woman became with child; and she sent word to David that she was with child. And David sent to Joab saying, Send Uriah the Hittite to me. And Joab sent Uriah to David. Now in the morning, David gave Uriah a letter to take to Joab. And in the letter he said, Take care to put Uriah in the very front of the line, where the fighting is most violent, and go back from him, so that he may be overcome and put to death. So while Joab was watching the town, he put Uriah in the place where it was clear to him the best fighters were. And the men of the town went out and had a fight with Joab: and a number of David's men came to their death in the fight, and with them Uriah the Hittite. And when the wife of Uriah had news that her husband was dead, she gave herself up to weeping for him. And when the days of weeping were past, David sent for her, and took her into his house, and she became his wife and gave him a son. But the Lord was not pleased with the thing David had done.

Saturday
Ps.103:1-17 (NHT)

Praise the Lord, my soul, and all that is within me, praise his holy name. Praise the Lord, my soul, and do not forget all his benefits; who forgives all your sins; who heals all your diseases; who redeems your life from destruction; who crowns you with loving kindness and tender mercies;

who satisfies your desire with good things; your youth is renewed like the eagle's. The Lord executes righteous acts, and justice for all who are oppressed. He made known his ways to Moses, his deeds to the children of Israel. The Lord is merciful and gracious, slow to anger, and abundant in loving kindness. He will not always accuse; neither will he stay angry forever. He has not dealt with us according to our sins, nor repaid us for our iniquities. For as the heavens are high above the earth, so great is his loving kindness toward those who fear him. As far as the east is from the west, so far has he removed our transgressions from us. Like a father has compassion on his children, so the Lord has compassion on those who fear him. For he knows how we are made. He remembers that we are dust. As for man, his days are like grass. As a flower of the field, so he flourishes. For the wind passes over it, and it is gone, and its place remembers it no more. But the Lord's loving kindness is from everlasting to everlasting with those who fear him, his righteousness to children's children;

Sunday

Luke 17:11-19 (NHT)

It happened as he was on his way to Jerusalem, that he was passing along the borders of Samaria and Galilee. As he entered into a certain village, ten men who were lepers met him, who stood at a distance. They lifted up their voices, saying, "Jesus, Master, have mercy on us." When he saw them, he said to them, "Go and show yourselves to the priests." It happened that as they went, they were cleansed. One of them, when he saw that he was healed, turned back, glorifying God with a loud voice. He fell on his face at Jesus' feet, giving him thanks; and he was a Samaritan. Jesus answered, "Weren't the ten cleansed? But where are the nine? Were there none found who returned to give glory to God, except this stranger?" Then he said to him, "Get up, and go your way. Your faith has healed you."

Week 33

Monday

Luke 15:11-32 (BBE)

And he said, "A certain man had two sons: And the younger of them said to his father, 'Father, give me that part of your property which will be mine.' And he made division of his goods between them. And not long after, the younger son got together everything which was his and took a journey into a far-away country, and there all his money went in foolish living. And when everything was gone, there was no food to be had in that country, and he was in need. And he went and put himself into the hands of one of the people of that country, and he sent him into his fields to give the pigs their food. And so great was his need that he would have been glad to take the pigs' food, and no one gave him anything. But when he came to his senses, he said, What numbers of my father's servants have bread enough, and more, while I am near to death here through need of food! I will get up and go to my father, and will say to him, 'Father, I have done wrong, against heaven and in your eyes: I am no longer good enough to be named your son: make me like one of your servants.' And he got up and went to his father. But while he was still far away, his father saw him and was moved with pity for him and went quickly and took him in his arms and gave him a kiss. And his son said to him, 'Father, I have done wrong, against heaven and in your eyes: I am no longer good enough to be named your son.' But the father said to his servants, 'Get out the first robe quickly, and put it on him, and put a ring on his hand and shoes on his feet: And get the fat young ox and put it to death, and let us have a feast, and be glad. For this, my son, who was dead, is living again; he had gone away from me, and has come back.' And they were full of joy. Now the older son was in the field: and when he came near the house, the sounds of music and dancing came to his ears. And he sent for one of the servants, questioning him about what it might be. And he said to him, 'Your brother has come; and your father has had the young ox put to death because he has come back safely.' But he was angry and would not go in; and his father came out and made a request to him to come in. But he made answer and said to his father, 'See, all these years I have been your servant, doing your orders in everything: and you never gave me even a young goat so that I might have a feast with my friends: But when this your son came, who has been wasting your property with bad women, you put to death the fat young ox for him.' And he said to him, 'Son, you are with me at all times, and all I have is yours. But it was right to be glad and to have a feast; for this your brother, who was dead, is living again; he had gone away and has come back.'"

Tuesday

Ezek.34:11-17,22-24 (BBE)

For this is what the Lord has said: Truly, I, even I, will go searching and looking for my sheep. As the keeper goes looking for his flock when he is among his wandering sheep, so I will go looking for my sheep, and will get them safely out of all the places where they have been sent wandering in the day of clouds and black night. And I will take them out from among the peoples, and get them together from the countries, and will take them into their land; and I will give them food on the mountains of Israel by the water-streams and wherever men are living in the country. I will give them good grass-land for their food, and their safe place will be the mountains of the high place of Israel: there they will take their rest in a good place, and on fat grass-land they will take their food on the mountains of Israel. I myself will give food to my flock, and I will give them rest, says the Lord. I will go in search of that which had gone wandering from the way, and will get back that which had been sent in flight, and will put bands on that which was broken, and give strength to that which was ill: but the fat and the strong I will give up to destruction; I will give them for their food the punishment which is theirs by right. And as for you, O my flock, says the Lord, truly, I will be judge between sheep and sheep, the he-sheep and the he-goats. I will make my flock safe, and they will no longer be taken away, and I will be judge between sheep and sheep. And I will put over them one keeper, and he will give them food, even my servant David; he will give them food and be their keeper. And I the Lord will be their God and my servant David their ruler; I the Lord have said it.

Wednesday

2 Thes.1:6,8-9; 2:13-15; 3:6-10

For it is an act of righteousness on God's part to give trouble as their reward to those who are troubling you, to give punishment to those who have no knowledge of God, and to those who do not give ear to the good news of our Lord Jesus: Whose reward will be eternal destruction from the face of the Lord and from the glory of his strength, But it is right for us to give praise to God at all times for you, brothers, loved by the Lord, because it was the purpose of God from the first that you might have salvation, being made holy by the Spirit and by faith in what is true: And in this purpose he gave you a part through the good news of which we were the preachers, even that you might have part in the glory of our Lord Jesus Christ. So then, brothers, be strong in purpose, and keep the teaching which has been given to you by word or by letter from us. Now we give you orders, brothers, in the name of our Lord Jesus Christ, to keep away from all those whose behaviour is not well ordered and in harmony with the teaching which they had from us. For you yourselves are used to taking us as your example, because our life among you was ruled by order, And we did not take food from any man for nothing, but were working hard night and day not to be a trouble to any of you: Not because we have not the right, but to make ourselves an example to you, so that you might do the same. For even when we were with you we gave you orders, saying, If any man does no work, let him not have food.

Thursday

Lev.18:1-5 (BBE)

And the Lord said to Moses, "Say to the children of Israel, I am the Lord your God. You may not do those things which were done in the land of Egypt where you were living; and you may not do those things which are done in the land of Canaan where I am taking you, or be guided in your behaviour by their rules. But you are to be guided by my decisions and keep my rules, and be guided by them: I am the Lord your God. So keep my rules and my decisions, which, if a man does them, will be life to him: I am the Lord."

Friday

2 Sam.12:1-10,15,18-23 (BBE)

And the Lord sent Nathan to David. And Nathan came to him and said, "There were two men in the same town: one a man of great wealth, and the other a poor man. The man of wealth had great numbers of flocks and herds; But the poor man had only one little she-lamb, which he had got and taken care of: from its birth it had been with him like one of his children; his meat was its food, and from his cup it took its drink, resting in his arms, and it was like a daughter to him. Now a traveller came to the house of the man of wealth, but he would not take anything from his flock or his herd to make a meal for the traveller who had come to him, but he took the poor man's lamb and made it ready for the man who had come." And David was full of wrath against that man; and he said to Nathan, "By the living Lord, death is the right punishment for the man who has done this: And he will have to give back four times the value of the lamb, because he has done this and because he had no pity." And Nathan said to David, "You are that man. The Lord God of Israel says, I made you king over Israel, putting holy oil on you, and I kept you safe from the hands of Saul; I gave you your master's daughter and your master's wives for yourself, and I gave you the daughters of Israel and Judah; and if that had not been enough, I would have given you such and such things. Why then have you had no respect for the word of the Lord, doing what is evil in his eyes? You have put Uriah the Hittite to death with the sword, and have taken his wife to be your wife; you have put him to death with the sword of the children of Ammon. So now the sword will never be turned away from your family; because you have had no respect for me, and have taken the wife of Uriah the Hittite to be your wife." Then Nathan went back to his house.

And the hand of the Lord was on David's son, the child of Uriah's wife, and it became very ill. And then on the seventh day the child's death took place. And David's servants were in fear of giving him the news of the child's death: for they said, "Truly, while the child was still living he gave no attention when we said anything to him: what will he do to himself if we give him word that the child is dead?" But when David saw that his servants were talking together quietly, he was certain that the child was dead: and he said to his servants," Is the child dead?" and they said, "He is." Then David got up from the earth, and after washing and rubbing himself with oil and changing his clothing, he went into the house of the Lord and gave worship: then he went back to his house, and at his order they put food before him and he had a meal. Then his servants said to him, "Why have you been acting in this way? you were weeping and going without food while the child was still living; but when the child was dead, you got up and had a meal." And he said, "While the child was still living I went without food and gave myself up to weeping: for I said, Who is able to say that the Lord will not have mercy on me and give the child life? But now that the child is dead there is no reason for me to go without food; am I able to make him come back to life? I will go to him, but he will never come back to me."

Saturday

Ps.104:1-5,10-14,24,31 (WBS)

Bless the Lord, O my soul. O Lord my God, thou art very great; thou art clothed with honour and majesty. Who coverest thyself with light as with a garment: who stretchest out the heavens like a curtain: Who layeth the beams of his chambers in the waters: who maketh the clouds his chariot: who walketh upon the wings of the wind: Who maketh his angels spirits; his ministers a flaming fire: Who laid the foundations of the earth, that it should not be removed for ever. He sendeth the springs into the valleys, which run among the hills. They give drink to every beast of the field: the wild asses quench their thirst. By them shall the fowls of the heaven have their habitation, which sing among the branches. He watereth the hills from his chambers: the earth is satisfied with the fruit of thy works. He causeth the grass to grow for the cattle, and herb for the service of man: that he may bring forth food out of the earth; O Lord, how manifold are thy works! in wisdom hast thou made them all: the earth is full of thy riches. The glory of the Lord shall endure for ever: the Lord shall rejoice in his works.

Sunday

John 4:1-26 (BBE)

Now when it was clear to the Lord that word had come to the ears of the Pharisees that Jesus was making more disciples than John and was giving them baptism (Though, in fact, it was his disciples who gave baptism, not Jesus himself), He went out of Judaea into Galilee again. And it was necessary for him to go through Samaria. So he came to a town of Samaria which was named Sychar, near to the bit of land which Jacob gave to his son Joseph: Now Jacob's fountain was there. Jesus, being tired after his journey, was resting by the fountain. It was about the sixth hour. A woman of Samaria came to get water, and Jesus said to her, "Give me some water." For his disciples had gone to the town to get food. The woman of Samaria said to him, "Why do you, a Jew, make a request for water to me, a woman of Samaria?" She said this because Jews have nothing to do with the people of Samaria. In answer Jesus said, "If you had knowledge of what God gives freely and who it is who says to you, 'Give me water', you would make your prayer to him, and he would give you living water." The woman said to him, "Sir, you have no vessel and the fountain is deep; from where will you get the living water? Are you greater than our father Jacob who gave us the fountain and took the water of it himself, with his children and his cattle?" Jesus said to her, "Everyone who takes this water will be in need of it again: But whoever takes the water I give him will never be in need of drink again; for the water I give him will become in him a fountain of eternal life." The woman said to him, "Sir, give me this water, so that I may not be in need again of drink and will not have to come all this way for it." Jesus said to her, "Go, get your husband and come back here with him." In answer, the woman said, "I have no husband." Jesus said to her, "You have said rightly, I have no husband: You have had five husbands, and the man you have now is not your husband: that was truly said." The woman said to him, "Sir, I see that you are a prophet. Our fathers gave worship on this mountain, but you Jews say that the right place for worship is in Jerusalem." Jesus said to her, "Woman, take my word for this; the time is coming when you will not give worship to the Father on this mountain or in Jerusalem. You give worship, but without knowledge of what you are worshipping: we give worship to what we have knowledge of: for salvation comes from the Jews. But the time is coming, and is even now here, when the true worshippers will give worship to the Father in the true way of the spirit, for these are the worshippers desired by the Father. God is Spirit: then let his worshippers give him worship in the true way of the spirit." The woman said to him, "I am certain that the Messiah, who is named Christ, is coming; when he comes he will make all things clear to us." Jesus said to her, "I, who am talking to you, am he."

Week 34

Monday

Luke 16:19-31 (BBE)

Now there was a certain man of great wealth, who was dressed in fair clothing of purple and delicate linen, and was shining and glad every day. And a certain poor man, named Lazarus, was stretched out at his door, full of wounds, Desiring the broken bits of food which came from the table of the man of wealth; and even the dogs came and put their tongues on his wounds. And in time the poor man came to his end, and angels took him to Abraham's breast. And the man of wealth came to his end, and was put in the earth. And in hell, being in great pain, lifting up his eyes he saw Abraham, far away, and Lazarus on his breast. And he gave a cry and said, "Father Abraham, have mercy on me and send Lazarus, so that he may put the end of his finger in water and put it on my tongue, for I am cruelly burning in this flame." But Abraham said, "Keep in mind, my son, that when you were living, you had your good things, while Lazarus had evil things: but now, he is comforted and you are in pain. And in addition, there is a deep division fixed between us and you, so that those who might go from here to you are not able to do so, and no one may come from you to us." And he said, "Father, it is my request that you will send him to my father's house; For I have five brothers; and let him give them an account of these things, so that they may not come to this place of pain." But Abraham said, "They have

Moses and the prophets; let them give ear to what they say." And he said, "No, father Abraham, but if someone went to them from the dead, their hearts would be changed." And he said to him, "If they will not give attention to Moses and the prophets, they will not be moved even if someone comes back from the dead."

Tuesday
Ezek.37:1-14 (BBE)

The hand of the Lord had been on me, and he took me out in the spirit of the Lord and put me down in the middle of the valley; and it was full of bones; And he made me go past them round about: and I saw that there was a very great number of them on the face of the wide valley, and they were very dry. And he said to me, Son of man, is it possible for these bones to come to life? And I made answer, and said, It is for you to say, O Lord. And again he said to me, Be a prophet to these bones, and say to them, O you dry bones, give ear to the word of the Lord. This is what the Lord has said to these bones: See, I will make breath come into you so that you may come to life; And I will put muscles on you and make flesh come on you, and put skin over you, and breath into you, so that you may have life; and you will be certain that I am the Lord. So I gave the word as I was ordered: and at my words there was a shaking of the earth, and the bones came together, bone to bone. And looking I saw that there were muscles on them and flesh came up, and they were covered with skin: but there was no breath in them. And he said to me, Be a prophet to the wind, be a prophet, son of man, and say to the wind, The Lord has said: Come from the four winds, O wind, breathing on these dead so that they may come to life. And I gave the word at his orders, and breath came into them, and they came to life and got up on their feet, a very great army. Then he said to me, Son of man, these bones are all the children of Israel: and see, they are saying, Our bones have become dry our hope is gone, we are cut off completely. For this cause be a prophet to them, and say, This is what the Lord has said: See, I am opening the resting-places of your dead, and I will make you come up out of your resting-places, O my people; and I will take you into the land of Israel. And you will be certain that I am the Lord by my opening the resting-places of your dead and making you come up out of your resting-places, O my people. And I will put my spirit in you, so that you may come to life, and I will give you a rest in your land: and you will be certain that I the Lord have said it and have done it, says the Lord.

Wednesday
1Tim 2:1-6,8-10; 4:1-5 (BBE)

My desire is, first of all, that you will make requests and prayers and give praise for all men; For kings and all those in authority; so that we may have a calm and quiet life in all fear of God and serious behaviour. This is good and pleasing in the eyes of God our Saviour; Whose desire is that all men may have salvation and come to the knowledge of what is true. For there is one God and one peacemaker between God and men, the man Christ Jesus, Who gave himself as an offering for all; It is my desire, then, that in every place men may give themselves to prayer, lifting up holy hands, without wrath or argument. And that women may be dressed in simple clothing, with a quiet and serious air; not with twisted hair and gold or jewels or robes of great price; But clothed with good works, as is right for women who are living in the fear of God. The Spirit says clearly that in later times some will be turned away from the faith, giving their minds to spirits of deceit, and the teachings of evil spirits, Through the false ways of men whose words are untrue, whose hearts are burned as with a heated iron; Who keep men from being married and from taking food which God made to be taken with praise by those who have faith and true knowledge. Because everything which God has made is good, and nothing is evil, if it is taken with praise: For it is made holy by the word of God and by prayer.

Thursday

Lev.18:6-19 (NHT)

None of you shall approach anyone who are his close relatives, to uncover their nakedness: I am the Lord. You shall not uncover the nakedness of your father, nor the nakedness of your mother: she is your mother. You shall not uncover her nakedness. You shall not uncover the nakedness of your fathers wife: it is your fathers nakedness. You shall not uncover the nakedness of your sister, the daughter of your father, or the daughter of your mother, whether born at home, or born abroad. You shall not uncover the nakedness of your sons daughter, or of your daughters daughter, even their nakedness: for theirs is your own nakedness. You shall not uncover the nakedness of your fathers wife's daughter, conceived by your father, since she is your sister, you shall not uncover her nakedness. You shall not uncover the nakedness of your fathers sister: she is your fathers flesh. You shall not uncover the nakedness of your mothers sister: for she is your mothers flesh You shall not uncover the nakedness of your fathers brother, you shall not approach his wife: she is your aunt. You shall not uncover the nakedness of your daughter-in-law: she is your sons wife. You shall not uncover her nakedness. You shall not uncover the nakedness of your brothers wife: it is your brothers nakedness. You shall not uncover the nakedness of a woman and her daughter. You shall not take her sons daughter, or her daughters daughter, to uncover her nakedness; they are near kinswomen: it is wickedness. You shall not take a wife to her sister, to be a rival, to uncover her nakedness, while her sister is yet alive. You shall not approach a woman to uncover her nakedness, as long as she is impure by her uncleanness.

Friday

1 Chr.29:10-20; 28:9 (WBS)

Wherefore David blessed the Lord before all the congregation: and David said, "Blessed be thou, Lord God of Israel our father, for ever and ever. Thine, O Lord, is the greatness, and the power, and the glory, and the victory, and the majesty: for all that is in the heaven and on the earth is thine; thine is the kingdom, O Lord, and thou art exalted as head above all. Both riches and honour come from thee, and thou reignest over all; and in thy hand is power and might; and in thy hand it is to make great, and to give strength to all. Now therefore, our God, we thank thee, and praise thy glorious name. But who am I, and what is my people, that we should be able to offer so willingly after this sort? for all things come from thee, and of thy own have we given thee. For we are strangers before thee, and sojourners, as were all our fathers: our days on the earth are as a shadow, and there is no abiding. O Lord our God, all this store that we have prepared to build thee a house for thy holy name cometh from thy hand, and is all thy own. I know also, my God, that thou triest the heart, and hast pleasure in uprightness. As for me, in the uprightness of my heart I have willingly offered all these things: and now have I seen with joy thy people, who are present here, to offer willingly to thee. O Lord God of Abraham, Isaac, and of Israel, our fathers, keep this for ever in the imagination of the thoughts of the heart of thy people, and prepare their heart to thee: And give to Solomon my son a perfect heart, to keep thy commandments, thy testimonies, and thy statutes, and to do all these things, and to build the palace, for which I have made provision. And David said to all the congregation, Now bless the Lord your God. And all the congregation blessed the Lord God of their fathers, and bowed their heads, and worshiped the Lord, and the king. And thou, Solomon my son, know thou the God of thy father, and serve him with a perfect heart, and with a willing mind: for the Lord searcheth all hearts and understandeth all the imaginations of the thoughts: if thou shalt seek him, he will be found of thee; but if thou shalt forsake him, he will cast thee off for ever."

Saturday

Ps.116:1-9,12-14 (WBS)

I love the Lord, because he hath heard my voice and my supplications. Because he hath inclined his ear to me, therefore will I call upon him as long as I live. The sorrows of death encompassed me, and the pains of hell came upon me: I found trouble and sorrow. Then I called upon the name of the Lord; O Lord, I beseech thee, deliver my soul. Gracious is the Lord, and righteous; yes, our God is merciful. The Lord preserveth the simple: I was brought low, and he helped me. Return to thy rest, O my soul; for the Lord hath dealt bountifully with thee. For thou hast delivered my soul from death, my eyes from tears, and my feet from falling. I will walk before the Lord in the land of the living. What shall I render to the Lord for all his benefits towards me? I will take the cup of salvation, and call upon the name of the Lord. I will pay my vows to the Lord now in the presence of all his people.

Sunday

John 8:1-11 (NHT)

Jesus went to the Mount of Olives. Now very early in the morning, he came again into the temple, and all the people came to him, and he sat down and taught them. Then the scribes and the Pharisees brought a woman taken in adultery, and having set her in the midst, they said to him, "Teacher, we found this woman in adultery, in the very act. Now in the Law, Moses commanded us to stone such. So what do you say?" Now they said this to test him, that they might have something to accuse him of. But Jesus stooped down, and wrote on the ground with his finger. But when they continued asking him, he looked up and said to them, "He who is without sin among you, let him throw the first stone at her." Again he stooped down, and with his finger wrote on the ground. But when they heard it, they went out one by one, beginning from the oldest, even to the last, and he was left alone with the woman where she was, in the middle. Then Jesus, standing up, said to her, "Woman, where are they? Did no one condemn you?" And she said, "No one, Lord." And Jesus said, "Neither do I condemn you. Go your way. From now on, sin no more."

Week 35

Monday

Luke 16:10-17 (BBE)

"He who is true in a little, is true in much; he who is false in small things, is false in great. If, then, you have not been true in your use of the wealth of this life, who will give into your care the true wealth? And if you have not been true in your care of the property of other people, who will give you that which is yours? No man may be a servant to two masters: for he will have hate for the one and love for the other; or he will keep to the one and have no respect for the other. You may not be servants of God and of wealth." And the Pharisees, who had a great love of money, hearing these things, were making sport of him. And he said, "You take care to seem right in the eyes of men, but God sees your hearts: and those things which are important in the opinion of men, are evil in the eyes of God. The law and the prophets were till John: but then came the preaching of the kingdom of God, and everyone makes his way into it by force. But heaven and earth will come to an end before the smallest letter of the law may be dropped out."

Tuesday

Jonah 2:2-9 (WBS)

I cried by reason of my affliction to the Lord, and he heard me; out of the belly of hell cried I, and thou heardst my voice. For thou hadst cast me into the deep, in the midst of the seas; and the floods encompassed me: all thy billows and thy waves passed over me. Then I said, "I am cast out of thy sight; yet I will look again towards thy holy temple. The waters encompassed me, even to the soul: the depth enclosed me on every side, the weeds were wrapped about my head. I went down to the bottoms of the mountains; the earth with her bars was about me for ever: yet hast thou brought up my life from corruption, O Lord my God. When my soul fainted within me I remembered the Lord: and my prayer came to thee, into thy holy temple. When my soul fainted within me I remembered the Lord: and my prayer came to thee, into thy holy temple. They that observe lying vanities forsake their own mercy. But I will sacrifice to thee with the voice of thanksgiving; I will pay that which I have vowed. Salvation is of the Lord.

Wednesday

1 Tim.6:6-14 (BBE)

But true faith, with peace of mind, is of great profit: for we came into the world with nothing, and we are not able to take anything out; but if we have food and a roof over us, let that be enough. But those who have a desire for wealth are falling into danger, and are taken as in a net by a number of foolish and damaging desires, through which men are overtaken by death and destruction. For the love of money is a root of all evil: and some whose hearts were fixed on it have been turned away from the faith, and been wounded with unnumbered sorrows. But you, O man of God, keep yourself from these things, and go after righteousness, religion, faith, love, a quiet mind, gentle behaviour. Be fighting the good fight of the faith; take for yourself the life eternal, for which you were marked out, and of which you gave witness in the eyes of all. I give you orders before God, the giver of life, and Christ Jesus, who before Pontius Pilate gave witness to the faith, to keep the word untouched by evil, clear from all shame, till the revelation of our Lord Jesus Christ:

Thursday

Lev.18:20-24,29-30 (NHT)

You shall not lie carnally with your neighbours wife, and defile yourself with her. You shall not give any of your children to sacrifice to Moloch; neither shall you profane the name of your God: I am the Lord. You shall not have sexual relations with a male, as with a woman. That is detestable. You shall not have sexual relations with any animal to become defiled with it, nor shall any woman give herself to an animal to have sexual relations with it. It is a perversion. Do not defile yourselves in any of these things: for in all these the nations which I am casting out before you were defiled. For whoever shall do any of these abominations, even the souls that do them shall be cut off from among their people. Therefore you shall keep my requirements, that you do not practice any of these abominable customs, which were practiced before you, and that you do not defile yourselves with them: I am the Lord your God.'"

Friday
2 Chr.17:1,3,6; 20:1,3-6,12-26 (BBE)

And Jehoshaphat his son became king in his place, and made himself strong against Israel. And the Lord was with Jehoshaphat, because he went in the early ways of his father, not turning to the Baals, His heart was lifted up in the ways of the Lord; and he went so far as to take away the high places and the wood pillars out of Judah. Now after this, the children of Moab and the children of Ammon, and with them some of the Meunim, made war against Jehoshaphat. Then Jehoshaphat, in his fear, went to the Lord for directions, and gave orders all through Judah for the people to go without food. And Judah came together to make prayer for help from the Lord; from every town of Judah they came to give worship to the Lord. And Jehoshaphat took his place in the meeting of Judah and Jerusalem, in the house of the Lord in front of the new open space, And said, "O Lord, the God of our fathers, are you not God in heaven? are you not ruler over all the kingdoms of the nations? and in your hands are power and strength so that no one is able to keep his place against you. O our God, will you not be their judge? for our strength is not equal to this great army which is coming against us; and we are at a loss what to do: but our eyes are on you." And all Judah were waiting before the Lord, with their little ones, their wives, and their children. Then, before all the meeting, the spirit of the Lord came on Jahaziel, the son of Zechariah, son of Benaiah, son of Jeiel, son of Mattaniah, a Levite and one of the family of Asaph; And he said, "Give ear, O Judah, and you people of Jerusalem, and you, King Jehoshaphat: the Lord says to you, have no fear and do not be troubled on account of this great army; for the fight is not yours but God's. Go down against them tomorrow: see, they are coming up by the slope of Ziz; at the end of the valley, before the waste land of Jeruel, you will come face to face with them. There will be no need for you to take up arms in this fight; put yourselves in position, and keep where you are, and you will see the salvation of the Lord with you, O Judah and Jerusalem: have no fear and do not be troubled: go out against them tomorrow, for the Lord is with you." Then Jehoshaphat went down with his face to the earth, and all Judah and the people of Jerusalem gave worship to the Lord, falling down before him. And the Levites, the children of the Kohathites and the Korahites, got to their feet and gave praise to the Lord, the God of Israel, with a loud voice. And early in the morning they got up and went out to the waste land of Tekoa: and when they were going out, Jehoshaphat took his station and said to them, "Give ear to me, O Judah and you people of Jerusalem: have faith in the Lord your God and you will be safe; have faith in his prophets and all will go well for you." And after discussion with the people, he put in their places those who were to make melody to the Lord, praising him in holy robes, while they went at the head of the army, and saying, "May the Lord be praised, for his mercy is unchanging for ever." And at the first notes of song and praise the Lord sent a surprise attack against the children of Ammon and Moab and the people of Mount Seir, who had come against Judah; and they were overcome. And the children of Ammon and Moab made an attack on the people of Mount Seir with a view to their complete destruction; and when they had put an end to the people of Seir, everyman's hand was turned against his neighbour for his destruction. And Judah came to the watchtower of the waste land, and looking in the direction of the army, they saw only dead bodies stretched on the earth; no living man was to be seen. And when Jehoshaphat and his people came to take their goods from them, they saw beasts in great numbers, and wealth and clothing and things of value, more than they were able to take away; all this they took for themselves, and they were three days getting it away, there was so much. On the fourth day they all came together in the Valley of Blessing, and there they gave blessing to the Lord; for which cause that place has been named the Valley of Blessing to this day.

Saturday
Ps.118:6,8,14,17-18,21-24,26,28-29 (WBS)

The Lord is on my side; I will not fear: what can man do to me? It is better to trust in the Lord than to put confidence in man. The Lord is my strength and song, and is become my salvation. I shall not die, but live, and declare the works of the Lord. The Lord hath chastened me severely: but he hath not given me over to death. I will praise thee: for thou hast heard me, and art become my salvation. The stone which the builders refused is become the head stone of the corner. This is the Lord'S doing; it is wonderful in our eyes. This is the day which the Lord hath made; we will rejoice and be glad in it. Blessed be he that cometh in the name of the Lord: we have blessed you out of the house of the Lord. Thou art my God, and I will praise thee: thou art my God, I will exalt thee. O give thanks to the Lord; for he is good: for his mercy endureth for ever.

Sunday
John 11:7-44 (NHT)

Then after this he said to the disciples, "Let us go into Judea again." The disciples told him, "Rabbi, the Jewish leaders were just trying to stone you, and are you going there again?" Jesus answered, "Are there not twelve hours of daylight? If anyone walks in the day, he does not stumble, because he sees the light of this world. But if anyone walks in the night, he stumbles, because the light is not in him." He said these things, and after that, he said to them, "Our friend, Lazarus, has fallen asleep, but I am going so that I may awake him out of sleep." Then the disciples said to him, "Lord, if he has fallen asleep, he will recover." Now Jesus had spoken of his death, but they thought that he spoke of taking rest in sleep. So Jesus said to them plainly then, "Lazarus is dead. I am glad for your sakes that I was not there, so that you may believe. Nevertheless, let us go to him." Thomas therefore, who is called Didymus, said to his fellow disciples, "Let us go also, that we may die with him." So when Jesus came, he found that he had been in the tomb four days already. Now Bethany was near Jerusalem, about fifteen staid away. Many of the Jewish people had come to Martha and Mary, to console them concerning their brother. Then when Martha heard that Jesus was coming, she went and met him, but Mary stayed in the house. Therefore Martha said to Jesus, "Lord, if you would have been here, my brother would not have died. Even now I know that whatever you ask of God, God will give you." Jesus said to her, "Your brother will rise again." Martha said to him, "I know that he will rise again in the resurrection at the last day." Jesus said to her, "I am the resurrection and the life. He who believes in me will still live, even if he dies. And whoever lives and believes in me will never die. Do you believe this?" She said to him, "Yes, Lord. I have come to believe that you are the Messiah, the Son of God, he who comes into the world." And when she had said this, she went away, and called Mary, her sister, secretly, saying, "The Teacher is here, and is calling you." When she heard this, she arose quickly, and went to him. Now Jesus had not yet come into the village, but was still in the place where Martha met him. Then the Judeans who were with her in the house, and were consoling her, when they saw Mary, that she rose up quickly and went out, followed her, supposing that she was going to the tomb to weep there. Therefore when Mary came to where Jesus was, and saw him, she fell down at his feet, saying to him, "Lord, if you would have been here, my brother would not have died." When Jesus therefore saw her weeping, and the Judeans weeping who came with her, he was deeply moved in spirit and was troubled, and said, "Where have you put him?" They told him, "Lord, come and see." Jesus wept. The Judeans therefore said, "See how he loved him." But some of them said, "Could not this man, who opened the eyes of him who was blind, have also kept this man from dying?" So Jesus, deeply moved again, came to the tomb. Now it was a cave, and a stone lay against it. Jesus said, "Take away the stone." Martha, the sister of the dead man, said to him, "Lord, by this time there is a stench, for he has been dead four days." Jesus said to her, "Did I not tell you that if you believed, you would see God's glory?" So they took away the stone. And Jesus lifted up his eyes, and said, "Father, I thank you that you listened to me. I know that you always listen to me, but because of the crowd that stands around I said this, that they may believe that you sent me." When he had said this, he shouted with a loud voice, "Lazarus, come out." The man who had died came out, bound hand and foot with wrappings, and his face was wrapped around with a cloth. Jesus said to them, "Free him, and let him go."

Week 36

Monday

Luke 17:3-9 (BBE)

"Give attention to yourselves: if your brother does wrong, say a sharp word to him; and if he has sorrow for his sin, let him have forgiveness. And if he does you wrong seven times in a day, and seven times comes to you and says, I have regret for what I have done; let him have forgiveness." And the twelve said to the Lord, "Make our faith greater." And the Lord said, "If your faith was only as great as a grain of mustard seed, you might say to this tree, be rooted up and planted in the sea; and it would be done. But which of you, having a servant who is ploughing or keeping sheep, will say to him, when he comes in from the field, 'come now and be seated and have a meal.' Will he not say, 'Get a meal for me, and make yourself ready and see to my needs till I have had my food and drink; and after that you may have yours?' Does he give praise to the servant because he did what was ordered?"

Tuesday

Dan.9:4-6,11,14,17-19 (WBS)

And I prayed to the Lord my God, and made my confession, and said, "O Lord, the great and dreadful God, keeping the covenant and mercy to them that love him, and to them that keep his commandments; We have sinned, and have committed iniquity, and have done wickedly, and have rebelled, even by departing from thy precepts and from thy judgments: Neither have we hearkened to thy servants the prophets, who spoke in thy name to our kings, our princes, and our fathers, and to all the people of the land. And all Israel have transgressed thy law, even by departing, that they might not obey thy voice; therefore the curse is poured upon us, and the oath that is written in the law of Moses the servant of God, because we have sinned against him. Therefore hath the Lord watched upon the evil, and brought it upon us: for the Lord our God is righteous in all his works which he doeth: for we have not obeyed his voice. Now therefore, O our God, hear the prayer of thy servant, and his supplications, and cause thy face to shine upon thy sanctuary that is desolate, for the Lord's sake. O my God, incline thy ear, and hear; open thy eyes, and behold our desolations, and the city which is called by thy name: for we do not present our supplications before thee for our righteousnesses, but for thy great mercies. O Lord, hear; O Lord, forgive; O Lord, hearken and do; defer not, for thy own sake, O my God: for thy city and thy people are called by thy name."

Wednesday
2 Tim.2:11-13,16,22-23 (BBE)

This is a true saying: If we undergo death with him, then will we be living with him: If we go on to the end, then we will be ruling with him: if we say we have no knowledge of him, then he will say he has no knowledge of us: If we are without faith, still he keeps faith, for he will never be untrue to himself.

Take no part in wrong and foolish talk, for those who do so will go farther into evil. Keep yourself from those desires of the flesh which are strong when the body is young, and go after righteousness, faith, love, peace, with those whose prayers go up to the Lord from a clean heart. and put away foolish and uncontrolled questionings, seeing that they are a cause of trouble.

Thursday
Ex.35:1-3 (NHT)

Moses assembled all the congregation of the children of Israel, and said to them, "These are the words which the Lord has commanded, that you should do them. 'Six days shall work be done, but on the seventh day there shall be a holy day for you, a Sabbath of solemn rest to the Lord: whoever does any work in it shall be put to death. You shall kindle no fire throughout your habitations on the Sabbath day.'"

Friday
1 Kings 3:5-28 (WBS)

In Gibson the Lord appeared to Solomon in a dream by night: and God said, "Ask what I shall give thee." And Solomon said, "Thou hast shown to thy servant David my father great mercy, according as he walked before thee in truth, and in righteousness, and in uprightness of heart with thee; and thou hast kept for him this great kindness, that thou hast given him a son to sit on his throne, as it is this day. And now, O Lord my God, thou hast made thy servant king instead of David my father: and I am but a little child: I know not how to go out or come in. And thy servant is in the midst of thy people which thou hast chosen, a great people, that cannot be numbered nor counted for multitude. Give therefore to thy servant an understanding heart to judge thy people, that I may discern between good and bad: for who is able to judge this thy so great a people?" And the speech pleased the Lord, that Solomon had asked this thing. And God said to him, "Because thou hast asked this thing, and hast not asked for thyself long life; neither hast asked riches for thyself, nor hast asked the life of thy enemies: but hast asked for thyself understanding to discern judgment; Behold, I have done according to thy words: lo, I have given thee a wise and an understanding heart; so that there hath been none like thee before thee, neither after thee shall any arise like to thee. And I have also given thee that which thou hast not asked, both riches, and honour: so that there shall not be any among the kings like to thee all thy days, And if thou wilt walk in my ways, to keep my statutes and my commandments, as thy father David did walk, then I will lengthen thy days." And Solomon awoke; and behold, it was a dream. And he came to Jerusalem, and stood before the ark of the covenant of the Lord, and offered up burnt-offerings, and offered peace-offerings, and made a feast to all his servants.

Then came there two women, that were harlots, to the king, and stood before him. And the one woman said, "O my lord, I and this woman dwell in one house; and I was delivered of a child with her in the house. And it came to pass the third day after I was delivered, that this woman was delivered also: and we were together; there was no stranger with us in the house, save us two in the house. And this woman's child died in the night; because she overlaid it. And she arose at midnight, and took my son from beside me, while thy handmaid slept, and laid it in her bosom, and laid her dead child in my bosom. And when I rose in the morning to nurse my child, behold, it was dead: but when I had considered it in the morning, behold, it was not my son, which I bore." And the other woman said, "No; but the living is my son, and the dead is thy son." And this said, "No; but the dead is thy son, and the living is my son." Thus they spoke before the king. Then said the king, "The one saith, This is my son that lived, and thy son is the dead; and the other saith, No; but thy son is the dead, and my son is the living." And the king said, "Bring me a sword." And they brought a sword before the king. And the king said, "Divide the living child in two, and give half to the one, and half to the other." Then spoke the woman whose the living child was to the king, for her bowels yearned upon her son, and she said, "O my lord, give her the living child, and in no wise slay it." But the other said, "Let it be neither mine nor thine, but divide it." Then the king answered and said, "Give her the living child, and in no wise slay it: she is the mother of it." And all Israel heard of the judgment which the king had judged; and they feared the king: for they saw that the wisdom of God was in him, to do judgment.

Saturday
Ps.119:1-8 (WBS)

Blessed are the undefiled in the way, who walk in the law of the Lord. Blessed are they that keep his testimonies, and that seek him with the whole heart. They also do no iniquity: they walk in his ways. Thou hast commanded us to keep thy precepts diligently. O that my ways were directed to keep thy statutes, then shall I not be ashamed, when I have respect to all thy commandments. I will praise thee with uprightness of heart, when I shall have learned thy righteous judgments. I will keep thy statutes: O forsake me not utterly.

Sunday

Matt.14:22-35 (BBE)

And straight away he made the disciples get into the boat and go before him to the other side, till he had sent the people away. And after he had sent the people away, he went up into the mountain by himself for prayer: and when evening was come, he was there by himself. But the boat was now in the middle of the sea, and was troubled by the waves: for the wind was against them. And in the fourth watch of the night he came to them, walking on the sea. And when they saw him walking on the sea, they were troubled, saying, "It is a spirit"; and they gave cries of fear. But straight away Jesus said to them, "Take heart; it is I, have no fear." And Peter, answering, said to him, "Lord, if it is you, give me the order to come to you on the water." And he said, "Come." And Peter got out of the boat, and walking on the water, went to Jesus. But when he saw the wind he was in fear and, starting to go down, he gave a cry, saying, "Help, Lord." And straight away Jesus put out his hand and took a grip of him, and said to him, "O man of little faith, why were you in doubt?" And when they had got into the boat, the wind went down. And those who were in the boat gave him worship, saying, "Truly you are the Son of God." And when they had gone across, they came to land at Gennesaret. And when the men of that place had news of him, they sent into all the country round about, and took to him all who were ill

Week 37

Monday

Luke 18:1-8 (BBE)

And he made a story for them, the point of which was that men were to go on making prayer and not get tired; saying, "There was a judge in a certain town, who had no fear of God or respect for man: and there was a widow in that town, and she kept on coming to him and saying, 'Give me my right against the man who has done me wrong.' And for a time he would not: but later, he said to himself, 'Though I have no fear of God or respect for man, because this widow is a trouble to me, I will give her her right; for if not, I will be completely tired out by her frequent coming.'" And the Lord said, "Give ear to the words of the evil judge. And will not God do right in the cause of his saints, whose cries come day and night to his ears, though he is long in doing it? I say to you that he will quickly do right in their cause. But when the Son of man comes, will there be any faith on earth?"

Tuesday

Dan.12:1-9,13 (BBE)

And at that time Michael will take up his place, the great angel, who is the supporter of the children of your people: and there will be a time of trouble, such as there never was from the time there was a nation even till that same time: and at that time your people will be kept safe, everyone who is recorded in the book. And a number of those who are sleeping in the dust of the earth will come out of their sleep, some to eternal life and some to eternal shame. And those who are wise will be shining like the light of the outstretched sky; and those by whom numbers have been turned to righteousness will be like the stars for ever and ever. But as for you, O Daniel, let the words be kept secret and the book rolled up and kept shut till the time of the end: numbers will be going out of the way and troubles will be increased. Then I, Daniel, looking, saw two others, one at the edge of the river on this side and one at the edge of the river on that side. And I said to the man clothed in linen, who was over the waters of the river, "How long will it be to the end of these wonders?" Then in my hearing the man clothed in linen, who was over the river, lifting up his right hand and his left hand to heaven, took an oath by him who is living for ever that it would be a time, times, and a half; and when the power of the crusher of the holy people comes to an end, all these things will be ended. And the words came to my ears, but the sense of them was not clear to me: then I said, "O my lord, what is the sense of these things?" And he said, "Go on your way, Daniel: for the words are secret and shut up till the time of the end; But you, go on your way and take your rest: for you will be in your place at the end of the days."

Wednesday

2 Tim.3:12-4:5 (BBE)

All whose purpose is to be living in the knowledge of God in Christ Jesus, will be cruelly attacked. Evil and false men will become worse and worse, using deceit and themselves overcome by deceit. But see that you keep to the teaching you have been given and the things of which you are certain, conscious of who has been your teacher; and that from the time when you were a child, you have had knowledge of the holy Writings, which are able to make you wise to salvation, through faith in Christ Jesus. Every holy Writing which comes from God is of profit for teaching, for training, for guiding, for education in righteousness so that the man of God may be complete, trained and made ready for every good work.

I give you orders, before God and Christ Jesus, who will be the judge of the living and the dead, and by his revelation and his kingdom. Be preaching the word at all times, in every place; make protests, say sharp words, give comfort, with long waiting and teaching; for the time will come when they will not take the true teaching; but, moved by their desires, they will get for themselves a great number of teachers for the pleasure of hearing them; and shutting their ears to what is true, will be turned away to belief in foolish stories. But be self-controlled in all things, do without comfort, go on preaching the good news, completing the work which has been given you to do.

Thursday

Lev.23:9-10, 33-35,42-43 (BBE)

And the Lord said to Moses, "Say to the children of Israel, 'When you have come to the land which I will give you, and have got in the grain from its fields, take some of the first-fruits of the grain to the priest.'" And the Lord said to Moses, "Say to the children of Israel, 'On the fifteenth day of this seventh month let the feast of tents be kept to the Lord for seven days. On the first day there will be a holy meeting: do no field-work. For seven days you will be living in tents; all those who are Israelites by birth are to make tents their living-places: So that future generations may keep in mind how I gave the children of Israel tents as their living-places when I took them out of the land of Egypt: I am the Lord your God.'"

Friday

2 Chr 5:2-5; 6:1-3,13b-15,18-19,21,30,36-37,39; 1 Kings 8:55-58 (WBS)

Then Solomon assembled the elders of Israel, and all the heads of the tribes, the chief of the fathers of the children of Israel, to Jerusalem, to bring up the ark of the covenant of the Lord from the city of David, which is Zion. Wherefore all the men of Israel assembled themselves to the king in the feast which was in the seventh month. And all the elders of Israel came; and the Levites took up the ark. And they brought up the ark, and the tabernacle of the congregation, and all the holy vessels that were in the tabernacle, these did the priests and the Levites bring up. Then said Solomon, "The Lord hath said that he would dwell in the thick darkness. But I have built a house of habitation for thee, and a place for thy dwelling for ever." And the king turned his face, and blessed the whole congregation of Israel: and all the congregation of Israel stood. He kneeled upon his knees before all the congregation of Israel, and spread forth his hands towards heaven and said, "O Lord God of Israel, there is no God like thee in the heaven, nor on the earth; who keepest covenant, and showest mercy to thy servants, that walk before thee with all their hearts: Thou who hast kept with thy servant David my father that which thou hast promised him; and hast spoken with thy mouth, and hast fulfilled it with thy hand, as it is this day. But will God in very deed dwell with men on the earth? behold, heaven and the heaven of heavens cannot contain thee; how much less this house which I have built! Have respect therefore to the prayer of thy servant, and to his supplication, O Lord my God, to hearken to the cry and the prayer which thy servant prayeth before thee: Hearken therefore to the supplications of thy servant, and of thy people Israel, which they shall make towards this place: hear thou from thy dwelling-place, even from heaven; and when thou hearest, forgive.Then hear thou from heaven thy dwelling-place, and forgive, and render to every man according to all his ways, whose heart thou knowest (for thou only knowest the hearts of the children of men:)If they sin against thee, (for there is no man who sinneth not,) and thou be angry with them, and deliver them over before their enemies, and they carry them away captives to a land far off or near; Yet if they bethink themselves in the land whither they are carried captive, and turn and pray to thee in the land of their captivity, saying, We have sinned, we have done amiss, and have dealt wickedly; Then hear thou from the heavens, even from thy dwelling-place, their prayer and their supplications, and maintain their cause, and forgive thy people who have sinned against thee." And he stood, and blessed all the congregation of Israel with a loud voice, saying, "Blessed be the Lord, that hath given rest to his people Israel, according to all that he promised: there hath not failed one word of all his good promise, which he promised by the hand of Moses his servant. The Lord our God be with us, as he was with our fathers: let him not leave us, nor forsake us: That he may incline our hearts to him, to walk in all his ways, and to keep his commandments, and his statutes, and his judgments, which he commanded our fathers."

Saturday

Ps.119:35-40 (WBS)

Make me to go in the path of thy commandments; for in that do I delight. Incline my heart to thy testimonies, and not to covetousness. Turn away my eyes from beholding vanity; and revive thou me in thy way. Establish thy word to thy servant, who is devoted to thy fear. Turn away my reproach which I fear: for thy judgments are good. Behold, I have longed after thy precepts: revive me in thy righteousness.

Sunday

Mark 8:27-37 (BBE)

And Jesus went out, with his disciples, into the little towns round Caesarea Philippi; and on the way he put a question to his disciples, saying, "Who do men say that I am?" And they made answer, "John the Baptist; and others, Elijah; but others, One of the prophets." And he said to them, "But who do you say I am?" Peter said in answer, "You are the Christ." And he put them under orders not to say this of him to anyone. And teaching them, he said that the Son of man would have to undergo much, and be hated by those in authority, and the chief priests, and the scribes, and be put to death, and after three days come back from the dead. And he said this openly. And Peter took him, and was protesting. But he, turning about, and seeing his disciples, said sharply to Peter, "Get out of my way, Satan: for your mind is not on the things of God, but on the things of men." And turning to the mass of people with his disciples, he said to them, "If any man has the desire to come after me, let him give up all other desires, and take up his cross and come after me. Whoever has a desire to keep his life, will have it taken from him; and whoever gives up his life because of me and the good news, will keep it. What profit has a man if he gets all the world with the loss of his life? And what would a man give in exchange for his life?"

Week 38

Monday

Luke 18:9-14 (BBE)

And he made this story for some people who were certain that they were good, and had a low opinion of others: Two men went up to the Temple for prayer; one a Pharisee, and the other a tax-farmer. The Pharisee, taking up his position, said to himself these words: "God, I give you praise because I am not like other men, who take more than their right, who are evil-doers, who are untrue to their wives, or even like this tax-farmer. Twice in the week I go without food; I give a tenth of all I have." The tax-farmer, on the other hand, keeping far away, and not lifting up even his eyes to heaven, made signs of grief and said, "God, have mercy on me, a sinner." I say to you, This man went back to his house with God's approval, and not the other: for everyone who makes himself high will be made low and whoever makes himself low will be made high.

Tuesday

Hosea 4:1-2,10-13; 7:13-16 (BBE)

Give ear to the word of the Lord, O children of Israel; for the Lord has a cause against the people of this land, because there is no good faith in it, and no mercy and no knowledge of God in the land. There is cursing and broken faith, violent death and attacks on property, men are untrue in married life, houses are broken into, and there is blood touching blood. They will have food, but they will not be full; they will be false to me, but they will not be increased, because they no longer give thought to the Lord. Loose ways and new wine take away wisdom. My people get knowledge from their tree*, and their rod gives them news; for a false spirit is the cause of their wandering, and they have been false to their God. They make offerings on the tops of mountains, burning perfumes in high places, under trees of every sort, because their shade is good: and so your daughters are given up to loose ways and your brides are false to their husbands. May trouble be theirs! for they have gone far away from me; and destruction, for they have been sinning against me; I was ready to be their saviour, but they said false words against me. And they have not made prayer to me in their hearts, but

they make loud cries on their beds; they are cutting themselves for food and wine, they are turned against me. Though I have given training and strength to their arms, they have evil designs against me. They have gone to what is of no value; they are like a false bow; their captains will come to destruction by the sword, and their ruler by my wrath; for this, the land of Egypt will make sport of them.
*wooden idols

Wednesday
Titus 2:11-14; 3:4-7 (BBE)

For the grace of God has come, giving salvation to all men, training us so that, turning away from evil and the desires of this world, we may be living wisely and uprightly in the knowledge of God in this present life; looking for the glad hope, the revelation of the glory of our great God and Saviour Jesus Christ who gave himself for us, so that he might make us free from all wrongdoing, and make for himself a people clean in heart and on fire with good works.

When the mercy of God our Saviour, and his love to man was seen, not by works of righteousness which we did ourselves, but in the measure of his mercy, he gave us salvation, through the washing of the new birth and the giving of new life in the Holy Spirit, which he gave us freely through Jesus Christ our Saviour; so that, having been given righteousness through grace, we might have a part in the heritage, the hope of eternal life.

Thursday
Lev.19:1-4,9-10 (BBE)

And the Lord said to Moses, "Say to all the people of Israel, You are to be holy, for I, the Lord your God, am holy. Let every man give honour to his mother and to his father and keep my Sabbaths: I am the Lord your God. Do not go after false gods, and do not make metal images of gods for yourselves: I am the Lord your God. And when you get in the grain from your land, do not let all the grain be cut from the edges of the field, or take up what has been dropped on the earth after the getting in of the grain. And do not take all the grapes from your vine-garden, or the fruit dropped on the earth; let the poor man, and the man from another country, have these: I am the Lord your God."

Friday
1 Kings 17:1-15 (BBE)

And Elijah the Tishbite, of Tishbe in Gilead, said to Ahab, "By the living Lord, the God of Israel, whose servant I am, there will be no dew or rain in these years, but only at my word." Then the word of the Lord came to him, saying, "Go from here in the direction of the east, and keep yourself in a secret place by the stream Cherith, east of Jordan. The water of the stream will be your drink, and by my orders the ravens will give you food there." So he went and did as the Lord said, living by the stream Cherith, east of Jordan. And the ravens took him bread in the morning and meat in the evening; and the water of the stream was his drink. Now after a time the stream became dry, because there was no rain in the land. Then the word of the Lord came to him, saying, "Up! go now to Zarephath, in Zidon, and make your living-place there; I have given orders to a widow woman there to see that you have food." So he got up and went to Zarephath; and when he came to the door of the town, he saw a widow woman getting sticks together; and crying out to her he said, "Will you give me a little water in a vessel for my drink?" And when she was going to get it, he said to her, "And get me with it a small bit of bread." Then she said, "By the life of the Lord your God, I have nothing but a little meal in my store, and a drop of oil in the bottle; and now I am getting two sticks together so that I may go in and make it ready for me and my son, so that we may have a meal before our death." And Elijah said to her, "Have no fear; go and do as you have said, but first make me a little cake of it and come and give it to me, and then make something for yourself and your son. For this is the word of the Lord, the God of Israel: The store of meal will not come to an end, and the bottle will never be without oil, till the day when the Lord sends rain on the earth." So she went and did as Elijah said; and she and he and her family had food for a long time.

Saturday
Ps.119:105-106,125,133-135,149,175-176 (WBS)

Thy word is a lamp to my feet, and a light to my path. I have sworn, and I will perform it, that I will keep thy righteous judgments. I am thy servant; give me understanding, that I may know thy testimonies. Order my steps in thy word: and let not any iniquity have dominion over me. Deliver me from the oppression of man: so will I keep thy precepts. Make thy face to shine upon thy servant: and teach me thy statutes. Hear my voice, according to thy loving-kindness: O Lord, revive me according to thy judgment. Let my soul live, and it shall praise thee; and let thy judgments help me. I have gone astray like a lost sheep; seek thy servant; for I do not forget thy commandments.

Sunday
Mark 9:2-13 (NHT)

After six days Jesus took with him Peter, James, and John, and brought them up onto a high mountain privately by themselves, and he was changed into another form in front of them. His clothing became glistening, exceedingly white, such as no launderer on earth can whiten them. Elijah and Moses appeared to them, and they were talking with Jesus. Peter said to

Jesus, "Rabbi, it is good for us to be here. Let us make three tents: one for you, one for Moses, and one for Elijah." For he did not know what to answer, for they became very afraid. A cloud came, overshadowing them, and a voice came out of the cloud, "This is my beloved Son. Listen to him." Suddenly looking around, they saw no one with them any more, except Jesus only. As they were coming down from the mountain, he commanded them that they should tell no one what things they had seen, until after the Son of Man had risen from the dead. They kept this saying to themselves, questioning what the "rising from the dead" meant. They asked him, saying, "Why do the scribes say that Elijah must come first?" And he said to them, "Elijah indeed comes first, and restores all things. And why is it written of the Son of Man that he should suffer many things and be rejected? But I tell you that Elijah has come, and they have also done to him whatever they wanted to, even as it is written about him."

Week 39

Monday

Luke 18:18-25 (NHT)

A certain ruler asked him, saying, "Good Teacher, what must I do to inherit everlasting life?" Jesus asked him, "Why do you call me good? No one is good, except one, God. You know the commandments: 'Do not commit adultery,' 'Do not murder,' 'Do not steal,' 'Do not give false testimony,' 'Honour your father and your mother.'" And he said, "I have kept all these things from my youth up." When Jesus heard it, he said to him, "You still lack one thing. Sell all that you have, and distribute it to the poor. You will have treasure in heaven. Come, follow me." But when he heard these things, he became very sad, for he was very rich. And Jesus, seeing that he became very sad, said, "How hard it is for those who have riches to enter into the Kingdom of God. For it is easier for a camel to enter in through a needle's eye, than for a rich person to enter into the Kingdom of God."

Tuesday

Hosea 8:2-3,7,12; 11:1-4,8-9; 14:4 (NHT)

They cry to me, 'My God, we Israel acknowledge you.' Israel has cast off that which is good. The enemy will pursue him. For they sow the wind, and they will reap the whirlwind. He has no standing grain. The stalk will yield no head. If it does yield, strangers will swallow it up. I wrote for him the many things of my law; but they were regarded as a strange thing. When Israel was a child, I loved him, and out of Egypt I called my son. As I called them, the farther they went from me. They sacrificed to the Baals, and burned incense to engraved images. Yet I taught Ephraim to walk. I took them in my arms; but they did not know that I healed them. I drew them with cords of a man, with ties of love; and I was to them like those who lift up the yoke on their necks; and I bent down to him and I fed him. "How can I give you up, Ephraim? How can I hand you over, Israel? How can I make you like Admah? How can I make you like Zeboiim? My heart is turned within me, my compassion is aroused. I will not execute the fierceness of my anger. I will not return to destroy Ephraim: for I am God, and not man; the Holy One in the midst of you; and I will not come in wrath. I will heal their waywardness. I will love them freely; for my anger is turned away from him..

Wednesday
Heb.1:1-3; 4:14-16 (BBE)

In times past the word of God came to our fathers through the prophets, in different parts and in different ways; but now, at the end of these days, it has come to us through his Son, to whom he has given all things for a heritage, and through whom he made the order of the generations; who, being the outshining of his glory, the true image of his substance, supporting all things by the word of his power, having given himself as an offering making clean from sins, took his seat at the right hand of God in heaven. Having then a great high priest, who has made his way through the heavens, even Jesus the Son of God, let us be strong in our faith. For we have not a high priest who is not able to be touched by the feelings of our feeble flesh; but we have one who has been tested in all points as we ourselves are tested, but without sin. Then let us come near to the seat of grace without fear, so that mercy may be given to us, and we may get grace for our help in time of need.

Thursday
Lev.19:11-16 (BBE)

Do not take anyone's property or be false in act or word to another. And do not take an oath in my name falsely, putting shame on the name of your God: I am the Lord. Do not be cruel to your neighbour or take what is his; do not keep back a servant's payment from him all night till the morning. Do not put a curse on those who have no hearing, or put a cause of falling in the way of the blind, but keep the fear of your God before you: I am the Lord. Do no wrong in your judging: do not give thought to the position of the poor, or honour to the position of the great; but be a judge to your neighbour in righteousness. Do not go about saying untrue things among your people, or take away the life of your neighbour by false witness: I am the Lord.

Friday
1 Kings 18:17-40 (BBE)

And when he saw Elijah, Ahab said to him, "Is it you, you troubler of Israel?" Then he said in answer, "I have not been troubling Israel, but you and your family; because, turning away from the orders of the Lord, you have gone after the Baals. Now send, and get Israel together before me at Mount Carmel, with the four hundred and fifty prophets of Baal who get their food at Jezebel's table." So Ahab sent for all the children of Israel, and got the prophets together at Mount Carmel. And Elijah came near to all the people and said, "How long will you go on balancing between two opinions? if the Lord is God, then give worship to him; but if Baal, give worship to him." And the people said not a word in answer. Then Elijah said to the people, "I, even I, am the only living prophet of the Lord; but Baal's prophets are four hundred and fifty men. Now, let them give us two oxen; and let them take one for themselves, and have it cut up, and put it on the wood, but put no fire under it; I will get the other ox ready, and put it on the wood, and put no fire under it. And do you make prayers to your god, and I will make a prayer to the Lord: and it will be clear that the one who gives an answer by fire is God." And all the people in answer said, "It is well said." Then Elijah said to the prophets of Baal, "Take one ox for yourselves and get it ready first, for there are more of you; and make your prayers to your god, but put no fire under." So they took the ox which was given them, and made it ready, crying out to Baal from morning till the middle of the day, and saying, "O Baal, give ear to us." But there was no voice and no answer. And they were jumping up and down before the altar they had made. And in the middle of the day, Elijah made sport of them, saying, "Give louder cries, for he is a god; he may be deep in thought, or he may have gone away for some purpose, or he may be on a journey, or by chance he is sleeping and has to be made awake." So they gave loud cries, cutting themselves with knives and swords, as was their way, till the blood came streaming out all over them. And from the middle of the day they went on with their prayers till the time of the offering; but there was no voice, or any answer, or any who gave attention to them. Then Elijah said to all the people, "Come near to me"; and all the people came near. And he put up again the altar of the Lord which had been broken down. And Elijah took twelve stones, the number of the tribes of the sons of Jacob, to whom the Lord had said, Israel will be your name: And with the stones he made an altar to the name of the Lord; and he made a deep drain all round the altar, great enough to take two measures of seed. And he put the wood in order, and, cutting up the ox, put it on the wood. Then he said, "Get four vessels full of water and put it on the burned offering and on the wood." And he said, "Do it a second time", and they did it a second time; And he said, "Do it a third time", and they did it a third time. And the water went all round the altar, till the drain was full. Then at the time of the offering, Elijah the prophet came near and said, "O Lord, the God of Abraham, of Isaac, and of Israel, let it be seen this day that you are God in Israel, and that I am your servant, and that I have done all these things by your order. Give me an answer, O Lord, give me an answer, so that this people may see that you are God, and that you have made their hearts come back again." Then the fire of the Lord came down, burning up the offering and the wood and the stones and the dust, and drinking up the water in the drain. And when the people saw it, they all went down on their faces, and said, "The Lord, he is God, the Lord, he is God." And Elijah said to them, "Take the prophets of Baal, let not one of them get away." So they took them, and Elijah made them go down to the stream Kishon, and put them to death there.

Saturday

Ps.121 (NHT)

I will lift up my eyes to the hills. Where does my help come from? My help comes from the Lord, who made heaven and earth. He will not allow your foot to be moved. He who keeps you will not slumber. Look, he who keeps Israel will neither slumber nor sleep. The Lord is your keeper. The Lord is your shade on your right hand. The sun will not harm you by day, nor the moon by night. The Lord will keep you from all evil. He will keep your soul. The Lord will keep your going out and your coming in, from this time forth, and forevermore

Sunday

Mark 10:46-52 (NHT)

They came to Jericho. As he went out from Jericho, with his disciples and a large crowd, Bartimaeus, the son of Timaeus, a blind beggar, was sitting by the road. When he heard that it was Jesus the Nazarene, he began to cry out, and say, "Jesus, Son of David, have mercy on me." Many rebuked him, that he should be quiet, but he shouted all the louder, "Son of David, have mercy on me." Jesus stood still, and said, "Call him." They called the blind man, saying to him, "Cheer up. Get up. He is calling you." He, casting away his cloak, jumped up, and came to Jesus. Jesus asked him, "What do you want me to do for you?" The blind man said to him, "Rabboni, that I may see again." Jesus said to him, "Go your way. Your faith has made you well." And immediately he received his sight, and followed him on the road.

Week 40

Monday

Luke 20:9-17 (BBE)

And he gave the people this story: A man made a vine-garden and gave the use of it to some field-workers and went into another country for a long time. And at the right time he sent a servant to the workers to get part of the fruit from the vines; but the workmen gave him blows and sent him away with nothing. And he sent another servant, and they gave blows to him in the same way, and put shame on him, and sent him away with nothing. And he sent a third, and they gave him wounds and put him out. And the lord of the garden said, 'What am I to do? I will send my dearly loved son; they may give respect to him.' But when the workmen saw him, they said to one another, 'This is he who will one day be the owner of the property: let us put him to death and the heritage will be ours.' And driving him out of the garden they put him to death. Now what will the lord do to these workmen? He will come and put them to destruction and give the garden to others. And when he said this, they said, May it not be so. But he, looking on them, said, Is it not in the Writings, 'The stone which the builders put on one side, the same has become the chief stone of the building?'

Tuesday

Hosea 13:4-9; 14:1-3,9 (BBE)

But I am the Lord your God, from the land of Egypt; you have knowledge of no other God and there is no saviour but me. I had knowledge of you in the waste land where no water was. When I gave them food they were full, and their hearts were full of pride, and they did not keep me in mind. So I will be like a lion to them; as a cruel beast I will keep watch by the road; I will come face to face with them like a bear whose young ones have been taken from her, and their inmost hearts will be broken; there the dogs will make a meal of them; they will be wounded by the beasts of the field. I have sent destruction on you, O Israel; who will be your helper? O Israel, come back to the Lord your God; for your evil-doing has been the cause of your fall. Take with you words, and come back to the Lord; say to him, Let there be forgiveness for all wrongdoing, so that we may take what is good, and give in payment the fruit of our lips.

Wednesday

Heb.9:11-15; 10:12-18 (BBE)

Christ has come as the high priest of the good things of the future, through this greater and better Tent, not made with hands, that is to say, not of this world, And has gone once and for ever into the holy place, having got eternal salvation, not through the blood of goats and young oxen, but through his blood. For if the blood of goats and oxen, and the dust from the burning of a young cow, being put on the unclean, make the flesh clean: How much more will the blood of Christ, who, being without sin, made an offering of himself to God through the Holy Spirit, make your hearts clean from dead works to be servants of the living God? And for this cause it is through him that a new agreement has come into being, so that after the errors under the first agreement had been taken away by his death, the word of God might have effect for those who were marked out for an eternal heritage. when Jesus had made one offering for sins for ever, he took his place at the right hand of God; And has been waiting there from that time, till all who are against him are made a foot-rest for his feet. Because by one offering he has made complete for ever those who are made holy. And the Holy Spirit is a witness for us: for after he had said, This is the agreement which I will make with them after those days, says the Lord; I will put my laws in their hearts, writing them in their minds; he said, And I will keep no more memory of their sins and of their evil-doings. Now where there is forgiveness of these, there is no more offering for sin.

Thursday
Lev.19:17-18,32-34 (BBE)

Let there be no hate in your heart for your brother; but you may make a protest to your neighbour, so that he may be stopped from doing evil. Do not make attempts to get equal with one who has done you wrong, or keep hard feelings against the children of your people, but have love for your neighbour as for yourself: I am the Lord. Get up from your seats before the white-haired, and give honour to the old, and let the fear of your God be before you: I am the Lord. And if a man from another country is living in your land with you, do not make life hard for him; Let him be to you as one of your countrymen and have love for him as for yourself; for you were living in a strange land, in the land of Egypt: I am the Lord your God.

Friday
1 Kings 19:2-16,18 (WBS)

Jezebel sent a messenger to Elijah, saying, "So let the gods do to me, and more also, if I make not thy life as the life of one of them by to-morrow about this time." And when he saw that, he arose, and went for his life, and came to Beer-sheba, which belongeth to Judah, and left his servant there. But he himself went a day's journey into the wilderness, and came and sat down under a juniper-tree: and he requested for himself that he might die; and said, "It is enough; now, O Lord, take away my life; for I am not better than my fathers." And as he lay and slept under a juniper-tree, behold, then an angel touched him, and said to him, "Arise and eat." And he looked, and behold, there was a cake baked on the coals, and a cruse of water at his head. And he ate and drank, and laid himself down again. And the angel of the Lord came again the second time, and touched him, and said, "Arise and eat, because the journey is too great for thee." And he arose, and ate and drank, and went in the strength of that food forty days and forty nights to Horeb the mount of God. And he came thither to a cave, and lodged there; and behold, the word of the Lord came to him, and he said to him, "What doest thou here, Elijah?" And he said, "I have been very jealous for the Lord God of hosts: for the children of Israel have forsaken thy covenant, thrown down thy altars, and slain thy prophets with the sword; and I, I only, am left; and they seek my life to take it away." And he said, "Go forth, and stand upon the mount before the Lord." And behold, the Lord passed by, and a great and strong wind rent the mountains, and broke in pieces the rocks before the Lord; but the Lord was not in the wind: and after the wind an earthquake; but the Lord was not in the earthquake: And after the earthquake a fire; but the Lord was not in the fire: and after the fire a still small voice. And it was so, when Elijah heard it, that he wrapped his face in his mantle, and went out, and stood in the entrance of the cave. And behold, there came a voice to him, and said, What doest thou here, Elijah? And he said, "I have been very jealous for the Lord God of hosts: because the children of Israel have forsaken thy covenant, thrown down thy altars, and slain thy prophets with the sword; and I, I only, am left; and they seek my life, to take it away." And the Lord said to him, "Go, return on thy way to the wilderness of Damascus: and when thou comest, anoint Hazael to be king over Syria: And Jehu the son of Nimshi shalt thou anoint to be king over Israel: and Elisha the son of Shaphat of Abel-meholah shalt thou anoint to be prophet in thy room. Yet I have left to me seven thousand in Israel, all the knees which have not bowed to Baal, and every mouth which hath not kissed him."

Saturday

Ps.130 (WBS)

Out of the depths have I cried to thee, O Lord. Lord, hear my voice: let thy ears be attentive to the voice of my supplications. If thou, Lord, shouldest mark iniquities, O Lord, who shall stand? But there is forgiveness with thee, that thou mayest be feared. I wait for the Lord, my soul doth wait, and in his word do I hope. My soul waiteth for the Lord more than they that watch for the morning: I say, more than they that watch for the morning. Let Israel hope in the Lord: for with the Lord there is mercy, and with him is plenteous redemption. And he shall redeem Israel from all his iniquities.

Sunday

Luke 20:20-28 (NHT)

They (the chief priests and the scribes) watched him, and sent out spies, who pretended to be righteous, that they might trap him in something he said, so as to deliver him up to the power and authority of the governor. They asked him, "Teacher, we know that you say and teach what is right, and are not partial to anyone, but truly teach the way of God. Is it lawful for us to pay taxes to Caesar, or not?" But he perceived their craftiness, and said to them, "Show me a denarius. Whose image and inscription are on it?" They answered, "Caesar's." He said to them, "Then give to Caesar the things that are Caesar's, and to God the things that are God's." They weren't able to trap him in his words before the people. They marvelled at his answer, and were silent.

Week 41

Monday

John 3:1-21 (BBE)

Now there was among the Pharisees a man named Nicodemus, who was one of the rulers of the Jews. He came to Jesus by night and said to him, "Rabbi, we are certain that you have come from God as a teacher, because no man would be able to do these signs which you do if God was not with him." Jesus said to him, "Truly, I say to you, Without a new birth no man is able to see the kingdom of God." Nicodemus said to him, "How is it possible for a man to be given birth when he is old? Is he able to go into his mother's body a second time and come to birth again?" Jesus said in answer, "Truly, I say to you, If a man's birth is not from water and from the Spirit, it is not possible for him to go into the kingdom of God. That which has birth from the flesh is flesh, and that which has birth from the Spirit is spirit. Do not be surprised that I say to you, It is necessary for you to have a second birth. The wind goes where its pleasure takes it, and the sound of it comes to your ears, but you are unable to say where it comes from and where it goes: so it is with everyone whose birth is from the Spirit." And Nicodemus said to him, "How is it possible for these things to be?" And Jesus, answering, said, "Are you the teacher of Israel and have no knowledge of these things? Truly, I say to you, We say that of which we have knowledge; we give witness of what we have seen; and you do not take our witness to be true. If you have no belief when my words are about the things of earth, how will you have belief if my words are about the things of heaven? And no one has ever gone up to heaven but he who came down from heaven, the Son of man. As the snake was lifted up by Moses in the waste land, even so it is necessary for the Son of man to be lifted up: So that whoever has faith may have in him eternal life. For God had such love for the world that he gave his only Son, so that whoever has faith in him may not come to destruction but have eternal life. God did not send his Son into the world to be judge of the world; he sent him so that the world might have salvation through him. The man who has faith in him does not come up to be judged; but he who has no faith in him has been judged even now, because he has no faith in the name of the only Son of God. And this is the test by which men are judged: the light has come into the world and men have more love for the dark than for the light, because their acts are evil. The light is hated by everyone whose acts are evil and he does not come to the light for fear that his acts will be seen. But he whose life is true comes to the light, so that it may be clearly seen that his acts have been done by the help of God."

Tuesday

Joel 2:1-3,13,28-32 (BBE)

Let the horn be sounded in Zion, and a war-cry in my holy mountain;

let all the people of the land be troubled: for the day of the Lord is coming; For a day of dark and deep shade is near, a day of cloud and black night: like a black cloud a great and strong people is covering the mountains; there has never been any like them and will not be after them again, from generation to generation. Before them fire sends destruction, and after them flame is burning: the land is like the garden of Eden before them, and after them an unpeopled waste; truly, nothing has been kept safe from them. Let your hearts be broken, and not your clothing, and come back to the Lord your God: for he is full of grace and pity, slow to be angry and great in mercy, ready to be turned from his purpose of punishment. And after that, it will come about, says the Lord, that I will send my spirit on all flesh; and your sons and your daughters will be prophets, your old men will have dreams, your young men will see visions: And on the servants and the servant-girls in those days I will send my spirit. And I will let wonders be seen in the heavens and on the earth, blood and fire and pillars of smoke. The sun will be made dark and the moon turned to blood, before the great day of the Lord comes, a day to be feared. And it will be that whoever makes his prayer to the name of the Lord will be kept safe: for in Mount Zion and in Jerusalem some will be kept safe, as the Lord has said, and will be among the small band marked out by the Lord.

Wednesday

Heb.10:19-20,22-25; 11:1-3; 12:6-8,11-12,14

So then, my brothers, being able to go into the holy place without fear, because of the blood of Jesus, by the new and living way which he made open for us through the veil, that is to say, his flesh. Let us go in with true hearts, in certain faith, having our hearts made free from the sense of sin and our bodies washed with clean water. Let us keep the witness of our hope strong and unshaking, for he is true who has given his word: and let us be moving one another at all times to love and good works, not giving up our meetings, as is the way of some, but keeping one another strong in faith; and all the more because you see the day coming near.

Now faith is the substance of things hoped for, and the sign that the things not seen are true for by it our fathers had God's approval. By faith it is clear to us that the order of events was fixed by the word of God, so that what is seen has not been made from things which only seem to be.

The Lord sends punishment on his loved ones; everyone whom he takes as his son has experience of his rod. It is for your training that you undergo these things; God is acting to you as a father does to his sons; for what son does not have punishment from his father? But if you have not that punishment of which we all have our part, then you are not true sons, but children of shame. At the time all punishment seems to be pain and not joy: but after, those who have been trained by it get from it the peace-giving fruit of righteousness. For this cause let the hands which are hanging down be lifted up, and let the feeble knees be made strong, Let your desire be for peace with all men, and to be made holy, without which no man may see the Lord;

Thursday

Lev.19:19,26,30,35-6 (BBE)

Let there be no hate in your heart for your brother; but you may make a protest to your neighbour, so that he may be stopped from doing evil. Do not make attempts to get equal with one who has done you wrong, or keep hard feelings against the children of your people, but have love for your neighbour as for yourself: I am the Lord.

Nothing may be used for food with its blood in it;

You may not make use of strange arts, or go in search of signs and wonders.

Keep my Sabbaths and have respect for my holy place: I am the Lord.

Do not make false decisions in questions of yard-sticks and weights and measures. Have true scales, true weights and measures for all things:

Friday

1 Kings 21:1-8,13-19,23 (NHT)

It happened after these things, that Naboth the Jezreelite had a vineyard, which was in Jezreel, near the palace of Ahab king of Samaria. Ahab spoke to Naboth, saying, "Give me your vineyard, that I may have it for a vegetable garden, because it is near to my house; and I will give you for it a better vineyard than it. Or, if it seems good to you, I will give you its worth in money." Naboth said to Ahab, "May the Lord forbid me, that I should give the inheritance of my fathers to you." Ahab came into his house sullen and angry because of the word which Naboth the Jezreelite had spoken to him; for he had said, "I will not give you the inheritance of my fathers." He laid himself down on his bed, and turned away his face, and would eat no bread. But Jezebel his wife came to him, and said to him, "Why is your spirit so sad, that you eat no bread?" He said to her, "Because I spoke to Naboth the Jezreelite, and said to him, 'Give me your vineyard for money; or else, if it pleases you, I will give you another vineyard for it.' He answered, 'I will not give you my vineyard.'" Jezebel his wife said to him, "Do you now govern the kingdom of Israel? Arise, and eat bread, and let your heart be merry. I will give you the vineyard of Naboth the Jezreelite." So she wrote letters in Ahab's name, and sealed them with his seal, and sent the letters to the elders and to the nobles who were in his city, who lived with Naboth. The two men, the base fellows, came in and sat before him. The base fellows testified against him, even against Naboth, in the presence of the people, saying, "Naboth cursed God and the king." Then they carried him out of the city, and stoned him to death with stones. Then they sent to Jezebel, saying, "Naboth has been stoned, and is dead." It happened, when Jezebel heard that Naboth was stoned, and was dead, that Jezebel said to Ahab, "Arise, take possession of the vineyard of Naboth the Jezreelite, which he refused to give you for money; for Naboth is not alive, but dead." It happened, when Ahab heard that Naboth was dead, that Ahab rose up to go down to the vineyard of Naboth the Jezreelite, to take possession of it. The word of the Lord came to Elijah the Tishbite, saying, "Arise, go down to meet Ahab king of Israel, who dwells in Samaria. Look, he is in the vineyard of Naboth, where he has gone down to take possession of it. You shall speak to him, saying, 'Thus says the Lord, "Have you killed and also taken possession?"' You shall speak to him, saying, 'Thus says the Lord, "In the place where dogs licked the blood of Naboth, dogs will lick your blood, even yours."'" The Lord also spoke of Jezebel, saying, "The dogs shall eat Jezebel in the district of Jezreel.

Saturday

Ps.138 (WBS)

I will praise thee with my whole heart: before the gods will I sing praise to thee. I will worship towards thy holy temple, and praise thy name for thy loving-kindness and for thy truth: for thou hast magnified thy word above all thy name. In the day when I cried thou didst answer me, and strengthen me with strength in my soul. All the kings of the earth shall praise thee, O Lord, when they hear the words of thy mouth. Yes, they shall sing in the ways of the Lord: for great is the glory of the Lord. Though the Lord is high, yet hath he respect to the lowly: but the proud he knoweth afar off. Though I walk in the midst of trouble, thou wilt revive me: thou wilt stretch forth thy hand against the wrath of my enemies, and thy right hand will save me. The Lord will perfect that which concerneth me: thy mercy, O Lord, endureth for ever: forsake not the works thy own hands.

Sunday

Luke 21:1-4 (BBE)

And looking up, he saw the men of wealth putting their offerings in the money-box. And he saw a certain poor widow putting in a farthing. And he said, "Truly I say to you, This poor widow has given more than all of them: For they gave out of their wealth, having more than enough for themselves: but she, even out of her need, has put in all her living."

Week 42

Monday

John 6:25-40 (BBE)

When they came across him on the other side of the sea they said,

"Rabbi, when did you come here?" Jesus, answering them, said, "Truly I say to you, You come after me, not because you saw signs, but because you were given the bread and had enough. Let your work not be for the food which comes to an end, but for the food which goes on for eternal life, which the Son of man will give to you, for on him has God the Father put his mark." Then they said to him, "How may we do the works of God?" Jesus, answering, said to them, "This is to do the work of God: to have faith in him whom God has sent." So they said, "What sign do you give us, so that we may see and have faith in you? What do you do? Our fathers had the manna in the waste land, as the Writings say, He gave them bread from heaven." Jesus then said to them, "Truly I say to you, What Moses gave you was not the bread from heaven; it is my Father who gives you the true bread from heaven. The bread of God is the bread which comes down out of heaven and gives life to the world." "Ah, Lord," they said, "give us that bread for ever!" And this was the answer of Jesus: "I am the bread of life. He who comes to me will never be in need of food, and he who has faith in me will never be in need of drink. But it is as I said to you: you have seen me, and still you have no faith. Whatever the Father gives to me will come to me; and I will not send away anyone who comes to me. For I have come down from heaven, not to do my pleasure, but the pleasure of him who sent me. And this is the pleasure of him who sent me, that I am not to let out of my hands anything which he has given me, but I am to give it new life on the last day. This, I say, is my Father's pleasure, that everyone who sees the Son and has faith in him may have eternal life: and I will take him up on the last day."

Tuesday
Amos 5:4,8,21-24 (NHT)

For thus says the Lord to the house of Israel: "Seek me, and you will live; seek him who made Kimah and Kesil, and turns the shadow of death into the morning, and makes the day dark with night; who calls for the waters of the sea, and pours them out on the surface of the earth, the Lord is his name, I hate, I despise your feasts, and I can't stand your solemn assemblies. Yes, though you offer me your burnt offerings and meal offerings, I will not accept them; neither will I regard the peace offerings of your fat animals. Take away from me the noise of your songs. I will not listen to the music of your harps. But let justice roll on like rivers, and righteousness like a mighty stream.

Wednesday
Heb.13:1-2,4-8,15-16 (BBE)

Let your desire be for peace with all men, and to be made holy, without which no man may see the Lord; Go on loving your brothers in the faith. Take care to keep open house: because in this way some have had angels as their guests, without being conscious of it. Keep in mind those who are in chains, as if you were chained with them, and those who are in trouble, as being yourselves in the body. Let married life be honoured among all of you and not made unclean; for men untrue in married life will be judged by God. Be free from the love of money and pleased with the things which you have; for he himself has said, I will be with you at all times. So that we say with a good heart, The Lord is my helper; I will have no fear: what is man able to do to me? Keep in mind those who were over you, and who gave you the word of God; seeing the outcome of their way of life, let your faith be like theirs. Jesus Christ is the same yesterday and today and for ever. Let us then make offerings of praise to God at all times through him, that is to say, the fruit of lips giving witness to his name. But go on doing good and giving to others, because God is well-pleased with such offerings.

Thursday
Lev.20:1,6-8,27 (BBE)

And the Lord said to Moses, And whoever goes after those who make use of spirits and wonder-workers, doing evil with them, against him will my face be turned, and he will be cut off from among his people. So make and keep yourselves holy, for I am the Lord your God. And keep my rules and do them: I am the Lord, who make you holy. Any man or woman who makes use of spirits, or who is a wonder-worker, is to be put to death: they are to be stoned with stones: their blood will be on them.

Friday
2 Kings 4:8-22,32-37 (NHT)

It fell on a day, that Elisha passed to Shunem, where there was a prominent woman; and she persuaded him to eat bread. So it was, that as often as he passed by, he turned in there to eat bread. She said to her husband, "See now, I perceive that this is a holy man of God, that passes by us continually. Please let us make a little room on the wall. Let us set for him there a bed, a table, a chair, and a lamp stand. It shall be, when he comes to us, that he shall turn in there." One day he came there, and he turned into the room and lay there. He said to Gehazi his servant, "Call this Shunammite." When he had called her, she stood before him. He said to him, "Say now to her, 'Look, you have cared for us with all this care. What is to be done for you? Would you like to be spoken for to the king, or to the captain of the army?'" She answered, "I dwell among my own people." He said, "What then is to be done for her?" Gehazi answered, "Most certainly she has no son, and her husband is old." He said, "Call her." When he had called her, she stood in the door. He said, "At this season, when the time comes around, you will embrace a son." She said, "No, my lord, you man of

God, do not lie to your handmaid." The woman conceived, and bore a son at that season, when the time came around, as Elisha had said to her. When the child was grown, it happened one day that he went out to his father to the reapers. He said to his father, "My head. My head." He said to his servant, "Carry him to his mother." When he had taken him, and brought him to his mother, he sat on her knees until noon, and then died. She went up and laid him on the bed of the man of God, and shut the door on him, and went out. She called to her husband, and said, "Please send me one of the servants, and one of the donkeys, that I may run to the man of God, and come again." When Elisha had come into the house, look, the child was dead, and lay on his bed. He went in therefore, and shut the door on them both, and prayed to the Lord. He went up, and lay on the child, and put his mouth on his mouth, and his eyes on his eyes, and his hands on his hands. He stretched himself on him; and the flesh of the child grew warm. Then he returned, and walked in the house once back and forth; and went up, and stretched himself on him. Then the child sneezed seven times, and the child opened his eyes. He called Gehazi, and said, "Call this Shunammite." So he called her. When she had come in to him, he said, "Take up your son." Then she went in, and fell at his feet, and bowed herself to the ground; and she took up her son, and went out.

Saturday
Ps.139:1-16 (WBS)

O Lord, thou hast searched me, and known me. Thou knowest my down-sitting and my up rising, thou understandest my thought afar off. Thou compassest my path and my lying down, and art acquainted with all my ways. For there is not a word on my tongue, but lo, O Lord, thou knowest it altogether. Thou hast beset me behind and before, and laid thy hand upon me. Such knowledge is too wonderful for me; it is high, I cannot attain to it. Whither shall I go from thy spirit? or whither shall I flee from thy presence? If I ascend into heaven, thou art there: if I make my bed in hell, behold, thou art there. If I take the wings of the morning, and dwell in the uttermost parts of the sea; Even there shall thy hand lead me, and thy right hand shall hold me. If I say, Surely the darkness shall cover me; even the night shall be light about me. Yes, the darkness hideth not from thee; but the night shineth as the day: the darkness and the light are both alike to thee. For thou hast possessed my reins: thou hast covered me in my mother's womb. I will praise thee: for I am fearfully and wonderfully made: wonderful are thy works; and that my soul well knoweth. My substance was not hid from thee when I was made in secret, and curiously formed in the lowest parts of the earth. Thy eyes saw my substance, yet being imperfect; and in thy book all my members were written, which in continuance were fashioned, when as yet there was none of them.

Sunday

John 13:1-17 (NHT)

Now before the feast of the Passover, Jesus, knowing that his time had come that he would depart from this world to the Father, having loved his own who were in the world, he loved them to the end. And during the meal, the devil had already put into the heart of Judas Iscariot, Simon's son, to betray him. Because he knew that the Father had given all things into his hands, and that he came forth from God, and was going to God, arose from the meal, and removed his outer garments. He took a towel, and wrapped a towel around his waist. Then he poured water into the basin, and began to wash the disciples' feet, and to wipe them with the towel that was wrapped around him. Then he came to Simon Peter. He said to him, "Lord, do you wash my feet?" Jesus answered him, "You do not know what I am doing now, but you will understand later." Peter said to him, "You will never wash my feet." Jesus answered him, "If I do not wash you, you have no part with me." Simon Peter said to him, "Lord, not my feet only, but also my hands and my head." Jesus said to him, "Someone who has bathed only needs to have his feet washed, but is completely clean. You are clean, but not all of you." For he knew him who would betray him, therefore he said, "You are not all clean." So when he had washed their feet, put his outer garment back on, and sat down again, he said to them, "Do you know what I have done to you? You call me, 'Teacher' and 'Lord.' You say so correctly, for so I am. If I then, the Lord and the Teacher, have washed your feet, you also ought to wash one another's feet. For I have given you an example, that you also should do as I have done to you. Truly, truly, I tell you, a servant is not greater than his master, neither one who is sent greater than he who sent him. If you know these things, blessed are you if you do them."

Week 43

Monday

John 6:41-57 (BBE)

Now the Jews said bitter things about Jesus because of his words, "I am the bread which came down from heaven." And they said, "Is not this Jesus, the son of Joseph, whose father and mother we have seen? How is it then that he now says, I have come down from heaven?" Jesus made answer and said, "Do not say things against me, one to another. No man is able to come to me if the Father who sent me does not give him the desire to come: and I will take him up from the dead on the last day. The writings of the prophets say, And they will all have teaching from God. Everyone whose ears have been open to the teaching of the Father comes to me. Not that anyone has ever seen the Father; only he who is from God, he has seen the Father. Truly I say to you, He who has faith in me has eternal life. I am the bread of life. Your fathers took the manna in the waste land and they are dead. The bread which comes from heaven is such bread that a man may take it for food and never see death. I am the living bread which has come from heaven: if any man takes this bread for food he will have life for ever: and more than this, the bread which I will give is my flesh which I will give for the life of the world. Then the Jews had an angry discussion among themselves, saying, How is it possible for this man to give us his flesh for food? Then Jesus said to them, Truly I say to you, If you do not take the flesh of the Son of man for food, and if you do not take his blood for drink, you have no life in you. He who takes my flesh for food and my blood for drink has eternal life: and I will take him up from the dead at the last day My flesh is true food and my blood is true drink. He who takes my flesh for food and my blood for drink is in me and I in him. As the living Father has sent me, and I have life because of the Father, even so he who takes me for his food will have life because of me."

Tuesday

Obad.1:3-4,12,15 (NHT)

The pride of your heart has deceived you, you who dwell in the clefts of the rock, whose habitation is high, who says in his heart, 'Who will bring me down to the ground?' Though you mount on high as the eagle, and though your nest is set among the stars, I will bring you down from there," says the Lord. But do not look down on your brother in the day of his disaster, and do not rejoice over the children of Judah in the day of their destruction. Do not speak proudly in the day of distress. For the day of the Lord is near all the nations. As you have done, it will be done to you. Your deeds will return upon your own head.

Wednesday

James 1:5-8,12-15,19-22 (NHT)

But if any of you lacks wisdom, let him ask of God, who gives to all liberally and without reproach; and it will be given to him. But let him ask in faith, without any doubting, for the one who doubts is like a wave of the sea, driven and tossed by the wind. For let that person not think that he will receive anything from the Lord. He is a double-minded person, unstable in all his ways. Blessed is the one who perseveres under trial, for when he has been approved, he will receive the crown of life, which he promised to those who love him. Let no one say when he is tempted, "I am tempted by God," for God cannot be tempted by evil, and he himself tempts no one. But each one is tempted, when he is drawn away by his own lust, and enticed. Then the lust, when it has conceived, bears sin; and the sin, when it is full grown, brings forth death. This you know, my beloved brothers. But let every person be swift to hear, slow to speak, and slow to anger; for human anger does not accomplish the righteousness of God. Therefore, putting away all filthiness and overflowing of wickedness, receive with humility the implanted word, which is able to save your souls. But be doers of the word, and not only hearers, deluding your own selves.

Thursday
Lev.20:10-16 (NHT)

"'The man who commits adultery with another man's wife shall surely be put to death, both the adulterer and the adulteress. The man who lies with his father's wife has uncovered his father's nakedness: both of them shall surely be put to death; their blood shall be upon them. "'If a man lies with his daughter-in-law, both of them shall surely be put to death: they have committed a perversion; their blood shall be upon them. "'If a man has sexual relations with a male, as with a woman, both of them have committed an abomination: they shall surely be put to death; their blood shall be upon them. "'If a man takes a wife and her mother, it is wickedness: they shall be burned with fire, both he and they; that there may be no wickedness among you. "'If a man lies with an animal, he shall surely be put to death; and you shall kill the animal. "'If a woman approaches any animal, and lies down with it, you shall kill the woman, and the animal: they shall surely be put to death; their blood shall be upon them.

Friday
2 Kings 5:1-3,9-16 (NHT)

Now Naaman, captain of the army of the king of Syria, was a great man with his master, and honourable, because by him the Lord had given victory to Syria: he was also a mighty man of valour, but he was a leper. The Syrians had gone out in bands, and had brought away captive out of the land of Israel a little maiden; and she waited on Naaman's wife. She said to her mistress, "I wish that my lord were with the prophet who is in Samaria. Then he would heal him of his leprosy." So Naaman came with his horses and with his chariots, and stood at the door of the house of Elisha. Elisha sent a messenger to him, saying, "Go and wash in the Jordan seven times, and your flesh shall come again to you, and you shall be clean." But Naaman was angry, and went away, and said, "Look, I thought, 'He will surely come out to me, and stand, and call on the name of the Lord his God, and wave his hand over the place, and heal the leper.' Aren't Abanah and Pharpar, the rivers of Damascus, better than all the waters of Israel? Couldn't I go wash in them, and be clean?" So he turned and went away in a rage. His servants came near, and spoke to him, and said, "My father, if the prophet had asked you to do some great thing, wouldn't you have done it? How much rather then, when he says to you, 'Wash, and be clean?'" Then went he down, and dipped himself seven times in the Jordan, according to the saying of the man of God; and his flesh was restored like the flesh of a little child, and he was clean. He returned to the man of God, he and all his company, and came, and stood before him; and he said, "See now, I know that there is no God in all the earth, but in Israel. Now therefore, please take a gift from your servant." But he said, "As the Lord lives, before whom I stand, I will receive none." He urged him to take it; but he refused.

Saturday
Ps.141:1-4,9 (WBS)

Lord, I cry to thee: make haste to me; give ear to my voice, when I cry to thee. Let my prayer be set forth before thee as incense; and the lifting up of my hands as the evening sacrifice. Set a watch, O Lord, before my mouth; keep the door of my lips. Incline not my heart to any evil thing, to practice wicked works with men that work iniquity: and let me not eat of their dainties. Keep me from the snare which they have laid for me, and the gins of the workers of iniquity.

Sunday
Luke 22:39-53 (NHT)

He came out, and went, as his custom was, to the Mount of Olives. His disciples also followed him. When he was at the place, he said to them, "Pray that you do not enter into temptation." He was withdrawn from them about a stone's throw, and he knelt down and prayed, saying, "Father, if you are willing, remove this cup from me. Nevertheless, not my will, but yours, be done." And an angel from heaven appeared to him, strengthening him. Being in agony he prayed more earnestly. His sweat became like great drops of blood falling down on the ground. When he rose up from his prayer, he came to the disciples, and found them sleeping because of grief, and said to them, "Why do you sleep? Rise and pray that you may not enter into temptation." While he was still speaking, look, a crowd came, and he who was called Judas, one of the twelve, was leading them. He came near to Jesus to kiss him. But Jesus said to him, "Judas, do you betray the Son of Man with a kiss?" When those who were around him saw what was about to happen, they said to him, "Lord, should we strike with the sword?" A certain one of them struck the servant of the high priest, and cut off his right ear. But Jesus answered and said, ï¿½No more of this.ï¿½ Then he touched his ear and healed him. Jesus said to the chief priests, captains of the temple, and elders, who had come against him, "Have you come out as against a robber, with swords and clubs? When I was with you in the temple daily, you did not stretch out your hands against me. But this is your hour, and the power of darkness."

Week 44

Monday

John 8:31-36,38,43,46-47 (BBE)

Then Jesus said to the Jews who had faith in him, "If you keep my word, then you are truly my disciples; And you will have knowledge of what is true, and that will make you free." They said to him in answer, "We are Abraham's seed and have never been any man's servant: why do you say, You will become free?" And this was the answer Jesus gave them: "Truly I say to you, Everyone who does evil is the servant of sin. Now the servant does not go on living in the house for ever, but the son does. If then the son makes you free, you will be truly free. I say the things which I have seen in my Father's house: and you do the things which come to you from your father's house". Why are my words not clear to you? It is because your ears are shut to my teaching. Which of you is able truly to say that I am a sinner? If I say what is true, why have you no belief in me? He who is a child of God gives ear to the words of God: your ears are not open to them because you are not from God.

Tuesday

Micah 4:1-7 (NHT)

But in the latter days, it will happen that the mountain of the Lord's temple will be established on the top of the mountains, and it will be exalted above the hills; and peoples will stream to it. Many nations will go and say, "Come, and let us go up to the mountain of the Lord, and to the house of the God of Jacob; and he will teach us of his ways, and we will walk in his paths." For out of Zion will go forth the law, and the word of the Lord from Jerusalem; and he will judge between many peoples, and will decide concerning strong nations afar off. They will beat their swords into ploughshares, and their spears into pruning hooks. Nation will not lift up sword against nation, neither will they learn war any more. But they will sit every man under his vine and under his fig tree; and no one will make them afraid: For the mouth of the Lord of hosts has spoken. Indeed all the nations may walk in the name of their gods; but we will walk in the name of the Lord our God forever and ever. "In that day," says the Lord, "I will assemble that which is lame, and I will gather that which is driven away, and that which I have afflicted; and I will make that which was lame a remnant, and that which was cast far off a strong nation: and the Lord will reign over them on Mount Zion from then on, even forever."

Wednesday

James 2:10-11; 4:4,7-8 (NHT)

For whoever keeps the whole law, and yet stumbles in one point, he has become guilty of all. For he who said, "Do not commit adultery," also said, "Do not commit murder." Now if you do not commit adultery, but murder, you have become a transgressor of the law. You adulterers and adulteresses, do you not know that friendship with the world is hostility toward God? Therefore whoever wants to be a friend of the world makes himself an enemy of God. Be subject therefore to God. But resist the devil, and he will flee from you. Draw near to God, and he will draw near to you. Cleanse your hands, you sinners; and purify your hearts, you double-minded.

Thursday
Ex.20:1-7 (NHT)

God spoke all these words, saying, "I am the Lord your God, who brought you out of the land of Egypt, out of the house of bondage. Do not have other gods before me. "Do not make for yourselves an idol, nor any image of anything that is in the heavens above, or that is in the earth beneath, or that is in the water under the earth: you must not bow yourself down to them, nor serve them, for I, the Lord your God, am a jealous God, visiting the iniquity of the fathers on the children, on the third and on the fourth generation of those who hate me, and showing loving kindness to thousands of those who love me and keep my commandments. "Do not take the name of the Lord your God in vain, for the Lord will not hold him guiltless who takes his name in vain.

Friday
2 Chr. 34:1-3,8-9a,14,19,21b,29-32; 35:1,18 (HB)

Josiah was eight years old when he began to reign; and he reigned thirty-one years in Jerusalem. He did that which was right in the eyes of the Lord, and walked in the ways of David his father, and did not turn aside to the right hand or to the left. For in the eighth year of his reign, while he was yet young, he began to seek after the God of David his father; and in the twelfth year he began to purge Judah and Jerusalem from the high places, and the Asherim, and the engraved images, and the molten images. Now in the eighteenth year of his reign, when he had purged the land and the house, he sent Shaphan the son of Azaliah, and Maaseiah the governor of the city, and Joah the son of Joahaz the recorder, to repair the house of the Lord his God. They came to Hilkiah the high priest, and delivered the money that was brought into God's house When they brought out the money that was brought into the house of the Lord, Hilkiah the priest found the scroll of the law of the Lord given by Moses It happened, when the king had heard the words of the law, that he tore his clothes. "for great is the wrath of the Lord that is poured out on us, because our fathers have not kept the word of the Lord, to do according to all that is written in this scroll." Then the king sent and gathered together all the elders of Judah and Jerusalem. The king went up to the house of the Lord, and all the men of Judah and the inhabitants of Jerusalem, and the priests, and the Levites, and all the people, both great and small: and he read in their ears all the words of the scroll of the covenant that was found in the house of the Lord. The king stood in his place, and made a covenant before the Lord, to walk after the Lord, and to keep his commandments, and his testimonies, and his statutes, with all his heart, and with all his soul, to perform the words of the covenant that were written in this scroll. He caused all who were found in Jerusalem and Benjamin to stand. The inhabitants of Jerusalem did according to the covenant of God, the God of their fathers. Josiah kept a Passover to the Lord in Jerusalem: and they killed the Passover on the fourteenth day of the first month. There was no Passover like that kept in Israel from the days of Samuel the prophet; neither did any of the kings of Israel keep such a Passover as Josiah kept, and the priests, and the Levites, and all Judah and Israel who were present, and the inhabitants of Jerusalem.

Saturday

Ps.143:1-2,5-11 (WBS)

Hear my prayer, O Lord, give ear to my supplications: in thy faithfulness answer me, and in thy righteousness. And enter not into judgment with thy servant: for in thy sight shall no man living be justified. I remember the days of old, I meditate on all thy works; I muse on the work of thy hands. I stretch forth my hands to thee: my soul thirsteth after thee, as a thirsty land. Hear me speedily, O Lord: my spirit faileth: hide not thy face from me, lest I be like them that go down into the pit. Cause me to hear thy loving-kindness in the morning; for in thee do I trust: cause me to know the way in which I should walk; for I lift up my soul to thee. Deliver me, O Lord, from my enemies: I flee to thee to hide me. Teach me to do thy will; for thou art my God: thy spirit is good; lead me into the land of uprightness. Revive me, O Lord, for thy name's sake: for thy righteousness' sake bring my soul out of trouble.

Sunday

Ex.20:8-17 (NHT)

"Remember the Sabbath day, to keep it holy. Six days you may labour, and do all your work, but the seventh day is a Sabbath to the Lord your God. You must not do any work in it, you, nor your son, nor your daughter, your male servant, nor your female servant, nor your livestock, nor your stranger who is within your gates; for in six days the Lord made heaven and earth, the sea, and all that is in them, and rested the seventh day; therefore the Lord blessed the seventh day, and made it holy. "Honour your father and your mother, that it may be well with you, that your days may be long in the land which the Lord your God gives you. "Do not commit adultery. "Do not murder. "Do not steal. "Do not give false testimony against your neighbour. "Do not covet your neighbour's house. Do not covet your neighbour's wife, nor his male servant, nor his female servant, nor his ox, nor his donkey, nor anything that is your neighbour's."

Week 45
Monday
John 10:7-18 (BBE)

So Jesus said again, "Truly I say to you, I am the door of the sheep. All who came before me are thieves and outlaws: but the sheep did not give ear to them. I am the door: if any man goes in through me he will have salvation, and will go in and go out, and will get food. The thief comes only to take the sheep and to put them to death: he comes for their destruction: I have come so that they may have life and have it in greater measure. I am the good keeper of sheep: the good keeper gives his life for the sheep. He who is a servant, and not the keeper or the owner of the sheep, sees the wolf coming and goes in flight, away from the sheep; and the wolf comes down on them and sends them in all directions: Because he is a servant he has no interest in the sheep. I am the good keeper; I have knowledge of my sheep, and they have knowledge of me, Even as the Father has knowledge of me and I of the Father; and I am giving my life for the sheep. And I have other sheep which are not of this field: I will be their guide in the same way, and they will give ear to my voice, so there will be one flock and one keeper. For this reason am I loved by the Father, because I give up my life so that I may take it again. No one takes it away from me; I give it up of myself. I have power to give it up, and I have power to take it again. These orders I have from my Father."

Tuesday
Nahum 1:1-8 (BBE)

The word about Nineveh. The book of the vision of Nahum the Elkoshite. The Lord is a God who takes care of his honour and gives punishment for wrong; the Lord gives punishment and is angry; the Lord sends punishment on those who are against him, being angry with his haters. The Lord is slow to get angry and great in power, and will not let the sinner go without punishment: the way of the Lord is in the wind and the storm, and the clouds are the dust of his feet. He says sharp words to the sea and makes it dry, drying up all the rivers: Bashan is feeble, and Carmel, and the flower of Lebanon is without strength. The mountains are shaking because of him, and the hills flowing away; the earth is falling to bits before him, the world and all who are in it. Who may keep his place before his wrath? and who may undergo the heat of his passion? his wrath is let loose like fire and the rocks are broken open by him. The Lord is good, a strong place in the day of trouble; and he has knowledge of those who take him for their safe cover. But like water overflowing he will take them away; he will put an end to those who come up against him, driving his haters into the dark.

Wednesday

James 2:14,26; 5:13-16; 4:13-17 (NHT)

What good is it, my brothers, if someone says he has faith, but has no works? Can faith save him? For as the body apart from the spirit is dead, even so faith apart from works is dead. Is any among you suffering? Let him pray. Is any cheerful? Let him sing praises. Is any among you sick? Let him call for the elders of the church, and let them pray over him, anointing him with oil in the name of the Lord, and the prayer of faith will save the one who is sick, and the Lord will raise him up. If he has committed sins, he will be forgiven. Therefore confess your sins to one another, and pray for one another, that you may be healed. The prayer of the righteous person is powerfully effective. Come now, you who say, "Today or tomorrow let us go into this city, and spend a year there, trade, and make a profit." Whereas you do not know what tomorrow will be like. What is your life? For you are a vapour that appears for a little time and then vanishes away. For you ought to say, "If the Lord wills, we will both live, and do this or that." But now you glory in your boasting. All such boasting is evil. To him therefore who knows to do good, and does not do it, to him it is sin.

Thursday

Lev.20:17-21 (NHT)

If a man takes his sister, his fathers daughter, or his mothers daughter, and sees her nakedness, and she sees his nakedness; it is a shameful thing; and they shall be cut off in the sight of the children of their people: he has uncovered his sisters nakedness; he shall bear his iniquity. If a man lies with a woman having her monthly period, and uncovers her nakedness; he has made naked her fountain, and she has uncovered the fountain of her blood: and both of them shall be cut off from among their people. You shall not uncover the nakedness of your mothers sister, nor of your fathers sister; for he has made naked his close relative: they shall bear their iniquity. If a man lies with his uncles wife, he has uncovered his uncles nakedness: they shall bear their sin; they shall die childless. If a man takes his brothers wife, it is an impurity: he has uncovered his brother's nakedness; they shall be childless.

Friday

Job 1:1-3,6-22 (BBE)

There was a man in the land of Uz whose name was Job. He was without sin and upright, fearing God and keeping himself far from evil and he had seven sons and three daughters. And of cattle he had seven thousand sheep and goats, and three thousand camels, and a thousand oxen, and five hundred she-asses, and a very great number of servants. And the man was greater than any of the sons of the east. And there was a day when the sons of the gods came together before the Lord, and the Satan came with them. And the Lord said to the Satan, "Where do you come from?" And the Satan said in answer, "From wandering this way and that on the earth, and walking about on it." And the Lord said to the Satan, "Have you taken note of my servant Job, for there is no one like him on the earth, a man without sin and upright, fearing God and keeping himself far from evil?" And the Satan said in answer to the Lord, "Is it for nothing that Job is a god-fearing man? Have you yourself not put a wall round him and his house and all he has on every side, blessing the work of his hands, and increasing his cattle in the land? But now, put out your hand against all he has, and he will be cursing you to your face." And the Lord said to the Satan, "See, I give all he has into your hands, only do not put a finger on the man himself." And the Satan went out from before the Lord. And there was a day when his sons and daughters were feasting in the house of their oldest brother, And a man came to Job, and said, "The oxen were ploughing, and the asses were taking their food by their side and the men of Sheba came against them and took them away, putting the young men to the sword, and I was the only one who got away safe to give you the news." And this one was still talking when another came, and said, "The fire of God came down from heaven, burning up the sheep and the goats and the young men completely, and I was the only one who got away safe to give you the news." And this one was still talking when another came, and said, "The Chaldaeans made themselves into three bands, and came down on the camels and took them away, putting the young men to the sword, and I was the only one who got away safe to give you the news." And this one was still talking when another came, and said, "Your sons and your daughters were feasting together in their oldest brother's house, when a great wind came rushing from the waste land against the four sides of the house, and it came down on the young men, and they are dead; and I was the only one who got away safe to give you the news." Then Job got up, and after parting his clothing and cutting off his hair, he went down on his face to the earth, and gave worship, and said, "With nothing I came out of my mother's body, and with nothing I will go back there; the Lord gave and the Lord has taken away; let the Lord's name be praised." In all this Job did no sin, and did not say that God's acts were foolish.

Saturday
Ps.145 (WBS)

I will extol thee, my God, O king; and I will bless thy name for ever and ever. Every day will I bless thee; and I will praise thy name for ever and ever. Great is the Lord, and greatly to be praised; and his greatness is unsearchable. One generation shall praise thy works to another, and shall declare thy mighty acts. I will speak of the glorious honour of thy majesty, and of thy wondrous works. And men shall speak of the might of thy terrible acts: and I will declare thy greatness. They shall abundantly utter the memory of thy great goodness, and shall sing of thy righteousness. The Lord is gracious, and full of compassion; slow to anger, and of great mercy. The Lord is good to all: and his tender mercies are over all his works. All thy works shall praise thee, O Lord; and thy saints shall bless thee. They shall speak of the glory of thy kingdom, and talk of thy power; To make known to the sons of men his mighty acts, and the glorious majesty of his kingdom. Thy kingdom is an everlasting kingdom, and thy dominion endureth throughout all generations. The Lord upholdeth all that fall, and raiseth up all those that are bowed down. The eyes of all wait upon thee; and thou givest them their food in due season. Thou openest thy hand, and satisfiest the desire of every living creature. The Lord is righteous in all his ways, and holy in all his works. The Lord is nigh to all them that call upon him, to all that call upon him in truth. He will fulfil the desire of them that fear him: he also will hear their cry, and will save them. The Lord preserveth all them that love him: but all the wicked will he destroy. My mouth shall speak the praise of the Lord: and let all flesh bless his holy name for ever and ever..

Sunday

Luke 22:54-62 (NHT)

They seized him, and led him away, and brought him into the high priest's house. But Peter followed from a distance. When they had kindled a fire in the middle of the courtyard, and had sat down together, Peter sat among them. A certain servant girl saw him as he sat in the light, and looking intently at him, said, "This man also was with him." But he denied it, saying, "Woman, I do not know him." After a little while someone else saw him, and said, "You also are one of them." But Peter answered, "Man, I am not." After about one hour passed, another confidently affirmed, saying, "Truly this man also was with him, for he is a Galilean." But Peter said, "Man, I do not know what you are talking about." Immediately, while he was still speaking, a rooster crowed. The Lord turned, and looked at Peter. Then Peter remembered the Lord's word, how he said to him, "Before the rooster crows today you will deny me three times" and he went out, and wept bitterly.

Week 46

Monday

John 14:1-10,13-14 (NHT)

"Do not let your heart be troubled. Believe in God. Believe also in me. In my Father's house are many dwelling places. If it weren't so, I would have told you; for I go to prepare a place for you. And if I go and prepare a place for you, I will come again, and will receive you to myself; that where I am, you may be there also. And you know the way where I am going." Thomas said to him, "Lord, we do not know where you are going. How can we know the way?" Jesus said to him, "I am the way, the truth, and the life. No one comes to the Father except through me. If you have known me, you will know my Father also. From now on you do know him and have seen him." Philip said to him, "Lord, show us the Father, and that will be enough for us." Jesus said to him, "Have I been with you all this time, and still you do not know me, Philip? He who has seen me has seen the Father. How can you say, 'Show us the Father?' Do you not believe that I am in the Father, and the Father is in me? The words that I say to you I do not speak from myself; but the Father who lives in me does his works. Believe me that I am in the Father, and the Father is in me; or else believe because of the works themselves. Truly, truly, I tell you, he who believes in me, the works that I do, he will do also; and he will do greater works than these, because I am going to the Father. And whatever you ask in my name, this I will do, that the Father may be glorified in the Son. If you ask me anything in my name, I will do it."

Tuesday
Zeph. 3:14-19 (NHT)

Sing, daughter of Zion. Shout, Israel. Be glad and rejoice with all your heart, daughter of Jerusalem. The Lord has taken away your judgments. He has thrown out your enemy. The King of Israel, the Lord, is in the midst of you. You will not be afraid of evil any more. In that day, it will be said to Jerusalem, "Do not be afraid, Zion. Do not let your hands be weak." The Lord your God is in your midst, a mighty one who will save. He will rejoice over you with joy. He will calm you in his love. He will rejoice over you with singing. I will remove those who grieve about the appointed feasts from you. They are a burden and a reproach to you. Look, at that time I will deal with all those who afflict you, and I will save those who are lame, and gather those who were driven away. I will give them praise and honour, whose shame has been in all the earth.

Wednesday
1 Pet 1:3-4,13-16,22-25 (BBE)

Praise be to the God and Father of our Lord Jesus Christ, who through his great mercy has given us a new birth and a living hope by the coming again of Jesus Christ from the dead, And a heritage fair, holy and for ever new, waiting in heaven for you, So make your minds ready, and keep on the watch, hoping with all your power for the grace which is to come to you at the revelation of Jesus Christ; Like children ruled by God, do not go back to the old desires of the time when you were without knowledge: But be holy in every detail of your lives, as he, whose servants you are, is holy; Because it has been said in the Writings, You are to be holy, for I am holy. And as you have made your souls clean, being ruled by what is true, and loving one another without deceit, see that your love is warm and from the heart: Because you have had a new birth, not from the seed of man, but from eternal seed, through the word of a living and unchanging God. For it is said, All flesh is like grass, and all its glory like the flower of the grass. The grass becomes dry and the flower dead: But the word of the Lord is eternal. And this is the word of the good news which was given to you.

Thursday
Lev.23:1-3,26-32 (BBE)

And the Lord said to Moses, "Say to the children of Israel, These are the fixed feasts of the Lord, which you will keep for holy meetings: these are my feasts. On six days work may be done; but the seventh day is a special day of rest, a time for worship; you may do no sort of work: it is a Sabbath to the Lord wherever you may be living." And the Lord said to Moses, "The tenth day of this seventh month is the day for the taking away of sin; let it be a holy day of worship; you are to keep from pleasure, and give to the Lord an offering made by fire. And on that day you may do no sort of work, for it is a day of taking away sin, to make you clean before the Lord your God. For any person, whoever he may be, who takes his pleasure on that day will be cut off from his people. And if any person, whoever he may be, on that day does any sort of work, I will send destruction on him from among his people. You may not do any sort of work: this is an order for ever through all your generations wherever you may be living. Let this be a Sabbath of special rest to you, and keep yourselves from all pleasure; on the ninth day of the month at nightfall from evening to evening, let this Sabbath be kept."

Friday
Job 29:1-8,18; 30:16-17; 38:1,4-7,12-31; 40:3,5; 42:2,5-6 (BBE)

And Job again took up the word and said, "If only I might again be as I was in the months which are past, in the days when God was watching over me! When his light was shining over my head, and when I went through the dark by his light. As I was in my flowering years, when my tent was covered by the hand of God; While the Ruler of all was still with me, and my children were round me; When my steps were washed with milk, and rivers of oil were flowing out of the rock for me. When I went out of my door to go up to the town, and took my seat in the public place, The young men saw me, and went away, and the old men got up from their seats; Then I said, I will come to my end with my children round me, my days will be as the sand in number; But now my soul is turned to water in me, days of trouble overtake me: The flesh is gone from my bones, and they give me no rest;

there is no end to my pains."

And the Lord made answer to Job out of the storm-wind, and said, "Where were you when I put the earth on its base? Say, if you have knowledge. By whom were its measures fixed? Say, if you have wisdom; or by whom was the line stretched out over it? On what were its pillars based, or who put down its angle-stone, When the morning stars made songs together, and all the sons of the gods gave cries of joy? Have you, from your earliest days, given orders to the morning, or made the dawn conscious of its place; So that it might take a grip of the skirts of the earth, shaking all the evil-doers out of it? It is changed like wet earth under a stamp, and is coloured like a robe; And from the evil-doers their light is kept back, and the arm of pride is broken. Have you come into the springs of the sea, walking in the secret places of the deep? Have the doors of death been open to you, or have the door-keepers of the dark ever seen you? Have you taken note of the wide limits of the earth? Say, if you have knowledge of it all. Which is the way to the resting-place of the light, and where is the store-house of the dark; So that you might take it to its limit, guiding it to its house? No doubt you have knowledge of it, for then you had come to birth, and the number of your days is great. Have you come into the secret place of snow, or have you seen the store-houses of the ice-drops, Which I have kept for the time of trouble, for the day of war and fighting? Which is the way to the place where the wind is measured out, and the east wind sent out over the earth? By whom has the way been cut for the flowing of the rain, and the flaming of the thunder; Causing rain to come on a land where no man is living, on the waste land which has no people; To give water to the land where there is waste and destruction, and to make the dry land green with young grass? Has the rain a father? or who gave birth to the drops of night mist? Out of whose body came the ice? and who gave birth to the cold mist of heaven? The waters are joined together, hard as a stone, and the face of the deep is covered. Are the bands of the Pleiades fixed by you, or are the cords of Orion made loose?"

And Job said in answer to the Lord, "I have said once, and even twice, what was in my mind, but I will not do so again. I see that you are able to do every thing, and to give effect to all your designs. Word of you had come to my ears, but now my eye has seen you. For this cause I give witness that what I said is false, and in sorrow I take my seat in the dust."

Saturday

Prov.3:1-12 (BBE)

My son, keep my teaching in your memory, and my rules in your heart for they will give you increase of days, years of life, and peace. Let not mercy and good faith go from you; let them be hanging round your neck, recorded on your heart; So you will have grace and a good name in the eyes of God and men. Put all your hope in God, not looking to your reason for support. In all your ways give ear to him, and he will make straight your footsteps. Put no high value on your wisdom: let the fear of the Lord be before you, and keep yourself from evil: This will give strength to your flesh, and new life to your bones. Give honour to the Lord with your wealth, and with the first-fruits of all your increase: So your store-houses will be full of grain, and your vessels overflowing with new wine. My son, do not make your heart hard against the Lord's teaching; do not be made angry by his training: For to those who are dear to him the Lord says sharp words, and makes the son in whom he has delight undergo pain.

Sunday

Luke 1:1-20 (NHT)

Since many have undertaken to set in order a narrative concerning those matters which have been fulfilled among us, even as those who from the beginning were eyewitnesses and servants of the word delivered them to us, it seemed good to me also, having traced the course of all things accurately from the first, to write to you in order, most excellent Theophilus; that you might know the certainty concerning the things in which you were instructed. There was in the days of Herod, the king of Judea, a certain priest named Zechariah, of the division of Abijah. He had a wife of the daughters of Aaron, and her name was Elizabeth. They were both righteous before God, walking blamelessly in all the commandments and ordinances of the Lord. But they had no child, because Elizabeth was barren, and they both were well advanced in years. Now it happened, while he was performing the priest's office before God in the order of his division, according to the custom of the priest's office, his lot was to enter into the temple of the Lord and burn incense. And the whole crowd of people were praying outside at the hour of incense. An angel of the Lord appeared to him, standing on the right side of the altar of incense. Zechariah was troubled when he saw him, and fear fell upon him. But the angel said to him, "Do not be afraid, Zechariah, because your request has been heard, and your wife, Elizabeth, will bear you a son, and you are to name him John. You will have joy and gladness; and many will rejoice at his birth. For he will be great in the sight of the Lord, and he will drink no wine nor strong drink. He will be filled with the Holy Spirit, even from his mother's womb. He will turn many of the sons of Israel to the Lord, their God. He will go before him in the spirit and power of Elijah, 'to turn the hearts of the fathers to the children,' and the disobedient to the wisdom of the just; to make ready a people prepared for the Lord." Zechariah said to the angel, "How can I be sure of this? For I am an old man, and my wife is well advanced in years." The angel answered him, "I am Gabriel, who stands in the presence of God. I was sent to speak to you, and to bring you this good news. And look, you will be silent and not able to speak, until the day that these things will happen, because you did not believe my words, which will be fulfilled in their proper time."

Week 47

Monday

John 15:1-8 (BBE)

I am the true vine and my Father is the gardener. He takes away every branch in me which has no fruit, and every branch which has fruit he makes clean, so that it may have more fruit. You are clean, even now, through the teaching which I have given you. Be in me at all times as I am in you. As the branch is not able to give fruit of itself, if it is not still on the vine, so you are not able to do so if you are not in me. I am the vine, you are the branches: he who is in me at all times as I am in him, gives much fruit, because without me you are able to do nothing. If a man does not keep himself in me, he becomes dead and is cut off like a dry branch; such branches are taken up and put in the fire and burned. If you are in me at all times, and my words are in you, then anything for which you make a request will be done for you. Here is my Father's glory, in that you give much fruit and so are my true disciples.

Tuesday

Haggai 1:2-9 (NHT)

This is what the Lord of hosts says: These people say, 'The time hasn't yet come, the time for the Lord's house to be built.' Then the word of the Lord came by Haggai, the prophet, saying, "Is it a time for you yourselves to dwell in your panelled houses, while this house lies waste? Now therefore this is what the Lord of hosts says: Consider your ways. You have sown much, and bring in little. You eat, but you do not have enough. You drink, but you aren't filled with drink. You clothe yourselves, but no one is warm, and he who earns wages earns wages to put them into a bag with holes in it." This is what the Lord of hosts says: "Consider your ways. Go up to the mountain, bring wood, and build the house. I will take pleasure in it, and I will be glorified," says the Lord. "You looked for much, and, look, it came to little; and when you brought it home, I blew it away. Why?" says the Lord of hosts, "Because of my house that lies waste, while each of you is busy with his own house.

Wednesday

1 Pet.2:19-25; 4:9-10; 5:5b,7-10 (BBE)

It is a sign of grace if a man, desiring to do right in the eyes of God, undergoes pain as punishment for something which he has not done. What credit is it if, when you have done evil, you take your punishment quietly? but if you are given punishment for doing right, and take it quietly, this is pleasing to God. This is God's purpose for you: because Jesus himself underwent punishment for you, giving you an example, so that you might go in his footsteps: who did no evil, and there was no deceit in his mouth: to sharp words he gave no sharp answer; when he was undergoing pain, no angry word came from his lips; but he put himself into the hands of the judge of righteousness: He took our sins on himself, giving his body to be nailed on the tree, so that we, being dead to sin, might have a new life in righteousness, and by his wounds we have been made well. Like sheep, you had gone out of the way; but now you have come back to him who keeps watch over your souls.

Keep open house for all with a glad heart making distribution among one another of whatever has been given to you, like true servants of the unmeasured grace of God;

Let all of you put away pride and make yourselves ready to be servants: for God is a hater of pride, but he gives grace to those who make themselves low. Put all your troubles on him, for he takes care of you. Be serious and keep watch; the Evil One, who is against you, goes about like a lion with open mouth in search of food. Do not give way to him but be strong in your faith, in the knowledge that your brothers who are in the world undergo the same troubles. And after you have undergone pain for a little time, the God of all grace who has given you a part in his eternal glory through Christ Jesus, will himself give you strength and support, and make you complete in every good thing;

Thursday
Num.27:8-11;36:8-9;30:3-6,11-12,14 (BBE)

And say to the children of Israel, If a man has no son at the time of his death, let his heritage go to his daughter. And if he has no daughter, then give his heritage to his brothers. And if he has no brothers, then give his heritage to his father's brothers. And if his father has no brothers, then give it to his nearest relation in the family, as his heritage: this is to be a decision made by law for the children of Israel, as the Lord gave orders to Moses. And every daughter owning property in any tribe of the children of Israel is to be married to one of the family of her father's tribe, so that every man of the children of Israel may keep the heritage of his fathers. And no property will be handed from one tribe to another, but every tribe of the children of Israel will keep its heritage.

If a woman, being young and under the authority of her father, takes an oath to the Lord or gives an undertaking; If her father, hearing of her oath or the undertaking she has given, says nothing to her, then all her oaths and every undertaking she has given will have force. But if her father, hearing of it, makes her take back her word, then the oaths or the undertakings she has given will have no force; and she will have forgiveness from the Lord, because her oath was broken by her father. And if she is married to a husband at the time when she is under an oath or an undertaking given without thought; And her husband, hearing of it, said nothing to her and did not put a stop to it, then all her oaths and every undertaking she gave will have force. But if her husband, on hearing of it, made them without force or effect, then whatever she has said about her oaths or her undertaking has no force: her husband has made them without effect, and she will have the Lord's forgiveness. But if the days go on, and her husband says nothing whatever to her, then he is giving the support of his authority to her oaths and undertakings, because at the time of hearing them he said nothing to her.

Friday

Jer. 52:1-13 (BBE)

Zedekiah was twenty-one years old when he became king; he was king for eleven years in Jerusalem: and his mother's name was Hamutal, the daughter of Jeremiah of Libnah. And he did evil in the eyes of the Lord, as Jehoiakim had done. And because of the wrath of the Lord this came about in Jerusalem and Judah, till he had sent them away from before him: and Zedekiah took up arms against the king of Babylon. And in the ninth year of his rule, on the tenth day of the tenth month, Nebuchadrezzar, king of Babylon, came against Jerusalem with all his army and took up his position before it, building earthworks all round it. So the town was shut in by their forces till the eleventh year of King Zedekiah. In the fourth month, on the ninth day of the month, the store of food in the town was almost gone, so that there was no food for the people of the land. Then an opening was made in the wall of the town, and all the men of war went in flight out of the town by night through the doorway between the two walls which was by the king's garden; (now the Chaldaeans were stationed round the town:) and they went by the way of the Arabah. And the Chaldaean army went after King Zedekiah and overtook him on the other side of Jericho, and all his army went in flight from him in every direction. Then they made the king a prisoner and took him up to the king of Babylon to Riblah in the land of Hamath to be judged. And the king of Babylon put the sons of Zedekiah to death before his eyes: and he put to death all the rulers of Judah in Riblah. And he put out Zedekiah's eyes; and the king of Babylon, chaining him in iron bands, took him to Babylon, and put him in prison till the day of his death. Now in the fifth month, on the tenth day of the month, in the nineteenth year of King Nebuchadrezzar, king of Babylon, Nebuzaradan, the captain of the armed men, a servant of the king of Babylon, came into Jerusalem. And he had the house of the Lord and the king's house and all the houses of Jerusalem, even every great house, burned with fire.

Saturday

Prov.6:16-19; 7:1-2; 9:10 (BBE)

Six things are hated by the Lord; seven things are disgusting to him: Eyes of pride, a false tongue, hands which take life without cause; a heart full of evil designs, feet which are quick in running after sin; a false witness, breathing out untrue words, and one who lets loose violent acts among brothers. My son, keep my sayings, and let my rules be stored up with you. Keep my rules and you will have life; let my teaching be to you as the light of your eyes. The fear of the Lord is the start of wisdom, and the knowledge of the Holy One gives a wise mind

Sunday

Luke 1:26-38 (NHT)

Now in the sixth month, the angel Gabriel was sent from God to a city of Galilee, named Nazareth, to a virgin pledged to be married to a man whose name was Joseph, of the house of David. The virgin's name was Mary. Having come in, the angel said to her, "Greetings, favoured one. The Lord is with you." But when she saw him, she was greatly troubled at the saying, and considered what kind of salutation this might be. The angel said to her, "Do not be afraid, Mary, for you have found favour with God. And look, you will conceive in your womb, and bring forth a son, and will call his name 'Jesus.' He will be great, and will be called the Son of the Most High. The Lord God will give him the throne of his father, David, and he will reign over the house of Jacob forever. There will be no end to his Kingdom." Mary said to the angel, "How can this be, seeing I am a virgin?" The angel answered her, "The Holy Spirit will come on you, and the power of the Most High will overshadow you. Therefore also the holy one who is born will be called the Son of God. And look, Elizabeth, your relative, also has conceived a son in her old age; and this is the sixth month with her who was called barren. For with God nothing will be impossible." And Mary said, "See, the handmaid of the Lord; be it to me according to your word." The angel departed from her.

Week 48

Monday

John 15:9-17 (BBE)

Even as the Father has given me his love, so I have given my love to you: be ever in my love. If you keep my laws, you will be ever in my love, even as I have kept my Father's laws, and am ever in his love. I have said these things to you so that I may have joy in you and so that your joy may be complete. This is the law I give you: Have love one for another, even as I have love for you. Greater love has no man than this, that a man gives up his life for his friends. You are my friends, if you do what I give you orders to do. No longer do I give you the name of servants; because a servant is without knowledge of what his master is doing: I give you the name of friends, because I have given you knowledge of all the things which my Father has said to me. You did not take me for yourselves, but I took you for myself; and I gave you the work of going about and producing fruit which will be for ever; so that whatever request you make to the Father in my name he may give it to you.   So this is my law for you: Have love one for another.

Tuesday
Mal.2:10-12,14-16 (NHT)

Do we not all have one father? Hasn't one God created us? Why do we deal treacherously every man against his brother, profaning the covenant of our fathers? Judah has dealt treacherously, and an abomination is committed in Israel and in Jerusalem; for Judah has profaned the holiness of the Lord which he loves, and has married the daughter of a foreign god. The Lord will cut off, to the man who does this, him who wakes and him who answers, out of the tents of Jacob, and him who offers an offering to the Lord of hosts. Yet you say, 'Why?' Because the Lord has been witness between you and the wife of your youth, against whom you have dealt treacherously, though she is your companion, and the wife of your covenant. Did he not make one, although he had the residue of the Spirit? Why one? He sought a godly seed. Therefore take heed to your spirit, and let none deal treacherously against the wife of his youth. For I hate divorce," says the Lord, the God of Israel, "and him who covers his garment with violence." says the Lord of hosts. "Therefore take heed to your spirit, that you do not deal treacherously.

Wednesday
2 Pet. 1:20-21, 3-9 (NHT)

No prophecy of Scripture is of private interpretation for no prophecy ever came by human will, but people spoke from God, being moved by the Holy Spirit.

His divine power has granted to us all things that pertain to life and godliness, through the knowledge of him who called us by his own glory and virtue; by which he has granted to us his precious and exceedingly great promises; that through these you may become partakers of the divine nature, having escaped from the corruption that is in the world by lust. Yes, and for this very cause adding on your part all diligence, in your faith supply moral excellence; and in moral excellence, knowledge; and in knowledge, self-control; and in self-control patience; and in patience godliness; and in godliness brotherly affection; and in brotherly affection, love. For if these things are yours and abound, they make you to be not idle nor unfruitful to the knowledge of our Lord Jesus Christ. For he who lacks these things is blind, seeing only what is near, having forgotten the cleansing from his old sins.

Thursday

Num.35:16,22-24,30-31 (BBE)

If a man gives another man a blow with an iron instrument, causing his death, he is a taker of life and is certainly to be put to death; but if a man has given a wound to another suddenly and not in hate, or without design has sent something against him, or has given him a blow with a stone, without seeing him, so causing his death, though he had nothing against him and no desire to do him evil: then let the meeting of the people be judge between the man responsible for the death and him who has the right of punishment for blood, acting by these rules: Anyone causing the death of another is himself to be put to death on the word of witnesses: but the word of one witness is not enough. Further, no price may be given for the life of one who has taken life and whose right reward is death: he is certainly to be put to death.

Friday

Dan.3:1,4-6,16-25,28 (NHT)

Nebuchadnezzar the king made an image of gold, whose height was sixty cubits, and its breadth six cubits: he set it up in the plain of Dura, in the province of Babylon. Then the herald cried aloud, "To you it is commanded, peoples, nations, and languages, that whenever you hear the sound of the horn, flute, zither, lyre, harp, pipe, and all kinds of music, you fall down and worship the golden image that Nebuchadnezzar the king has set up; and whoever doesn't fall down and worship shall the same hour be cast into the midst of a burning fiery furnace." Shadrach, Meshach, and Abednego answered the king, "Nebuchadnezzar, we have no need to answer you in this matter. If it be so, our God whom we serve is able to deliver us from the burning fiery furnace; and he will deliver us out of your hand, O king. But if not, be it known to you, O king, that we will not serve your gods, nor worship the golden image which you have set up." Then was Nebuchadnezzar full of fury, and the expression of his face was changed against Shadrach, Meshach, and Abednego. Therefore he spoke, and commanded that they should heat the furnace seven times more than it was usually heated. He commanded certain mighty men who were in his army to bind Shadrach, Meshach, and Abednego, and to cast them into the burning fiery furnace. Then these men were bound in their cloaks, trousers, their turbans, and their other garments, and were cast into the midst of the burning fiery furnace. Therefore because the king's commandment was urgent, and the furnace exceeding hot, the flame of the fire killed those men who took up Shadrach, Meshach, and Abednego. These three men, Shadrach, Meshach, and Abednego, fell down bound into the midst of the burning fiery furnace. Then Nebuchadnezzar the king was astonished, and rose up quickly. He spoke and said to his ministers, "Did we not cast three men bound into the midst of the fire?" They answered the king, "True, O king." He answered, "Look, I see four men loose, walking in the midst of the fire, and they are unharmed; and the aspect of the fourth is like a son of the gods." Nebuchadnezzar spoke and said, "Blessed be the God of Shadrach, Meshach, and Abednego, who has sent his angel, and delivered his servants who trusted in him, and have changed the king's word, and have yielded their bodies, that they might not serve nor worship any god, except their own God.

Saturday
Prov.31:10-31 (BBE)

Who may make discovery of a woman of virtue? For her price is much higher than jewels. The heart of her husband has faith in her, and he will have profit in full measure. She does him good and not evil all the days of her life. She gets wool and linen, working at the business of her hands. She is like the trading-ships, getting food from far away. She gets up while it is still night, and gives meat to her family, and their food to her servant-girls. After looking at a field with care, she gets it for a price, planting a vine-garden with the profit of her work. She puts a band of strength round her, and makes her arms strong. She sees that her marketing is of profit to her: her light does not go out by night. She puts her hands to the cloth-working rod, and her fingers take the wheel. Her hands are stretched out to the poor; yes, she is open-handed to those who are in need. She has no fear of the snow for her family, for all those in her house are clothed in red. She makes for herself cushions of needlework; her clothing is fair linen and purple. Her husband is a man of note in the public place, when he takes his seat among the responsible men of the land. She makes linen robes and gets a price for them, and traders take her cloth bands for a price. Strength and self-respect are her clothing; she is facing the future with a smile. Her mouth is open to give out wisdom, and the law of mercy is on her tongue. She gives attention to the ways of her family, she does not take her food without working for it. Her children get up and give her honour, and her husband gives her praise, saying, Unnumbered women have done well, but you are better than all of them. Fair looks are a deceit, and a beautiful form is of no value; but a woman who has the fear of the Lord is to be praised. Give her credit for what her hands have made: let her be praised by her works in the public place

Sunday
Luke 1:39-55 (NHT)

Mary arose in those days and went into the hill country with haste, into a city of Judah, and entered into the house of Zechariah and greeted Elizabeth. It happened, when Elizabeth heard Mary's greeting, that the baby leaped in her womb, and Elizabeth was filled with the Holy Spirit. She called out with a loud voice, and said, "Blessed are you among women, and blessed is the fruit of your womb. Why am I so favoured, that the mother of my Lord should come to me? For look, when the voice of your greeting came into my ears, the baby leaped in my womb for joy. Blessed is she who believed, for there will be a fulfilment of the things which have been spoken to her from the Lord." Mary said, "My soul magnifies the Lord. And my spirit rejoices in God my Saviour, for he has looked at the humble state of his servant girl. For look, from now on all generations will call me blessed. For he who is mighty has done great things for me, and holy is his name. His mercy is for generations of generations on those who fear him. He has shown strength with his arm. He has scattered the proud in the imagination of their hearts. He has put down princes from their thrones. And has exalted the lowly. He has filled the hungry with good things. He has sent the rich away empty. He has given help to Israel, his servant, that he might remember mercy, As he spoke to our fathers, to Abraham and his offspring forever."

Week 49

Monday

John 15:18-23; 16:1-4 (BBE)

If you are hated by the world, keep in mind that I was hated by the world before you. If you were of the world, you would be loved by the world: but because you are not of the world, but I have taken you out of the world, you are hated by the world. Keep in mind the words I said to you, 'A servant is not greater than his lord.' If they were cruel to me, they will be cruel to you; if they kept my words, they will keep yours. They will do all this to you because of my name, because they have no knowledge of him who sent me. If I had not come and been their teacher they would have had no sin: but now they have no reason to give for their sin. He who has hate for me has hate for my Father. I have said these things to you so that you may not be in doubt. They will put you out of the Synagogues: yes, the time is coming when whoever puts you to death will have the belief that he is doing God's pleasure. They will do these things to you because they have not had knowledge of the Father or of me. I have said these things to you so that when the time comes, what I have said may come to your mind. I did not say them to you at the first, because then I was still with you.

Tuesday

Mal.3:1-3,5: 4:1-5 (NHT)

"Look, I send my messenger, and he will prepare the way before me; and the Lord, whom you seek, will suddenly come to his temple; and the messenger of the covenant, whom you desire, look, he comes." says the Lord of hosts. But who can endure the day of his coming? And who will stand when he appears? For he is coming like a refiner's fire, and like launderer's soap. And he will sit as a refiner and purifier of silver, and he will purify the sons of Levi, and refine them as gold and silver; and they shall offer to the Lord offerings in righteousness. I will come near to you to judgment; and I will be a swift witness against the sorcerers, and against the adulterers, and against the perjurers, and against those who oppress the hireling in his wages, the widow, and the fatherless, and who deprive the foreigner of justice, and do not fear me," says the Lord of hosts. "For, look, the day comes, it burns as a furnace; and all the proud, and all who work wickedness, will be stubble; and the day that comes will burn them up," says the Lord of hosts, "that it shall leave them neither root nor branch. But to you who fear my name shall the sun of righteousness arise with healing in its wings. You will go out, and leap like calves of the stall. You shall tread down the wicked; for they will be ashes under the soles of your feet in the day that I make," says the Lord of hosts. "Remember the Law of Moses my servant, which I commanded to him in Horeb for all Israel, even statutes and ordinances. Look, I will send you Elijah the prophet before the great and awesome day of the Lord comes."

Wednesday

1 John 1:5-10; 2:1-2 (NHT)

This is the message which we have heard from him and announce to you, that God is light, and in him is no darkness at all. If we say that we have fellowship with him and walk in the darkness, we lie, and do not tell the truth. But if we walk in the light, as he is in the light, we have fellowship with one another, and the blood of Jesus, his Son, cleanses us from all sin. If we say that we have no sin, we deceive ourselves, and the truth is not in us. If we confess our sins, he is faithful and righteous to forgive us the sins, and to cleanse us from all unrighteousness. If we say that we have not sinned, we make him a liar, and his word is not in us. My little children, I write these things to you so that you may not sin. If anyone sins, we have an advocate with the Father, Jesus Christ, the righteous. And he is the atoning sacrifice for our sins, and not for ours only, but also for the whole world.

Thursday

Lev.22:17-20,31-32 (BBE)

And the Lord said to Moses, Say to Aaron and to his sons and to all the children of Israel, If any man of the children of Israel, or of another nation living in Israel, makes an offering, given because of an oath or freely given to the Lord for a burned offering; So that it may be pleasing to the Lord, let him give a male, without any mark, from among the oxen or the sheep or the goats. But anything which has a mark you may not give; it will not make you pleasing to the Lord.

So then, keep my orders and do them: I am the Lord. And do not make my holy name common; so that it may be kept holy by the children of Israel: I am the Lord who make you holy,

Friday
Dan.6:7,10-13,16,19-23 (NHT)

All the administrators of the kingdom, the deputies and the satraps, the counsellors and the governors, have consulted together to establish a royal statute, and to make a strong decree, that whoever shall ask a petition of any god or man for thirty days, except of you, O king, he shall be cast into the den of lions. When Daniel knew that the writing was signed, he went into his house (now his windows were open in his chamber toward Jerusalem) and he kneeled on his knees three times a day, and prayed, and gave thanks before his God, as he did before. Then these men assembled together, and found Daniel making petition and petition before his God. Then they came near, and spoke before the king concerning the king's decree. "Haven't you signed a decree, that every man who shall make petition to any god or man within thirty days, except to you, O king, shall be cast into the den of lions?" The king answered, "The thing is true, according to the law of the Medes and Persians, which cannot be changed." Then they answered and said before the king, "That Daniel, who is of the children of the captivity of Judah, doesn't regard you, O king, nor the decree that you have signed, but makes his petition three times a day." Then the king commanded, and they brought Daniel, and cast him into the den of lions. Now the king spoke and said to Daniel, "Your God whom you serve continually, he will deliver you." Then the king arose very early in the morning, and went in haste to the den of lions. When he came near to the den to Daniel, he cried with a lamentable voice. The king spoke and said to Daniel, "Daniel, servant of the living God. Is your God, whom you serve continually, able to deliver you from the lions?" Then said Daniel to the king, "O king, live forever. My God has sent his angel, and has shut the lions' mouths, and they have not hurt me; because before him innocence was found in me; and also before you, O king, have I done no wrong." Then was the king exceedingly glad, and commanded that they should take Daniel up out of the den. So Daniel was taken up out of the den, and no manner of hurt was found on him, because he had trusted in his God.

Saturday
Prov. 17:1,13-14; 19:17; 20:22; 23:17-18; 24:17-20; 30:5-9 (BBE)

Have no envy of sinners in your heart, but keep in the fear of the Lord all through the day; for without doubt there is a future, and your hope will not be cut off.

Do not be glad at the fall of your hater, and let not your heart have joy at his downfall: for fear that the Lord may see it, and it may be evil in his eyes, and his wrath may be turned away from him.

Do not be troubled because of evil-doers, or have envy of sinners: for there will be no future for the evil man; the light of sinners will be put out.

If anyone gives back evil for good, evil will never go away from his house. The start of fighting is like the letting out of water: so give up before it comes to blows. Do not say, I will give punishment for evil: go on waiting for the Lord, and he will be your saviour

Every word of God is tested: he is a breastplate to those who put their faith in him. Make no addition to his words, or he will make clear your error, and you will be seen to be false.

I have made request to you for two things; do not keep them from me before my death: Put far from me all false and foolish things: do not give me great wealth or let me be in need, but give me only enough food: for fear that if I am full, I may be false to you and say, Who is the Lord? or if I am poor, I may become a thief, using the name of my God wrongly.

He who has pity on the poor gives to the Lord, and the Lord will give him his reward.

Better a bit of dry bread in peace, than a house full of feasting and violent behaviour

Sunday

Luke 1:57-79 (NHT)

Now the time that Elizabeth should give birth was fulfilled, and she brought forth a son. Her neighbours and her relatives heard that the Lord had magnified his mercy towards her, and they rejoiced with her. It happened on the eighth day, that they came to circumcise the child; and they would have called him Zechariah, after the name of the father. His mother answered, "Not so; but he will be called John." They said to her, "There is no one among your relatives who is called by this name." They made signs to his father, what he would have him called. And he asked for a writing tablet, and wrote, "His name is John." And they were all amazed. His mouth was opened immediately, and his tongue freed, and he spoke, blessing God. Fear came on all who lived around them, and all these sayings were talked about throughout all the hill country of Judea. All who heard them laid them up in their heart, saying, "What then will this child be?" The hand of the Lord was with him. His father, Zechariah, was filled with the Holy Spirit, and prophesied, saying, "Blessed be the Lord, the God of Israel, for he has visited and worked redemption for his people; and has raised up a horn of salvation for us in the house of his servant David (as he spoke by the mouth of his holy prophets who have been from of old), salvation from our enemies, and from the hand of all who hate us; to show mercy towards our fathers, to remember his holy covenant, the oath which he spoke to Abraham, our father, to grant to us that we, being delivered out of the hand of our enemies, should serve him without fear, In holiness and righteousness before him all our days. And you, child, will be called a prophet of the Most High, for you will go before the Lord to make ready his ways, to give knowledge of salvation to his people by the remission of their sins, because of the tender mercy of our God, whereby the dawn from on high will visit us, to shine on those who sit in darkness and the shadow of death; to guide our feet into the way of peace."

Week 50

Monday

John 15:26-27; 16:8, 13-15 (BBE)

When the Helper comes, whom I will send to you from the Father even the Spirit of true knowledge who comes from the Father, he will give witness about me. And you, in addition, will give witness because you have been with me from the first. And he, when he comes, will make the world conscious of sin, and of righteousness, and of being judged: However, when he, the Spirit of true knowledge, has come, he will be your guide into all true knowledge: for his words will not come from himself, but whatever has come to his hearing, that he will say: and he will make clear to you the things to come. He will give me glory, because he will take of what is mine, and make it clear to you. Everything which the Father has is mine: that is why I say, He will take of what is mine and will make it clear to you.

Tuesday

Isa.11:1-9 (NHT)

A branch will come out of the stock of Jesse, and a shoot out of his roots will bear fruit. The Spirit of the Lord will rest on him: the spirit of wisdom and understanding, the spirit of counsel and might, the spirit of knowledge and of the fear of the Lord. His delight will be in the fear of the Lord. He will not judge by the sight of his eyes, neither decide by the hearing of his ears; but with righteousness he will judge the poor, and decide with equity for the humble of the earth. He will strike the earth with the rod of his mouth; and with the breath of his lips he will kill the wicked. Righteousness will be the belt of his waist, and faithfulness the belt of his waist. The wolf will live with the lamb, and the leopard will lie down with the young goat; The calf and the young lion will graze together; and a little child will lead them. The cow and the bear will graze. Their young ones will lie down together. The lion will eat straw like the ox. The nursing child will play near a cobra's hole, and the weaned child will put his hand on the viper's den. They will not hurt nor destroy in all my holy mountain; for the earth will be full of the knowledge of the Lord, as the waters cover the sea.

Wednesday

1 John 4:1,5; 2:15-17; 3:13-18 (BBE)

My loved ones, do not put your faith in every spirit, but put them to the test, to see if they are from God: because a great number of false prophets have gone out into the world. They are of the world, so their talk is the world's talk, and the world gives ear to them. Have no love for the world or for the things which are in the world. If any man has love for the world, the love of the Father is not in him because everything in the world, the desire of the flesh, the desire of the eyes, and the pride of life, is not of the Father but of the world. And the world and its desires is coming to an end: but he who does God's pleasure is living for ever. Do not be surprised, my brothers, if the world has no love for you. We are conscious that we have come out of death into life because of our love for the brothers. He who has no love is still in death. Anyone who has hate for his brother is a taker of life, and you may be certain that no taker of life has eternal life in him. In this we see what love is, because he gave his life for us; and it is right for us to give our lives for the brothers. But if a man has this world's goods, and sees that his brother is in need, and keeps his heart shut against his brother, how is it possible for the love of God to be in him? My little children, do not let our love be in word and in tongue, but let it be in act and in good faith.

Thursday

Lev.20:22-26 (BBE)

So then, keep my rules and my decisions and do them, so that the land which I am giving you as your resting-place may not violently send you out again. And do not keep the rules of the nations which I am driving out before you; for they did all these things, and for that reason my soul was turned against them. But I have said to you, You will take their land and I will give it to you for your heritage, a land flowing with milk and honey: I am the Lord your God who have made you separate from all other peoples. So then, make division between the clean beast and the unclean, and between the clean bird and the unclean: do not make yourselves disgusting by any beast or bird or anything which goes flat on the earth, which has been marked by me as unclean for you. And you are to be holy to me; for I the Lord am holy and have made you separate from the nations, so that you may be my people.

Friday

Est.3:8-10; 4:1-3; 5:1-4; 7:1-4; 8:6-11 (NHT)

Haman said to King Ahasuerus, "There is a certain people scattered abroad and dispersed among the peoples in all the provinces of your kingdom, and their laws are different than other people's. They do not keep the king's laws. Therefore it is not for the king's profit to allow them to remain.

If it pleases the king, let it be written that they be destroyed; and I will pay ten thousand talents of silver into the hands of those who are in charge of the king's business, to bring it into the king's treasuries." The king took his ring from his hand, and gave it to Haman the son of Hammedatha the Agagite, the Jews' enemy. Now when Mordecai found out all that was done, Mordecai tore his clothes, and put on sackcloth with ashes, and went out into the midst of the city, and wailed loudly and a bitterly. He came even before the King's Gate, for no one is allowed inside the King's Gate clothed with sackcloth. In every province, wherever the king's commandment and his decree came, there was great mourning among the Jews, and fasting, and weeping, and wailing; and many lay in sackcloth and ashes.

Now it happened on the third day that Esther put on her royal clothing, and stood in the inner court of the king's house, next to the king's house. The king sat on his royal throne in the royal house, next to the entrance of the house. When the king saw Esther the queen standing in the court, she obtained favour in his sight; and the king held out to Esther the golden sceptre that was in his hand. So Esther came near, and touched the top of the sceptre. Then the king asked her, "What would you like, queen Esther? What is your request? It shall be given you even to the half of the kingdom." Esther said, "If it seems good to the king, let the king and Haman come today to the banquet that I have prepared for him." So the king and Haman came to banquet with Esther the queen. The king said again to Esther on the second day at the banquet of wine, "What is your petition, queen Esther? It shall be granted you. What is your request? Even to the half of the kingdom it shall be performed." Then Esther the queen answered, "If I have found favour in your sight, O king, and if it please the king, let my life be given me at my petition, and my people at my request. For we are sold, I and my people, to be destroyed, to be slain, and to perish. But if we had been sold for bondservants and bondmaids, I would have held my peace, although the adversary could not have compensated for the king's loss." For how can I endure to see the disaster that would come to my people? How can I endure to see the destruction of my relatives?" Then King Ahasuerus said to Esther the queen and to Mordecai the Jew, "See, I have given Esther the house of Haman, and him they have hanged on the gallows, because he laid his hand on the Jews. Write also to the Jews, as it pleases you, in the king's name, and seal it with the king's ring; for the writing which is written in the king's name, and sealed with the king's ring, may not be reversed by any man." Then the king's scribes were called at that time, in the third month Sivan, on the twenty-third day of the month; and it was written according to all that Mordecai commanded to the Jews, and to the satraps, and the governors and officials of the provinces which are from India to Ethiopia, one hundred twenty-seven provinces, to every province according to its writing, and to every people in their language, and to the Jews in their writing, and in their language. He wrote in the name of King

Ahasuerus, and sealed it with the king's ring, and sent letters by courier on horseback, riding on royal horses that were bread from swift steeds. In those letters, the king granted the Jews who were in every city to gather themselves together, and to defend their life, to destroy, to kill, and to cause to perish, all the power of the people and province that would assault them, their little ones and women, and to plunder their possessions.

Saturday
Ecc.2:4,10a,11,18,20; 5:10a,15; 9:11; 7:25,14; 11:5; 5:19; 12:13-14 (NHT)

I made myself great works. I built myself houses. I planted myself vineyards. Whatever my eyes desired, I did not keep from them. I did not withhold my heart from any joy, Then I looked at all the works that my hands had worked, and at the labour that I had laboured to do; and look, all was vanity and a chasing after wind, and there was no profit under the sun. I hated all my labour in which I laboured under the sun, seeing that I must leave it to the man who comes after me. Therefore I began to cause my heart to despair concerning all the labour in which I had laboured under the sun. He who loves silver shall not be satisfied with silver; As he came forth from his mother's womb, naked shall he go again as he came, and shall take nothing for his labour, which he may carry away in his hand. I returned, and saw under the sun, that the race is not to the swift, nor the battle to the strong, neither yet bread to the wise, nor yet riches to men of understanding, nor yet favour to men of skill; but time and chance happen to them all.
I turned around, and my heart sought to know and to search out, and to seek wisdom and the scheme of things, and to know that wickedness is stupidity, and that foolishness is madness. In the day of prosperity be joyful, and in the day of adversity consider; yes, God has made the one side by side with the other, to the end that man should not find out anything after him As you do not know what is the way of the wind, nor how the bones grow in the womb of her who is with child; even so you do not know the work of God who does all. Every man also to whom God has given riches and wealth, and has given him power to eat of it, and to take his portion, and to rejoice in his labour, this is the gift of God. This is the end of the matter.

All has been heard. Fear God, and keep his commandments; for this is the whole duty of man. For God will bring every work into judgment, with every hidden thing, whether it is good, or whether it is evil.

Sunday
Matt.1:18-25 (NHT)

Now the birth of Jesus Christ happened like this. His mother Mary had been engaged to Joseph, and before they came together, she was found to be with child from the Holy Spirit. And Joseph, her husband, being a righteous man, and not willing to make her a public example, intended to put her away secretly. But when he thought about these things, look, an angel of the Lord appeared to him in a dream, saying, "Joseph, son of David, do not be afraid to take to yourself Mary, your wife, for that which is conceived in her is of the Holy Spirit. And she will bring forth a son, and you are to name him Jesus, for he will save his people from their sins." Now all this has happened, that it might be fulfilled which was spoken by the Lord through the prophet, saying, "Look, the virgin will conceive and bear a son, and they will call his name Immanuel;" which is translated, "God with us." And Joseph arose from his sleep, and did as the angel of the Lord commanded him, and took his wife to himself; and had no marital relations with her until she had brought forth a son; and he named him Jesus.

Week 51

Monday

John 17:13-23 (BBE)

And now I come to you; and these things I say in the world so that they may have my joy complete in them. I have given your word to them; and they are hated by the world, because they are not of the world, even as I am not of the world. My prayer is not that you will take them out of the world, but that you will keep them from the Evil One. They are not of the world any more than I am of the world. Make them holy by the true word: your word is the true word. Even as you have sent me into the world, so I have sent them into the world. And for them I make myself holy, so that they may be made truly holy. My prayer is not for them only, but for all who will have faith in me through their word; May they all be one! Even as you, Father, are in me and I am in you, so let them be in us, so that all men may come to have faith that you sent me. And the glory which you have given to me I have given to them, so that they may be one even as we are one; I in them, and you in me, so that they may be made completely one, and so that it may become clear to all men that you have sent me and that they are loved by you as I am loved by you

Tuesday

Isa.9:2-7 (NHT)

The people who walked in darkness have seen a great light. Those who lived in the land of the shadow of death, on them the light has shined. You have multiplied the nation. You have increased their joy. They rejoice before you according to the joy in harvest, as men rejoice when they divide the spoil. For the yoke of his burden, and the staff of his shoulder, the rod of his oppressor, you have broken as in the day of Midian. For all the armour of the armed man in the noisy battle, and the garments rolled in blood, will be for burning, fuel for the fire. For to us a child is born. To us a son is given; and the government will be on his shoulders. His name will be called

Wonderful Counsellor, Mighty God, Everlasting Father, Prince of Peace. Of the increase of his government and of peace there shall be no end, on the throne of David, and on his kingdom, to establish it, and to uphold it with justice and with righteousness from that time on, even forever. The zeal of the Lord of hosts will perform this.

Wednesday
1 John 4:4-21 (BBE)

You are of God, my little children, and you have overcome them because he who is in you is greater than he who is in the world. They are of the world, so their talk is the world's talk, and the world gives ear to them. We are of God: he who has the knowledge of God gives ear to us; he who is not of God does not give ear to us. By this we may see which is the true spirit, and which is the spirit of error.

My loved ones, let us have love for one another: because love is of God, and everyone who has love is a child of God and has knowledge of God. He who has no love has no knowledge of God, because God is love. And the love of God was made clear to us when he sent his only Son into the world so that we might have life through him. And this is love, not that we had love for God, but that he had love for us, and sent his Son to be an offering for our sins. My loved ones, if God had such love for us, it is right for us to have love for one another. No man has ever seen God: if we have love for one another, God is in us and his love is made complete in us: And his Spirit which he has given us is the witness that we are in him and he is in us.

And we have seen and give witness that the Father sent the Son to be the Saviour of the world. Everyone who says openly that Jesus is the Son of God, has God in him and is in God. And we have seen and had faith in the love which God has for us. God is love, and everyone who has love is in God, and God is in him. In this way love is made complete in us, so that we may be without fear on the day of judging, because as he is, so are we in this world. There is no fear in love: true love has no room for fear, because where fear is, there is pain; and he who is not free from fear is not complete in love. We have the power of loving, because he first had love for us. If a man says, I have love for God, and has hate for his brother, his words are false: for how is the man who has no love for his brother whom he has seen, able to have love for God whom he has not seen? And this is the word which we have from him, that he who has love for God is to have the same love for his brother.

Thursday
Lev.24:15-22 (BBE)

And say to the children of Israel, As for any man cursing God, his sin will be on his head. And he who says evil against the name of the Lord will certainly be put to death; he will be stoned by all the people; the man who is not of your nation and one who is an Israelite by birth, whoever says evil against the holy Name is to be put to death. And anyone who takes another's life is certainly to be put to death. And anyone wounding a beast and causing its death, will have to make payment for it: a life for a life. And if a man does damage to his neighbour, as he has done, so let it be done to him; wound for wound, eye for eye, tooth for tooth; whatever damage he has done, so let it be done to him. He who puts a beast to death will have to make payment for it; he who puts a man to death will himself be put to death. You are to have the same law for a man of another nation living among you as for an Israelite; for I am the Lord your God.

Friday

Jonah 3:1-5,10; 4:1-11 (WBS)

And the word of the Lord came to Jonah the second time, saying, "Arise, go to Nineveh, that great city, and preach to it the preaching that I bid thee.! So Jonah arose, and went to Nineveh, according to the word of the Lord. Now Nineveh was an exceeding great city of three days' journey. And Jonah began to enter into the city a day's journey, and he cried, and said, !Yet forty days, and Nineveh shall be overthrown." So the people of Nineveh believed God, and proclaimed a fast, and put on sackcloth, from the greatest of them even to the least of them. And God saw their works, that they turned from their evil way; and God repented of the evil, that he had said that he would do to them; and he did it not. But it displeased Jonah exceedingly, and he was very angry. And he prayed to the Lord, and said, "I pray thee, O Lord was not this my saying, when I was yet in my country? Therefore I fled before to Tarshish: for I knew that thou art a gracious God, and merciful, slow to anger, and of great kindness, and repentest of the evil. Therefore now, O Lord, take, I beseech thee, my life from me; for it is better for me to die than to live." Then said the Lord, "Doest thou well to be angry?" So Jonah went out of the city, and sat on the east side of the city, and there made him a booth, and sat under it in the shade, till he might see what would become of the city. And the Lord God prepared a gourd, and made it to come up over Jonah, that it might be a shade over his head, to deliver him from his grief. So Jonah was exceeding glad of the gourd. But God prepared a worm when the morning rose the next day, and it smote the gourd that it withered. And it came to pass, when the sun rose that God prepared a vehement east wind; and the sun beat upon the head of Jonah, that he fainted, and wished in himself to die, and said, "It is better for me to die than to live." And God said to Jonah, "Doest thou well to be angry for the gourd?" And he said, "I do well to be angry, even to death." Then said the Lord, "Thou hast had pity on the gourd, for which thou hast not laboured, neither made it grow; which came up in a night, and perished in a night: And should not I spare Nineveh, that great city, in which are more than a hundred and twenty thousand persons that cannot discern between their right hand and their left hand, and also many cattle?"

Saturday
Ecc.3:1-8 (NHT)

For everything there is a season, and a time for every purpose under heaven: a time to be born, and a time to die; a time to plant, and a time to pluck up that which is planted; a time to kill, and a time to heal; a time to break down, and a time to build up; a time to weep, and a time to laugh; a time to mourn, and a time to dance; a time to cast away stones, and a time to gather stones together; a time to embrace, and a time to refrain from embracing; a time to seek, and a time to lose; a time to keep, and a time to cast away; a time to tear, and a time to sew; a time to keep silence, and a time to speak; a time to love, and a time to hate; a time for war, and a time for peace.

Sunday
Luke 2:1-20 (WBS)

Now it happened in those days, that a decree went out from Caesar Augustus that all the world should be enrolled. This was the first enrolment made when Quirinius was governor of Syria. All went to enrol themselves, everyone to his own city. Joseph also went up from Galilee, out of the city of Nazareth, into Judea, to the city of David, which is called Bethlehem, because he was of the house and family of David; to enrol himself with Mary, who was pledged to be married to him, being pregnant. It happened, while they were there, that the day had come that she should give birth. She brought forth her firstborn son, and she wrapped him in bands of cloth, and placed him in a feeding trough, because there was no room for them in the inn. There were shepherds in the same country staying in the field, and keeping watch by night over their flock. And look, an angel of the Lord stood by them, and the glory of the Lord shone around them, and they were terrified. The angel said to them, "Do not be afraid, for see, I bring you good news of great joy which will be to all the people. For there is born to you, this day, in the city of David, a Saviour, who is Messiah, the Lord. This is the sign to you: you will find a baby wrapped in strips of cloth, lying in a feeding trough." Suddenly, there was with the angel a multitude of the heavenly host praising God, and saying, "Glory to God in the highest, and on earth peace, good will toward humanity." And it happened that when the angels went away from them into the sky, the shepherds said one to another, "Let us go to Bethlehem, now, and see this thing that has happened, which the Lord has made known to us." They came with haste, and found both Mary and Joseph, and the baby was lying in the feeding trough. When they saw it, they made known the saying which was spoken to them about this child. All who heard it wondered at the things which were spoken to them by the shepherds. But Mary kept all these sayings, pondering them in her heart. The shepherds returned, glorifying and praising God for all the things that they had heard and seen, just as it was told them.

Week 52

Monday

Luke 12:4-12 (BBE)

And I say to you, my friends, "Have no fear of those who may put the body to death, and are able to do no more than that. But I will make clear to you of whom you are to be in fear: of him who after death has power to send you to hell; yes, truly I say, Have fear of him. Are not five sparrows given in exchange for two farthings? and God has every one of them in mind. But even the hairs of your head are numbered. Have no fear: you are of more value than a flock of sparrows. And I say to you that to everyone who gives witness to me before men, the Son of man will give witness before the angels of God. But if anyone says before men that he has no knowledge of me, I will say that I have no knowledge of him before the angels of God. And if anyone says a word against the Son of man, he will have forgiveness: but for him who says evil words against the Holy Spirit, there will be no forgiveness. And when they take you before the Synagogues and the authorities and the rulers, take no thought about what answers you will give, or what you will say: For the Holy Spirit will make clear to you in that very hour what to say."

Tuesday

Hab.1:1-5; 3:1-2,17-19 (WBS)

The burden which Habakkuk the prophet saw. O Lord, how long shall I cry, and thou wilt not hear! even cry out to thee of violence, and thou wilt not save! Why dost thou show me iniquity, and cause me to behold grievance? for devastation and violence are before me: and there are that raise strife and contention. Therefore the law is slackened, and judgment doth never go forth: for the wicked doth encompass the righteous; therefore wrong judgment proceedeth. Behold ye among the heathen, and regard, and wonder marvellously: for I will work a work in your days, which ye will not believe though it be told you.

A prayer of Habakkuk the prophet. O Lord, I have heard thy speech, and was afraid: O Lord, revive thy work in the midst of the years, in the midst of the years make known; in wrath remember mercy. Although the fig-tree shall not blossom, neither shall fruit be in the vines; the labour of the olive shall fail, and the fields shall yield no food; the flock shall be cut off from the fold, and there shall be no herd in the stalls: Yet I will rejoice in the Lord, I will joy in the God of my salvation. The Lord God is my strength, and he will make my feet like hinds' feet, and he will make me to walk upon my high places.

Wednesday
Rev. 21:1-8; 22:16,18-19 (NHT)

I saw a new heaven and a new earth: for the first heaven and the first earth have passed away, and the sea is no more. I saw the holy city, New Jerusalem, coming down out of heaven from God, made ready like a bride adorned for her husband. I heard a loud voice from the throne saying, "Look, the tabernacle of God is with humans, and he will dwell with them, and they will be his people, and God himself will be with them and be their God. And he will wipe away every tear from their eyes, and death will be no more, nor will there be mourning, nor crying, nor pain anymore, for the first things have passed away." He who sits on the throne said, "Look, I am making all things new." He said, "Write, for these words are faithful and true." He said to me, "It is done. I am the Alpha and the Omega, the Beginning and the End. I will give freely to him who is thirsty from the spring of the water of life. He who overcomes, I will give him these things. I will be his God, and he will be my son. But for the cowardly, unbelieving, abominable, murderers, sexually immoral, sorcerers, idolaters, and all liars, their part is in the lake that burns with fire and sulphur, which is the second death." I, Jesus, have sent my angel to testify these things to you for the churches. I am the root and the offspring of David; the bright morning star." I testify to everyone who hears the words of the prophecy of this book, if anyone adds to them, God will add to him the plagues which are written in this book. If anyone takes away from the words of the book of this prophecy, God will take away his part from the tree of life, and out of the holy city, which are written in this book.

Thursday
Deut.10:12,20; 11:26-28;12:32 (NHT)

Now, Israel, what does the Lord your God require of you, but to fear the Lord your God, to walk in all his ways, and to love him, and to serve the Lord your God with all your heart and with all your soul, You shall fear the Lord your God; you shall serve him; and you shall cling to him, and you shall swear by his name. Look, I set before you this day a blessing and a curse: the blessing, if you shall listen to the commandments of the Lord your God, which I command you this day; and the curse, if you shall not listen to the commandments of the Lord your God, but turn aside out of the way which I command you this day, to go after other gods, which you have not known. Whatever thing I command you, that you shall observe to do: you shall not add thereto, nor diminish from it.

Friday

Neh.2:1-6; 8:1-3; 9:1-2,38; 10:28-29; 13:15-22 (BBE)

And it came about in the month Nisan, in the twentieth year of Artaxerxes the king, when wine was before him, that I took up the wine and gave it to the king. Now I had never before been sad when the king was present. And the king said to me, "Why is your face sad, seeing that you are not ill? this is nothing but sorrow of heart." Then I was full of fear and said to the king, "May the king be living for ever: is it not natural for my face to be sad, when the town, the place where the bodies of my fathers are at rest, has been made waste and its doorways burned with fire?" Then the king said to me, "What is your desire?" So I made prayer to the God of heaven and I said to the king, "If it is the king's pleasure, and if your servant has your approval, send me to Judah, to the town where the bodies of my fathers are at rest, so that I may take in hand the building of it." And the king said to me (the queen being seated by his side), "How long will your journey take, and when will you come back?" So the king was pleased to send me, and I gave him a fixed time.

And when the seventh month came, the children of Israel were in their towns. And all the people came together like one man into the wide place in front of the water-doorway; and they made a request to Ezra the scribe that he would put before them the book of the law of Moses which the Lord had given to Israel. And Ezra the priest put the law before the meeting of the people, before the men and women and all those who were able to take it in, on the first day of the seventh month. He was reading it in the wide place in front of the water-doorway, from early morning till the middle of the day, in the hearing of all those men and women whose minds were able to take it in; and the ears of all the people were open to the book of the law. Now on the twenty-fourth day of this month the children of Israel came together, taking no food and putting haircloth and dust on their bodies. And the seed of Israel made themselves separate from all the men of other nations, publicly requesting forgiveness for their sins and the wrongdoing of their fathers. And because of all this we are making an agreement in good faith, and putting it in writing; and our rulers, our Levites, and our priests are putting their names to it. And the rest of the people, the priests, the Levites, the door-keepers, the music-makers, the Nethinim, and all those who had made themselves separate from the peoples of the lands, to keep the law of God, their wives, their sons, and their daughters, everyone who had knowledge and wisdom; They were united with their brothers, their rulers, and put themselves under a curse and an oath, to keep their steps in the way of God's law, which was given by Moses, the servant of God, and to keep and do all the orders of the Lord, our Lord, and his decisions and his rules.

In those days, I saw in Judah some who were crushing grapes on the Sabbath, and getting in grain and putting it on asses; as well as wine and grapes and figs and all sorts of goods which they took into Jerusalem on the Sabbath day: and I gave witness against them on the day when they were marketing food. And there were men of Tyre there, who came with fish and all sorts of goods, trading with the children of Judah and in Jerusalem on the Sabbath. Then I made protests to the chiefs of Judah, and said to them, What is this evil which you are doing, not keeping the Sabbath day holy? Did not your fathers do the same, and did not our God send all this evil on us and on this town? but you are causing more wrath to come on Israel by not keeping the Sabbath holy. And so, when the streets of Jerusalem were getting dark before the Sabbath, I gave orders for the doors to be shut and not to be open again till after the Sabbath: and I put some of my servants by the door so that nothing might be taken in on the Sabbath day. So the traders in all sorts of goods took their night's rest outside Jerusalem once or twice. Then I gave witness against them and said, Why are you waiting all night by the wall? if you do so again I will have you taken prisoners. From that time they did not come again on the Sabbath. And I gave the Levites orders to make themselves clean and come and keep the doors and make the Sabbath holy. Keep this in mind to my credit, O my God, and have mercy on me

Saturday
Prov. 10:19,23; 11:25; 12:15,25; 15:1,3,17; 16:2-3,9,18; 19:17,21; 20:4-6,13; 21:3 (BBE)

Where there is much talk there will be no end to sin, but he who keeps his mouth shut does wisely. By a soft answer wrath is turned away, but a bitter word is a cause of angry feelings. Better is a simple meal where love is, than a fat ox and hate with it.

It is sport to the foolish man to do evil, but the man of good sense takes delight in wisdom.
He who gives blessing will be made fat, but the curser will himself be cursed. He who has pity on the poor gives to the Lord, and the Lord will give him his reward.

The way of the foolish man seems right to him but the wise man gives ear to suggestions. Pride goes before destruction, and a stiff spirit before a fall.

Most men make no secret of their kind acts: but where is a man of good faith to be seen? Care in the heart of a man makes it weighted down, but a good word makes it glad.

All a man's ways are clean to himself; but the Lord puts men's spirits into his scales. The purpose in the heart of a man is like deep water, but a man of good sense will get it out.

A man's heart may be full of designs, but the purpose of the Lord is unchanging. Put your works into the hands of the Lord, and your purposes will be made certain. A man may make designs for his way, but the Lord is the guide of his steps.

Do not be a lover of sleep, or you will become poor: keep your eyes open, and you will have bread enough. The hater of work will not do his ploughing because of the winter; so at the time of grain-cutting he will be requesting food and will get nothing.

Sunday
Matt.2:1-16 (NHT)

Now when Jesus was born in Bethlehem of Judea in the days of Herod the king, look, wise men from the east came to Jerusalem, saying, "Where is he who is born King of the Jews? For we saw his star in the east, and have come to worship him." And when King Herod heard it, he was troubled, and all Jerusalem with him. And gathering together all the chief priests and scribes of the people, he asked them where the Messiah would be born. And they said to him, "In Bethlehem of Judea, for thus it is written through the prophet, 'And you, Bethlehem, land of Judah, are in no way least among the rulers of Judah; for out of you will come forth a ruler who will shepherd my people, Israel.'" Then Herod secretly called the wise men, and learned from them exactly what time the star appeared. And he sent them to Bethlehem, and said, "Go and search diligently for the young child, and when you have found him, bring me word, so that I also may come and worship him." And they, having heard the king, went their way; and look, the star which they saw in the east went before them, until it came and stood over where the young child was. And when they saw the star, they rejoiced with exceedingly great joy. And they came into the house and saw the young child with Mary, his mother, and they fell down and worshiped him. Then, opening their treasures, they offered to him gifts: gold, frankincense, and myrrh. Being warned in a dream that they should not return to Herod, they went back to their own country another way. Now when they had departed, look, an angel of the Lord appeared to Joseph in a dream, saying, "Arise and take the young child and his mother, and flee into Egypt, and stay there until I tell you, for Herod will seek the young child to destroy him." And he arose and took the young child and his mother by night, and departed into Egypt, and was there until the death of Herod; that it might be fulfilled which was spoken by the Lord through the prophet, saying, "Out of Egypt I called my son." Then Herod, when he saw that he was mocked by the wise men, was exceedingly angry, and sent out, and killed all the male children who were in Bethlehem and in all the surrounding countryside, from two years old and under, according to the exact time which he had learned from the wise men.

Day 366

Judg.13:2-5,24;16:4-10,16-30 (BBE)

Now there was a certain man of Zorah of the family of the Danites, and his name was Manoah; and his wife had never given birth to a child. And the angel of the Lord came to the woman, and said to her, "See now, though you have never given birth to children, you will be with child and give birth to a son. Now then take care to have no wine or strong drink and to take no unclean thing for food for you are with child and will give birth to a son; his hair is never to be cut, for the child is to be separate to God from his birth; and he will take up the work of freeing Israel from the hands of the Philistines." So the woman gave birth to a son, and gave him the name Samson; and he became a man and the blessing of the Lord was on him.

Now after this, he was in love with a woman in the valley of Sorek, named Delilah. And the chiefs of the Philistines came up to her, and said to her, "Make use of your power over him and see what is the secret of his great strength, and how we may get the better of him, and put bands on him, so that we may make him feeble; and every one of us will give you eleven hundred shekels of silver." So Delilah said to Samson, "Make clear to me now what is the secret of your great strength, and how you may be put in bands and made feeble." And Samson said to her, "If seven new bow-cords which have never been made dry are knotted round me, I will become feeble and will be like any other man." So the chiefs of the Philistines gave her seven new bow-cords which had never been made dry, and she had them tightly knotted round him. Now she had men waiting secretly in the inner room; and she said to him, "The Philistines are on you, Samson." And the cords were broken by him as a twist of thread is broken when touched by a flame. So the secret of his strength did not come to light. Then Delilah said to Samson, "See, you have been making sport of me with false words; now, say truly how may you be put in bands?" So day after day she gave him no peace, for ever questioning him till his soul was troubled to death. And opening all his heart to her, he said to her, "My head has never been touched by a blade, for I have been separate to God from the day of my birth: if my hair is cut off, then my strength will go from me and I will become feeble, and will be like any other man." And when Delilah saw that he had let her see into his heart, she sent word to the chiefs of the Philistines saying, "Come up this time, for he has let out all his heart to me." Then the chiefs of the Philistines came to her, with the money in their hands. And she made Samson go to sleep on her knees; and she sent for a man and had his seven twists of hair cut off; and while it was being done he became feeble and his strength went from him. Then she said, "The Philistines are on you, Samson." And awaking from his sleep, he said, "I will go out" as at other times, shaking myself free. But he was not conscious that the Lord had gone from him.

So the Philistines took him and put out his eyes; then they took him down to Gaza, and, chaining him with bands of brass, put him to work crushing grain in the prison-house; but the growth of his hair was starting again after it had been cut off. And the chiefs of the Philistines came together to make a great offering to Dagon their god, and to be glad; for they said, "Our god has given into our hands Samson our hater." And when the people saw him, they gave praise to their god; for they said, "Our god has given into our hands the one who was fighting against us, who made our country waste, and who put great numbers of us to death." Now when their hearts were full of joy, they said, "Send for Samson to make sport for us." And they sent for Samson out of the prison-house, and he made sport before them; and they put him between the pillars. And Samson said to the boy who took him by the hand, "Let me put my hand on the pillars supporting the house, so that I may put my back against them." Now the house was full of men and women; and all the lords of the Philistines were there; and about three thousand men and women were on the roof, looking on while Samson made sport. And Samson, crying out to the Lord, said, "O Lord God, do have me now in mind, and do make me strong only this once, O God, so that I may take one last payment from the Philistines for my two eyes." Then Samson put his arms round the two middle pillars supporting the house, putting his weight on them, on one with his right hand and on the other with his left. And Samson said, "Let death overtake me with the Philistines." And he put out all his strength, and the house came down on the chiefs and on all the people who were in it. So the dead whom he sent to destruction by his death were more than all those on whom he had sent destruction in his life.